Win or Go Home

For Joy

Win or Go Home
Sudden Death Baseball

Gary R. Parker

Forewords by Carl Erskine
and Clem Labine

McFarland & Company, Inc., Publishers
Jefferson, North Carolina, and London

Library of Congress Cataloguing-in-Publication Data

Parker, Gary R., 1950 July 12–
    Win or go home : sudden death baseball / by Gary R. Parker ;
forewords by Carl Erskine and Clem Labine.
      p.   cm.
    Includes bibliographical references and index.
    ISBN 0-7864-1096-5 (softcover : 50# alkaline paper)∞
    1. Baseball — United States — History — 20th century.   I. Title:
Sudden death baseball.   II. Title.
    GV863.A1P37   2002
    796.357'0973 — dc21   2001052120

British Library cataloguing data are available

Manufactured in the United States of America

Cover photograph: Bobby Thomson's "Shot Heard Round the World," 1951

McFarland & Company, Inc., Publishers
  Box 611, Jefferson, North Carolina 28640
  www.mcfarlandpub.com

Contents

Acknowledgments

Sincere thanks go to the following people, without whose support and inspiration this book might never have seen the light of day:

Jim Cypher, Frank LaCorte, Rick and Shirley Tuber, Tim Mead, John Sevano, Dennis Hayes, Jack Harvey, Rex Hudler, Bill Schlansky, Tom Boswell, Stan Williams, Clem and Barbara Labine, Barbara Kingsolver, Carl Erskine, Sam Garfield, Don Demeter, Pat Kines, Marty Marion, Shirley Mullin Rhodes, Larraine Daniel, and Mike Powers.

Foreword by
Carl Erskine

The final basket. The last field goal. The final pitch. It has always amazed me how many times the outcome of a game or match is decided by one of these events. And when the contest is crucial to deciding which team will advance to a playoff or World Series, the event takes on an added importance.

During my 12 years in the major leagues, I was fortunate to have pitched in many exciting pennant races for the Brooklyn Dodgers. None was more dramatic than the historic playoff between the Dodgers and the New York Giants, which culminated with Bobby Thomson's "shot heard 'Round the world" in 1951. That year, I was part of a Dodger team that, at one point in August, had a 13½–game lead over New York. As everyone knows, the Giants played outstanding ball during the season's final weeks and finally caught the Dodgers, forcing a best-of-three playoff for the pennant.

During game three of that famous series, I was in the bullpen throwing alongside Ralph Branca. When Don Newcombe ran into trouble in the bottom of the ninth, Charlie Dressen, our manager, called Clyde Sukeforth, our coach, and asked, "Are they ready? Sukey told him we were and added, "Erskine is bouncing his curve ball occasionally." "Then let me have Branca" was Charlie's reply. On Ralph's second pitch, Thomson hit his historic home run to clinch the pennant for the Giants. Even now, when I'm asked by fans or interviewers what my best pitch was, I say with all honesty, "The curve ball that I bounced in the Polo Grounds' bullpen."

That afternoon, I was one of the first Dodgers to enter the Brooklyn clubhouse following the devastating blow by Thomson. It was like a tomb in there because all of the bedlam was outside. Our guys came in, one at a time, with their heads down. I watched Charlie Dressen rip off his uniform top without unbuttoning it. I saw Jackie Robinson fire his glove into the back of his locker with terrific force. Then Ralph Branca came in. There's this famous picture of Ralph sitting on the clubhouse steps, pitched forward, with his arms between his knees, his head down, and a big number 13 shining on his back. I remember looking at all that and thinking to myself, "We're on the losing side, but this is a historic moment."

This book you are now holding is full of historic moments. It tells the story of all eight of major league baseball's sudden-death playoffs. I hope you enjoy it.

Foreword by
Clem Labine

As a member of the Brooklyn Dodgers, I followed Carl Erskine to the mound on many occasions. Now we're teaming once again to provide forewords for this new book.

In its long history, baseball has had just eight regular season playoffs to determine a pennant or division winner. I was fortunate enough to play in two. For me, nothing can match the excitement of the 1951 pennant race and playoff between the Brooklyn Dodgers and the New York Giants. History tells it well. As late as August, the Dodgers had a 13½–game lead over the Giants. New York caught us in September, and suddenly, we were in the position of being eliminated if we lost to Philadelphia on the final day of the season. In a game that might have been more nerve-racking than the playoff games themselves, Jackie Robinson came through with a great play at second base in the 12th inning, then won the game for us with a clutch home run.

In the playoff against the Giants, I always thought our manager, Charlie Dressen, made the first error. After winning the coin toss, Dressen decided that we would play the first game at Ebbets Field and the next two at the Polo Grounds. To this day, I still don't understand Charlie's decision. The Dodgers were such a good hitting team on our own field, it made no sense to play any more games than we had to at the Polo Grounds. In game one, Ralph Branca pitched very well, but in a glimpse of what would happen two days later, Bobby Thomson hit a home run to beat us 3–2.

Dressen's decision to start me in game two against the Giants came as quite a surprise. I had been in Charlie's doghouse for some time, and over the season's final days, I had pitched just one inning of relief on the season's final day. When Charlie told me I was going to be his starter in game two, I remember feeling shocked and a little bit nervous but definitely happy to at last be pitching in a game with so much importance. Today, not many people remember, but we beat the Giants 10–0 in game two and evened the series. If there was a turning point in that game, it was my striking out Bobby Thomson with the bases loaded in the early innings.

With the series now tied, we squared off against New York in game three at the Polo Grounds. Before the game, Charlie asked me, "Can you pitch if I need you?" I said, "Yes." How could anyone not want to be part of the final game? Once the game was underway, Newcombe pitched well, as he had all season. But because Dressen had used him so often during the season's final weeks, Newk grew tired in the ninth and ran into trouble. In the bullpen, Charlie had Branca and Erskine warming up. In all honesty, I had mixed feelings. All my life, I had dreamed of being on the mound and getting the last out that would clinch a pennant or World Series. Still, I was confident that either Carl or Ralph could do the job. Ralph was called into the game, and as we all know, the mighty Thomson did *not* strike out!

Here, at last, is a book that covers every regular season playoff in baseball history. I think you will enjoy it.

Introduction

No one ever forgets his first pennant race. Mine came in the summer of 1959, courtesy of perhaps the unlikeliest band of pennant contenders in baseball history. In March of that year, the Los Angeles Dodgers, a team of fading stars and unproven rookies, had been the unanimous choice of sportswriters to be National League doormats. A year earlier, demoralized by the loss of Roy Campanella and disoriented by the sprawling landscape of Los Angeles, the club had performed dismally, fighting all season long just to stay out of the National League cellar. Ashamed and embarrassed, the once-proud team vowed to do better in 1959, but no one had paid much attention. To wit: a poll of 50 sportswriters conducted prior to the 1959 season showed that an overwhelming majority expected the club to finish no better than fifth.

As a fourth-grader living in southern California during 1959, I had little grasp of abstract concepts like punditry, history, and failure. That the Dodgers had broken Brooklyn's heart by moving west in 1958 meant little to me. That the team had finished in seventh place the year before counted for even less. What *did* matter to me was that the Dodgers were winning, and winning often, during the summer of 1959. Throughout the season, they ran straight and true, employing a mixture of youth and experience to overcome decidedly superior opponents.

As the days of summer dwindled and fall drew near, I was spellbound as the Dodgers warred ferociously with the Milwaukee Braves and the surprising San Francisco Giants for the National League pennant. When the Giants were finally eliminated in a rain-punctuated showdown with the Dodgers at Seals Stadium in late September, Los Angeles and Milwaukee stood eye to eye, ready to usher baseball into its rarest and most exciting spectacle, a sudden-death playoff for the National League pennant. I didn't realize it then, but for only the fourth time in baseball history, two teams would battle beyond the season's final day to determine a pennant winner and I was determined to watch it all unfold on TV.

Unfortunately, my parents had other ideas. As luck would have it, game one of the best-two-of-three playoff series was scheduled for Monday September 28, 1959, a school day. Try as I might, I was unable to convince my mother of the obvious fact that a battle for the National League pennant was far more important to my life than the lesson on California missions that my teacher had scheduled for that day. Resigned to my fate, I shuffled off to school. Upon returning home later that afternoon, I was greeted with the welcome news that the Dodgers had prevailed in game one.

With my team now just one win away from the pennant, I pleaded my case again the following morning. Marshaling as much logic and persuasive power as my nine-year-old brain could muster, I launched into my spiel: "The pennant's on the line today. The pennant! The game starts at 1 PM. I won't get out of school until three. By the time I get home, it'll be over. You've got to let me stay home!"

As it turned out, no, she didn't, and I again trudged off to school in a sullen haze. Throughout the day, I did my best to concentrate on my lessons, but my heart wasn't in it. While my teacher droned on about the missions, my mind was on what was transpiring at the ballpark. At noon, I visualized Hodges and Snider in the cage at the Los Angeles Coliseum taking batting practice. At 12:45, Dodger starter Don Drysdale would be warming up in the bullpen. At 1 PM I nearly groaned out loud. At that moment, Braves lead-off hitter Bill Bruton would be digging in at the plate to face Drysdale.

When the dismissal bell finally rang two hours later, I tucked my Dixon number 2 Ticonderoga pencil inside the magnetized chamber of my Nifty notebook, rose from my desk, and ducked out into the warmth of an early fall day for the half-mile walk home.

Assuming that the playoff game was over, or would be by the time I reached my house, I adopted a leisurely pace. I detoured by the local drugstore for a pack of baseball cards, opting for the wax pack because the gum sounded good. Perusing my cards as I made my way down Del Rosa Avenue, I finally reached my street. On the corner stood Hi Duden's house. Hi was a kid about my age whose blond hair seemed to always be shaved to a nub atop his round head. He was nowhere in sight today, but I knew someone was home because I could hear the sound of the Duden television wafting through the open front door.

"Bases loaded, nobody out," I heard Vin Scully say. "We're in the ninth."

The game was still on! Almost choking on my gum in surprise, I raced up the block to my house, shoved my key inside the lock, and burst through the door. After heaving my books in the general direction of the living room couch, I bolted into the den and switched on the set.

More than 40 years have passed, but today, a lingering grayness still colors my memories of that wonderful afternoon. Shaded images of Henry Aaron, Johnny Logan, Norm Larker, and Carl Furillo flickering from my family's black-and-white television; gray shadows of October slowly creeping across the expanse of the Coliseum playing field.

In the 9th the Dodgers rallied to tie the score, and the pressure-packed contest moved into the 10th and then the 11th innings. Finally, in the 12th a bounder from the bat of Carl Furillo scored Gil Hodges, and the issue of the National League pennant was settled once and for all when Vin Scully said the words I'd been waiting to hear: "We go to Chicago!"

During the four years that I spent working on this book, I've been asked by a number of well-intentioned people, "Does the world really need another baseball book?" Well, it might be the height of hubris, but I'm going to go out on a limb and say, "Yes, it needs this one." Like many fans, I have grown disillusioned with the recent direction of major league baseball. For more than 100 years, the baseball season was imbued with a fundamental sanity and order. Beginning on opening day, teams engaged in a grueling, summer-long test of skill and desire from which only one would emerge victorious. As summer turned to fall and the pretenders fell by the wayside, the resolute and the strong soldiered on, warring for first place and the right to represent their division or league in the playoffs. Unlike the NBA and the NHL, *the season* was the thing in baseball, an affirmation of excellence that rewarded the superior and penalized the mediocre.

In what can only be construed as an act of self-flagellation, the bumblers in charge of major league baseball jettisoned all of that in 1994 when they introduced the wild card playoff structure to the sport. A contrivance of men unable to distinguish change from progress, the wild card has knocked a century of baseball tradition on its ear and in the process, done irreparable damage to a vital component of the game's timeless appeal: its pennant races.

Of all the arguments that have been offered against the wild card, I find the ones addressing its impact on incentive to be the most compelling. Like the kid in gym class who stops at 100 situps because that is what's required to earn an A, a second-place team with a playoff berth guaranteed under the wild card system has no incentive to elevate its performance. If a good old-fashioned pennant race is what gets your juices flowing, then you had to have a sick feeling in your stomach on September 29, 1996. On that day, the Los Angeles Dodgers and the San Diego Padres, deadlocked after 161 games, squared off for the National League Western Division title — and neither one cared. With playoff berths assured under the wild card system, the two teams engaged in what essentially was a meaningless exhibition in which their stars either didn't play or were lifted after making token appearances.

With pennant races virtually extinct and the concepts of sustained excellence and consistency apparently passé in today's "whatever" society, it's no surprise that many longtime baseball fans find their minds drifting back to the dramatic pennant races of earlier years. In that spirit, I offer this book. Less a critique of what the game has become than a celebration of what it once was, it chronicles that most rare and exciting of spectacles: sudden-death baseball. And when I say rare, I'm using the word advisedly. In baseball's 120-odd-year history, it's happened just eight times. They're all here, from the give-and-take tension of the 1946 battle between Brooklyn and St. Louis to the crash-and-burn dynamics of the American League Western Division race of 1995. A brief word about the playoff formats you'll encounter in this book: Given their contentious history, you probably won't be surprised to find that the National and American Leagues relied on different playoff structures for most of their histories to determine a pennant winner in the event of a tie. In the National League, a best of three format was utilized while the American League relied on just a single game to crown a winner. That all changed with the advent of divisional play in 1969 and the National League joined the junior circuit in adopting the single game format. Whatever its structure, sudden death baseball occupies a unique and legendary place in baseball history. During the preparation of this book, I, at times, let my imagination roam free, dreaming of a day when baseball reconnects with its past and the vital component that made it one of the defining American phenomenons of the 20th century: its pennant races. In my imagination I visualize a landscape unlittered with wildcards and continued competition, where teams have no recourse but to win or go home. A dream? Probably. But who's to say?

Gary Parker
October 2001

1

1946: Brooklyn Dodgers vs. St. Louis Cardinals

After a four-year absence, major league baseball was back in 1946. To be sure, teams had competed under the major league banner during the war years, but impostors had frequented the diamond. Men too young, too old, or too infirm to qualify for military service had filled the vacancies created on major league rosters when hundreds of big leaguers and thousands of minor leaguers marched off to war between 1942 and 1945. Desperate to keep the game in the public eye during wartime, baseball owners beat the bushes for anyone with skill enough to maintain the illusion of big league play, but by late in the war years the talent pool had grown so shallow that a 15-year-old boy was pitching for the Cincinnati Reds and a one-armed man was playing outfield for the St. Louis Browns.

The war's end in 1945 signaled an end to the charade. Returning home would be more than 500 major leaguers, including many of the game's greatest stars. Among those away the longest was Bob Feller, who had enlisted in the navy within 24 hours of the Japanese bombing of Pearl Harbor. During his stint in the service, Feller had seen action in the South Pacific as a member of the USS *Alabama*'s antiaircraft gun crew. Feller had stayed in shape by pitching in pickup games while on shore leave and through a rigorous regimen of calisthenics. When he was finally discharged in August 1945, he immediately returned to Cleveland, where he received a hero's welcome from more than 47,000 fans who had gathered at Municipal Stadium to welcome him home.

Other players soon left the service and joined Feller stateside. In New York, excitement over the return of Joe DiMaggio was at a fever pitch in the fall of 1945. Discharged from the army in September, the great center fielder returned to New York soon after, but he surprised many of his contemporaries when he refused to rejoin the Yankees for a few late-season games. "I don't care what they do, they won't get me on a ballfield until I'm ready," the fiercely proud DiMaggio told a friend. The outfielder had heard stories about some of his fellow veterans taking the field before they were ready, inflicting, DiMaggio felt, permanent harm to their reputations. While he awaited the start of spring training, the Yankee center fielder spent the winter months working his way back into shape at the New York Athletic Club.

Among National League stars, no one was more eager to get home than 26-year-old Stan Musial. Musial had been luckier than most; during his year in the navy he'd been stationed in the Hawaiian Islands where he worked for a ship repair unit at Pearl Harbor. When time allowed, he played in pickup games with other professional ballplayers who also had been fortunate enough to draw Hawaiian duty. Musial's time in the service may not have been arduous, but it had succeeded in halting the career of one of baseball's blossoming superstars. In just his second full season with the St. Louis Cardinals in 1943, the 22-year-old lefty led the National League in average, slugging, hits, doubles, and triples. When Musial's father fell ill in the fall of 1945, Stan was shipped to Philadelphia, where he spent the remainder of his service time until his discharge in March 1946. After spending a week with family and friends, Musial packed his bags and headed for spring training.

As the Musials, Fellers, and DiMaggios gradually trickled home from duty, the lesser lights who'd populated major league rosters during the war were dispatched to whence they'd come. Major league owners, who'd fretted that the diluted product of the wartime years might adversely affect the game's fan base, were relieved when large crowds gathered for pre–spring training workout camps early in 1946. The camps, which were held by a smattering of big league clubs to help returning players round themselves into shape before the actual start of spring training, were kicked off by the Cubs on California's Catalina Island in mid-January. Soon, other teams, including the Dodgers, Cardinals, Senators, and Yankees, followed suit. When the official training camps opened in the spring, the reception by the fans was enthusiastic. In ballparks throughout Arizona and Florida, record crowds were on hand to welcome the returning players—and real baseball—back to the diamonds of America.

For all of its shortcomings, wartime baseball had represented an era of unparalleled success for the St. Louis Cardinals. Between 1942 and 1944, the club, which had been able to retain such key players as shortstop Marty Marion, third baseman Whitey Kurowski, and Stan Musial, had won three

Willard Mullin's classic illustration from the April 18, 1946, issue of *The Sporting News* tells the story: with the end of World War II, real baseball was back. (Shirley Mullin Rhodes and the Estate of Willard Mullin.)

National League pennants and two World Series. With Musial in the service, the team had to settle for second place in 1945, three games behind the league-leading Cubs. Now, with Harry Walker, team leader Terry Moore, and Musial returning for the 1946 season, expectations were at an all-time high. Also rejoining the club for spring training was outfielder Enos Slaughter, who'd missed the lion's share of three seasons serving in the army air corps. "I'd been away for three years, but it's funny, the layoff didn't bother me at all," says Slaughter today. "I was ready to go in spring training and once the season started, I think I was just as good as before I left."

As wartime baseball's top dog, and with a cadre of proven stars back in the fold, it's no surprise that the Cardinals were the odds-on favorite to win the National League pennant in 1946. A preseason poll of 115 Associated Press writers showed that a whopping 97 percent picked St. Louis to finish atop the National League standings. For first-year manager Eddie Dyer, such high expectations were anything but welcome. Dyer had been around baseball long enough to know that preseason hype was at best a distraction and, at worst, could lull a team into a sense of complacency and entitlement.

Enos Slaughter discounts reports that the 1946 St. Louis Cardinals were taking their competition too lightly:

> I don't think we were overconfident. Nobody really knew what was going to happen, because Terry Moore, [Johnny] Beazley, and a few others had been gone for three years. Now Stan [Musial], he'd been gone for just the one year, but the rest of us had been gone for three years. So, we didn't know what was going to happen. We just came back, put our noses to the grindstone, and let things play themselves out.

In the New York borough of Brooklyn, overconfidence was the last thing on Dodger manager Leo Durocher's mind. In the five years since the club's last pennant, the Dodgers had been unable to climb any higher than second place in the National League. A youth movement initiated during the war by Dodger president Branch Rickey was starting to pay dividends, however, and in 1946, a fresh crop of rookies arrived at spring training ready to prove themselves at the big league level. Even the skeptics conceded that the raw recruits had talent, and it was clear that Dodger veterans like Eddie Stanky, Dixie Walker, and Augie Galan would be pushed to retain their jobs.

When pressed by reporters during spring training for the direction his club would take in '46, Durocher blew hot and cold. He would praise his veterans and the stability they brought to the organization with one breath, then with his next, speak glowingly of the club's rookies and the spirit of youth that was infusing the club. Arthur Daley of the *New York Times* summed up the situation in Brooklyn best when he wrote on opening day:

> Our Dodgers can finish anywhere from second to fifth. Yet before you can even attempt to figure out the Brooks, you first have to figure out Durocher, and that's more than the atomic bomb research staff can do. If he goes all out for second, he might make it. But if he dallies around with his youth movement, he can wind up fifth.

"Branch Rickey, the team president, wanted the younger guys to play," remembers Brooklyn first baseman Howie Schultz:

> He was developing a young, strong ballclub, and he felt the only way they were going to get good was through playing time. And that proved to be true, because within a year or two, all the veterans were gone. There weren't any of them left. But whatever approach Durocher adopted for the team, we always felt we had a pretty darn good ballclub. Pee Wee Reese and Pete Reiser and a few of those other guys came out of the service. Dixie Walker was still there. The pitching wasn't all that deep, but there were some pretty good young pitchers, [Rex] Barney, [Hal] Gregg, and those guys. We knew we had the stuff to compete in 1946.

THE RACE

Opening day of 1946 belonged to the returning heroes as GIs were feted in ballparks throughout America. In Washington, D.C., the ceremonies were especially festive as President Harry Truman, resuming a tradition suspended in 1942 by Franklin Roosevelt, threw out the ceremonial first pitch for the Senators and Red Sox opener. On the field, Ted Williams, Bob Feller, and Joe DiMaggio wasted little time in reclaiming their rightful place among the game's elite. Against the Senators, Williams hammered one of the longest home runs ever hit at Griffith Stadium, while in Chicago, Feller twirled a three-hitter against the White Sox. Not to be outdone, DiMaggio powered a two-run homer that provided the winning margin for the Yankees in their season opener against the Philadelphia Athletics.

In Boston, Leo Durocher and the Dodgers were preparing to meet the Braves for their National League opener. Prior to the game, the Dodger manager met with members of the press, and as it had been all spring, the burgeoning Dodger youth movement was the primary topic of discussion. Yes, Durocher told a reporter, the Dodger youth movement was moving forward. Ever the gambler, Durocher had elected to roll the dice with his season opening lineup, penciling in the names of Carl Furillo, Dick Whitman, Ferrell Anderson, and Gene Hermanski to play against the Braves. But the Dodger manager also cautioned reporters not to read too much significance into his new lineup. Nothing was carved in stone, he told reporters; if the kids came through, fine. If not, he had Walker, Stanky, and Galan waiting in the wings.

As colorful and exciting as opening day invariably is, it generally reveals little of what baseball's long season portends for its teams and players. On this particular opening day, the Dodgers and the Cardinals would begin the season just as they would end it: with losses. But between those two events, the 1946 season would have more than its share of unexpected twists and turns and would provide both fans and players with many memorable and exciting moments.

Almost from the start of the season, Brooklyn played with a grit and determination that surprised their National League rivals. During the season's initial weeks, the team battled St. Louis for first place, then ultimately claimed sole possession of the top spot in May and June. Kirby Higbe, the southern boy whose "aw shucks" manner and ribald humor helped keep the Brooklyn clubhouse loose, was the staff ace, winning his first eight decisions without a loss. His stock-in-trade was a hard knuckleball, which he'd perfected while playing for a service team in Manila during the war. "Higbe could throw a knuckleball as hard as most people could throw a fastball," recalls Brooklyn first baseman Ed Stevens. "And that's what made him effective, because hitters thought it was a fastball." Also turning in quality starts for the Dodger pitching staff was southpaw Joe Hatten, who was delivering on the promise he'd shown during service ball, little Vic Lombardi, who offset his diminutive stature with a fierce will to win, and rookie right-hander Hank Behrman.

Heading the Brooklyn offense was outfielder Dixie Walker. Despite leading the National League in runs batted in during 1945, he'd been written off by Branch Rickey as too old to play every day, and at 36, "The People's Cherce" had been relegated during the spring to a supporting role behind the club's rookie outfielders. In many ways, Rickey's appraisal of the veteran was right on the mark; Walker had slowed down over the previous three years, becoming ponderously slow on the basepaths and in the outfield. But he still retained a keen batting eye and by early in the season, he'd parlayed a torrid hitting streak into an everyday job in the Brooklyn lineup.

Walker's offensive onslaught was helping to ease the pressure on a teammate of whom much more was expected, outfielder Pete Reiser. The slugger was hitting over .300, but a succession of injuries was threatening to end his season. Reiser's problems could be traced back to the spring, when in an ill-advised attempt to shore up his infield, Durocher had tried Reiser at third base. The experiment failed when Reiser hurt his arm attempting a long throw to first base. He was back in the lineup soon afterward, but it was clear to everyone that he was not fully healed. Giving up on his efforts at making Reiser a third baseman, Durocher returned Pete to the outfield, but nagging injuries continued to plague the slugger until by early summer, Durocher wasn't sure if he'd ever be able to pencil Reiser's name onto a lineup card again.

Reiser's woes aside, things were coming up roses for Brooklyn. A seven-game winning streak in early July opened up some daylight between the team and its competition, and by early summer, the red-hot Dodgers were atop the National League standings with a comfortable 7½–game lead.

In St. Louis, the uneven play of the heavily favored Cardinals stood in stark contrast to the surging Dodgers. While most observers around the league pointed to inconsistent starting pitching as the cause of the club's troubles, simmering tensions and off-field distractions were also exacting a toll. Still smarting over the "take it or leave it" contract negotiation tactics employed by Cardinal president Sam Breadon during the spring, third baseman Whitey Kurowski was seriously entertaining an offer from the upstart Mexican League to play south of the border in 1946.

Kurowski wasn't the only Cardinal disenchanted with the Cardinal president. Star pitcher Max Lanier had also grown weary of Breadon's parsimonious ways and was looking for a way out of St. Louis. On May 23, infielder Red Schoendienst returned to the New York hotel room he shared with Lanier during the Cardinals' road trip and found a note from his teammate. "So long, Red," the message said. "Keep hitting those line drives. I'll see you next winter and we'll go hunting." Lanier, along with pitcher Freddie Martin and infielder Lou Klein, had bolted for the Mexican League, lured by the larger salaries being dangled before American players. With the departure of Lanier, Klein, and Martin, rumors soon began circulating that Jorgé Posada, the wealthy mastermind behind the Mexican League raids on American baseball, was now targeting Stan Musial.

Troubling as they were, none of these developments diminished the expectations that Sam Breadon and the people of St. Louis held for rookie manager Eddie Dyer. Dyer had arrived in the major leagues with all the proper credentials. As a manager in the Cardinal farm system he'd won nine minor league pennants; following that, he had great success overseeing the entire Cardinal minor league system. But Cardinal fans had little

Known around Brooklyn as "The People's Cherce," Dixie Walker had been written off by Branch Rickey prior to the start of the 1946 season. It was one of the few times in Rickey's fabled career that his baseball intuition failed him. (Shirley Mullin Rhodes and the Estate of Willard Mullin.)

interest in Dyer's prior successes; they wanted the club's new manager to get the Cardinals on the winning track now. By early May, patience in St. Louis with the uneven play of the Cardinals was wearing thin, and after a particularly sluggish performance on July 2, a concerned Sam Breadon summoned team captain Terry Moore and shortstop Marty Marion to the front office to talk about the team — and Eddie Dyer. "Dyer had kind of a tough start," remembers Marty Marion:

At one point in his first year, Mr. Breadon called me and Terry Moore into his office to talk about the ballclub and ask what we thought of Dyer. It was obvious that they were worried about the club and the job that Dyer was doing. We told him we all thought he was a good manager. I'm a great believer that managers don't have much to do with winning and losing anyway. But being a rookie manager with a veteran ballclub, Eddie was definitely on the hot seat.

"We all thought he was a good manager," says Enos Slaughter. "See, he'd managed me in '36 in the minor leagues. I always had confidence in him, and I think he knew baseball very well. And he was an easy manager to get along with."

So robust was the endorsement of Dyer by Marion and Moore that Breadon elected to do nothing for the time being. With the All-Star break just a week away, he'd let the team regroup and start fresh, then he'd reevaluate the situation. Marion and Moore never told Dyer of their meeting with Breadon.

In midsummer, Leo Durocher and the Dodgers were in New York's Polo Grounds for a Fourth of July doubleheader against the Giants. Standing with his back to the Dodger bench as he watched his team during its pregame workout, Durocher turned to coach Charlie Dressen and asked, "How many games we got left to play?" With his club perched atop the National League standings and riding a seven-game winning streak, Durocher was allowing himself the luxury of a daydream. "Eighty-six," said Dressen.

"That's more than I thought," the Dodger skipper responded. "All I hope is that we have a half-game lead into the home stretch. You know what I mean — 8½ with eight to go, 10½ with ten to go."

Throughout baseball history, few men have engendered stronger feelings from players and fellow managers than Leo Durocher. Certainly, few managers can boast of more success. During the early months of 1946, it was widely acknowledged that Brooklyn's first-half surge was due as much to Durocher's deft handling of his personnel as it was to the club's performance on the field. During April, May, and June, the Dodger skipper had shuffled his players, using a platoon system to maximize the performance from his infield and skillfully juggling veterans and rookies in the outfield. By midsummer, Durocher's sleight-of-hand had proved so successful that some observers were postulating that the Dodger manager might be able to lead his club all the way to the pennant.

What Durocher couldn't do, many believed, was maintain harmony between himself and his players. At least, some of his players. Throughout his career as a big league manager, Durocher remained singularly incapable of distinguishing between the player who responded to a pat on the back or the one who required a kick in the butt. Brooklyn first baseman Ed Stevens stands as a prime example. As a green rookie, Stevens had consistently been on the receiving end of Durocher's needling. Once, during an exhibition game in the spring of 1945, the Dodger manager had been particularly vicious, riding Stevens nonstop from the first inning. Late in the game, Durocher's voice finally gave out, and he turned to Dressen and said, "Charlie, you take him from here." A rookie with great promise, Stevens was so incensed by Durocher's treatment that he refused to report when called up to the Dodgers later in the 1945 season.

"Well, Durocher is dead and gone," says Stevens today:

> and I don't want to be too hard on him. As a manager, he had some ability, but at the time, Charlie Dressen was his number one coach, and Charlie pretty well ran the ballclub. Durocher would show up maybe 15 minutes before game time and ask Charlie, "What kind of lineup we got going today?" Durocher very seldom showed up in time for batting practice because he had other things going on. Of course, when the game got started, Leo was then kind of in charge of everything.

"Well, Durocher was a darned good manager as far as the game was concerned," recalls Howie Schultz, who platooned with Stevens at first base:

> He was a very bright person and he managed very, very well. But Leo was also impatient. I think he probably didn't handle the younger players as well as he could have. He would say things that probably didn't sit well with a young inexperienced player, while the veterans knew him and understood him, and it probably rolled off their backs. I know he was tough on some of the younger players. I know he was tough on Ed Stevens. He was tough on a few of the other guys. Not that they didn't like him, but he was a little harder to play for than some of the other guys who might've been more gentle or more encouraging.

Durocher's in-your-face managerial style did more than negatively affect his own team; it raised the hackles of opposing players as well. Harry Walker of the Cardinals swore for years that Durocher's brusque style so alienated the Cardinals that they raised their level of play whenever they faced him just for the satisfaction of beating him. Antipathy toward Durocher among the Cardinals didn't extend to Enos Slaughter, however, who professes a distinct kinship with Durocher's take-no-prisoners approach to the game. "Durocher played the kind of baseball I liked," says Slaughter. "All out. He liked to win. Ask no quarter and give none. I'd have liked to have played for Leo."

Restrictions on wartime travel had prevented baseball from staging an All-Star contest, so on Tuesday, July 9, baseball's best gathered in Boston for the first midsummer classic in two years. Ted Williams' four hits, including a home run on a Rip Sewell "eephus" pitch, paced the American Leaguers to an embarrassing 12–0 rout over the Nationals. Following the game, the players dispersed to rejoin their teams, and the curtain rose on the second act of the 1946 season.

When the Cardinals and Dodgers met for games one and two of a key four-game series on July 14, Brooklyn's lead over St. Louis stood at 4½ games. Humidity and summer heat had descended on Sportsman's Park, and the capacity crowd sweltered in the sauna-like conditions. In game one, the Dodgers struck first, pushing across a run on two walks, an infield out, and a balk by Johnny Beazley. In the bottom of the first, St. Louis posted two runs against Kirby Higbe. Then, with Musial at second and Enos Slaughter at first, Eddie Dyer called for a double steal. The Dodger catcher fired the ball to second in an attempt to cut down Slaughter, but Enos beat the throw, slamming into Dodger second baseman Eddie Stanky with a bone-crushing takeout. Although Stanky held onto the ball and prevented Musial from scoring, he had to be taken to the hospital for X-rays. It was just another example of the clean-hit, no-holds-barred brand of baseball that Slaughter personified throughout his career.

"I always played the game hard," Slaughter says today:

> The turning point for me was back in 1936 when I was playing in Georgia. What happened was the third base dugout was a long way back from the playing field and I ran in until I hit the foul line and then I walked the rest of the way back into the dugout. And Eddie Dyer said, "If you're tired, I'll get you some help." And from that day on, I never walked on a baseball field.

Although the Dodgers managed to knot the score in the fifth, key hits by Musial and Slaughter in the eighth inning put the game away for the Cards. In game two, Musial broke up a 1–1 deadlock in the 12th inning with a homer off Vic Lombardi that clinched a sweep for the Cardinals. With the losses, Brooklyn's first-place lead was cut to just 2½ games.

In game three the following day, things grew worse for the Dodgers. Before a boisterous crowd of 28,000, Musial, Moore, and Marion pounded five Brooklyn pitchers for ten runs. Durocher, still stewing over the Cardinals' sweep of the day before, came completely unraveled when umpire Al Barlick ruled that Pete Reiser had trapped and not caught a drive from the bat of Slaughter. The Dodger manager bolted from the dugout, confronted Barlick, and then proceeded to scream obscenities at him for the next five minutes. Barlick listened for awhile before finally ejecting

Durocher from the game. Leo sat out the rest of the contest in the Brooklyn clubhouse, his mood growing darker as his team absorbed yet another tough loss. Following the game, National League president Ford Frick, reacting to a report that Barlick filed with the league office over the incident, suspended Durocher for five days.

With his suspension in effect, Durocher hopped a flight to Brooklyn to meet with the team president, Branch Rickey. With the National League pennant race tightening with each day, Rickey and Durocher huddled to devise strategies for keeping the Dodgers in first place. Throughout the meeting, the concentration of the two men was broken only by the sound of Red Barber's voice, emanating from a radio in the corner that was tuned to the Dodgers-Cardinals game in St. Louis.

At Sportsman's Park, the Dodgers had pieced together a pair of singles and two walks in the first inning for a run. The Cardinals countered with two runs of their own in the bottom of the inning. Brooklyn battled back with two more runs in the fifth and another in the eighth to make it 4–2. In the ninth, Dodger pitcher Joe Hatten was just three outs away from a complete game when he stumbled. After plunking Marion with an errant pitch, the left-hander then yielded a single to Clyde Kluttz. Sensing an opportunity, Dyer sent Erv Dusak to the plate to hit for Pollet. After missing a bunt attempt, then fouling off another pitch, Dusak powered a Hatten offering into the left-field stands for the game-winning homer. Dusak's homer was no paint-by-the-numbers job; it carried halfway up the bleachers before careening off a seat and coming to rest in the lap of a St. Louis fan. With the blast, the sweep was complete, and the Cardinals were within a half game of the first-place Dodgers.

Reeling from the lambasting administered by St. Louis, Brooklyn moved on to Cincinnati, where the team promptly dropped two games to the Reds. With the losses, St. Louis was able to take sole possession of first place. However, the return of Durocher at month's end buoyed the club, and the play of the Dodgers improved. The Cardinals, who'd looked so strong against Brooklyn just a week earlier, suddenly resumed their inconsistent play against the second-division Phillies and Giants, and by the end of July, Brooklyn had not only regained first place but had staked itself to a 3½–game lead over its on-again, off-again rivals.

Relief in Brooklyn over the resurgent Dodgers was tempered by the events of Thursday, August 1. In the rubber game of a three-game set against St. Louis, Peter Reiser was chasing a fly ball off the bat of Whitey Kurowski when he collided with the left centerfield wall and suffered a concussion. Lying dazed on a stretcher, Reiser was led past a battery of Dodgers who may have been wondering what possible misfortune would next befall their teammate. They didn't have to wait long to find out. Shortly after his release from the hospital, Reiser burned his arm attempting to light the kitchen stove at his home, extending his stay on the disabled list. It was yet another bizarre twist in the star-crossed career of one of baseball's most gifted players.

"I thought Pete Reiser had as much natural talent as anybody I'd ever seen," recalls Howie Schultz:

> He could run like a deer, he had good power, and was a darn good fielder until he beat himself up in the outfield, running into walls and things, which shortened his career. I placed him right behind Musial during that time. Reiser had some of the skills that Musial didn't have, such as his ability to run.

With Reiser out of commission, the Dodgers were left to ponder their fate. "Hey, it was a loss," says Ed Stevens. "Anytime you lose a fellow like that — he could steal bases, make things happen, well it hurts."

On August 11, pennant race pressure and the loss of Reiser were preying on the mind of Leo Durocher. During what would turn out to be a doubleheader shellacking by the Phillies, the Dodger manager nearly came to blows with home plate umpire George Magerkurth over a called third strike to Eddie Stanky. Durocher was restrained by his team before he could reach the umpire, but Magerkurth ejected Durocher, Stanky, Ralph Branca, and Hank Behrman from the contest. When razzing from the Dodger dugout continued after the incident, Magerkurth ordered that the entire Brooklyn bench be cleared. To add insult to injury, news of the Cardinals' doubleheader sweep of Cincinnati was posted on the Philadelphia scoreboard just as Durocher and his team left the field. The Brooklyn lead was now just a half game.

Following Durocher's latest escapade, the guessing game around the league wasn't whether Durocher would be suspended but for how long. As the architect of the Dodgers' sudden success, the feeling in Brooklyn was that a long suspension would surely doom the club's chances. While chatting with reporters on Tuesday, August 13, Durocher was handed a telegram from National League president Ford Frick. The room fell quiet as Durocher opened the message. The Dodger manager read the telegram in silence, looked up at the reporters without saying anything, then read the contents again.

"Is it from Frick?" a reporter ventured.

"Yes, it's from Frick," Durocher responded.

"What about?"

"I can't tell you."

"Why not?"

"Because it's confidential."

"Were you fined?"

"Can't say."

At that moment, another writer walked into Durocher's office and informed his colleagues that he'd just spoken with Frick and been told that Durocher had been "heavily fined" for his near-brawl with Magerkurth three days earlier, but there would be no suspension. Rocking back in his chair, Durocher exhaled deeply. With that issue settled, he could return his thoughts to the simmering National League pennant race.

While controversy was swirling around Durocher and the Dodgers, the Cardinals were tending to business. In mid-August, Musial, Slaughter, and Kurowski were hitting the cover off the ball, and Brazle, Pollet, and Brecheen were racking up victory after victory. On August 12, the Redbirds, paced by Musial's torrid bat, won their fifth straight game to stay within a half game of the Dodgers. Musial, who'd connected for his 12th hit in 14 at-bats during the game, was talking to reporters in a jovial Cardinal clubhouse. Straining to be heard over a portable phonograph that was grinding out rumba music, Musial said, "Yeah, 12 hits in 14 trips is pretty hot for two days. But what really counts is now we're playing the kind of ball we're capable of. This team is starting to gel."

"We didn't worry about any particular team." Enos Slaughter says today:

> I think in baseball, the bottom team can knock off the top team as well as vice versa. You can't set up for one team and not set up for the other. You've got to be ready to play everyday. And that's what the '46 Cardinals did.

Seasoned professionals, the Cardinals were close on the field but rarely saw each other socially. "It was kind of a clique-ish team," remembers Marty Marion:

> We had two cliques: the "good boys," those of us that went to the movies a lot, which Harry Walker, Pollet, myself, and a few others belonged to. And the "bad boys," who were the card players. They played cards all the time. We traveled by train a lot, and card playing was a big thing to kill time. It's a funny thing about a baseball team. You have a situation usually when you come to the ballpark you have a camaraderie where you kind of depend on other guys on the team. They'd help you out and you'd help them out. But once [we left] the field, we hardly ever saw each other. I hardly ever saw Musial or Schoendienst. They're great friends of mine, but I hardly ever saw them.

In late August, the Dodgers and the Cardinals met in St. Louis for a crucial four-game series. With the two teams in a flat-footed tie for first place, all four games had long since sold out, and ticket scalpers were scoring heavily prior to each game. The two teams would face off in a doubleheader on Sunday, with single games on subsequent days.

On Sunday, August 25, Hank Behrman outdueled Howie Pollet as the Dodgers won 3–2. The nightcap proved to be a three-hour nightmare for Brooklyn as the Cardinals batted around in the sixth inning and rang up a total of 14 runs. On Monday, Murry Dickson mesmerized the Dodgers with a baffling array of off-speed stuff, and the Cardinals won 2–1. "You talk about a pitcher," says Marty Marion of Dickson:

> If he got two strikes on anybody, you didn't have to worry about a thing until it got to three and two. He was always going to go to 3–2 before anything happened. He made me so mad playing back of him. He never got any quick outs. You like a pitcher that keeps you on your toes and ready to move, and not on your heels. But Murry was a very successful little pitcher, and a good athlete too.

Dickson's victory boosted the Cardinals into first place by one game over the Dodgers, but on Tuesday, Kirby Higbe outdueled Harry Brecheen, 7–3. Over four bruising games the two clubs had battled to a draw, and the National League pennant race remained deadlocked.

Over the next three days, a crippling series of one-run losses to the Cubs and Giants combined to drop the Dodgers 2½ games behind St. Louis. With just over three weeks to play, Brooklyn's shot at the National League pennant was fading with the summer light. On Sunday, September 1, reporters gathered around Durocher following a tough 2–1 loss to the Giants that had left his club searching for answers.

"These are the most important days of the season for you, Leo," a reporter said. "They can turn the whole race topsy-turvy."

"They're just days to me. I take each one as it comes," Durocher snapped in response. "Look," he continued, "when I was with the Cardinals in 1934, the Giants had something like a seven-game lead on us on Labor Day. And we caught them."

Overhearing Durocher's response was Dodger right fielder Dixie Walker, who had just entered the office. "There's nothing wrong with us," he said, making his way through the crowd of writers, "that an old-fashioned Dodger winning streak couldn't cure."

As it turns out, an "old-fashioned Dodger winning streak" was just around the corner. After splitting a doubleheader with the Phillies on Monday, September 2, the Dodgers got hot, winning eight of their next ten. Just as hot was St. Louis, which matched Brooklyn win for win during the stretch. By the time the two teams squared off for a critical three-game series in mid-September, the Cardinals were clinging to a scant 1½-game lead over the Dodgers.

On September 12, more than 31,000 fans elbowed their way into Ebbets Field to witness the showdown between the two bitter rivals. Upstairs, the tiny press box was straining at the seams as more than 100 sportswriters from around the country were on hand to keep the nation updated on the sizzling National League pennant race.

In game one, the Cardinals went on the attack in the first inning. After retiring the first two hitters he faced, Kirby Higbe surrendered a double to Musial, then walked Slaughter on four consecutive pitches. The next hitter was Whitey Kurowski, who topped a ball that skittered toward third base, just out of Lavagetto's reach. With the bases juiced, Dick Sisler ripped a single off of Ed Stevens' glove that drove home two runs. Higbe only made matters worse for himself when he hung a curve ball to Joe Garagiola that the catcher hammered into the bleachers for a three-run homer. The seats weren't even warm yet, and the Cardinals had already staked themselves to a comfortable 5–0 lead.

The Redbirds drove Higbe to cover in the third, then proceeded to pummel a succession of Dodger pitchers for five additional runs over the next seven innings. When the dust cleared, the Cardinals had tallied ten runs to just two for Brooklyn. On Friday, Brooklyn responded in kind, jumping all over Cardinal starter Red Munger in the first inning for four runs. Over the ensuing innings, however, Cardinal batters pecked away at Vic Lombardi, until by the seventh, the score stood 4–3. Yesterday's goat, Kirby Higbe, was summoned in relief by Durocher, and he shut the Redbirds down over the final frames. Brooklyn's joy over the big win was tempered by yet another injury to the jinxed Pete Reiser, who pulled a hamstring running out a base hit.

For game three on Saturday, Leo Durocher surprised fans in Brooklyn when he announced that Ralph Branca would start. After a particularly nasty contract dispute with Branch Rickey prior to the season, Branca had fallen into disfavor with the club and had been relegated to mop-up relief. The irregular work cost Branca his rhythm, and before long, he began to experience a series of minor injuries. To many, Branca's relative anonymity during 1946 made him an unlikely choice to start Brooklyn's biggest game of the year, but in truth, Durocher had an ace up his sleeve. The Dodger manager, in an effort to decoy Eddie Dyer, was using Branca as a shill. After Dyer finished packing his lineup with left-handed hitters to face Branca, Durocher planned to lift his right-hander from the game during the first inning and insert lefty Vic Lombardi.

Already stewing at the way he'd been treated during the season, this latest development proved to be the last straw for Branca. The big righty walked resolutely to the mound in the first inning and retired the first three Redbird hitters to face him on just five pitches. Impressed by Branca's performance, Durocher decided to give the righty one more inning. In the second, Branca was no less powerful. Inning after inning rolled by, and by the time the game ended, Branca had yielded just three hits and no runs as the Dodgers coasted, 5–0. With only 16 games left on its schedule, Brooklyn was just a half game away from first place.

The tough losses to Brooklyn might have broken the spirits of some teams, but not the St. Louis Cardinals. On Sunday, September 15, the Redbirds rallied behind the stellar pitching of Murry Dickson and Al Brazle to sweep a doubleheader from the Giants. Back in Brooklyn, the Dodgers could only manage a split of their twin bill against the Cubs. Game two was called after the sixth inning with the Dodgers leading 2–0 when a swarm of insects descended on the stands and the field, turning players and spectators alike into a dodging, swatting throng.

On September 21, the Dodgers turned up the heat on St. Louis when they hammered Warren Spahn and the Braves for a 6–2 victory. In a tense, dramatic struggle against the Cubs at Wrigley Field, St. Louis rallied in the ninth inning to steal a 2–1 victory from Chicago. Speaking to reporters following the game, Eddie Dyer was optimistic: "That was a tough one. But we've got five left to play, and we're in first place. As long as we take care of business and not worry what the other guy is doing, we'll be all right."

The following day, the Cubs proved just how fickle baseball fate can be. With 20-game winner Howie Pollet on the mound, the Cardinals were heavily favored to widen their league lead. But a three-run homer by Bob Sturgeon in the sixth inning opened the floodgates, and the Cubs pushed across another four runs to defeat St. Louis 7–2. For the Dodgers, a split of a doubleheader with Boston enabled them to again climb to within a half game of the Cardinals.

On Tuesday, September 23, National League president Ford Frick, with Leo Durocher at his side, placed a phone call to Cardinal president Sam Breadon. The task at hand was unprecedented: to establish a playoff plan in the unlikely event that Brooklyn and St. Louis ended the 1946 season in a tie for first place. Frick and baseball commissioner Happy Chandler had already determined that the two clubs would vie in a best-of-three series for the pennant. Now a coin flip would determine in which city the series would begin.

"In the 70-year history of the National League, we've never had two teams tie for the pennant," Frick said in his statement to the press. "But

whatever the likelihood, we've got to make arrangements just in case."
With Breadon on the phone, Frick flipped the coin. Breadon called,
"Heads." The coin came down tails.

"Leo won the flip of the coin," remembers Marty Marion. "And he
elected to start the series on the road, figuring that even if his club dropped
the first game, they'd be home for the deciding two."

With the Cardinals and the Dodgers separated by just a half game and
the season winding down, the fiery National League pennant race was now
the talk of baseball. An article that appeared in the Tuesday, September
24, edition of the *New York Times* provides a glimpse of the fervor that
was gripping fans in Brooklyn:

MINISTER ASKS PRAYERS FOR SUCCESS OF DODGERS

The Rev. Benney J. C. Benson, chaplain of the Kings County American Legion
Posts, yesterday called upon the people of Brooklyn to observe a minute of
prayer at noon each day this week for the success of the National League
pennant-chasing Dodgers.

"We've prayed for military victories and everything else, so why not pray
for the Dodgers?" said the Rev. Mr. Benson. The Rev. Mr. Benson said he
would ask John Cashmore, Borough President of Brooklyn, today to conduct brief public mass meetings on the Borough Hall steps at noon each day
until the Dodgers are "in."

Whether providence was a baseball fan, much less a Brooklyn Dodgers
fan, remained unresolved after both the Dodgers and the Cardinals won
their games on Monday. The Dodgers knocked off the Phillies 6–1 behind
clutch hitting by Dixie Walker. In Chicago, the Cardinals behind Harry
Brecheen outlasted the Cubs 1–0. Brecheen, nicknamed "The Cat" because
of his unique on-field presence, turned back one Chicago charge after
another and also drove in the only Cardinal run with a single in the third,
which scored Joe Garagiola. A key fielding play by Brecheen in the third
slammed the door on a potential Chicago rally.

"They didn't call this guy 'The Cat' for nothing," recalls Marty Marion. "He got his nickname in the minor leagues. He looked kind of like a
cat out there. He kind of sneaked around, he looked like he was crouch-
ing all the time. And he was quick, quick as a cat."

If Brecheen possessed nine lives, then so did the Cardinals. The win
had been a close call, but somehow they'd survived. Now with just five
games remaining, their tenuous half-game advantage over Brooklyn
remained intact. On Tuesday, a persistent downpour postponed the scheduled contest between the Phillies and the Dodgers at Ebbets Field. The
game was rescheduled for Wednesday, originally an off day for both clubs.

Quick as a feline, Harry Brecheen was known as "The Cat." With Howie Pollet and Murray Dickson as teammates, it's no wonder that the Cardinal pitching staff gave opposing hitters fits during 1946. (National Baseball Hall of Fame Library, Cooperstown, N.Y.)

While posing for photographers at the edge of muddy Ebbets Field, Durocher responded to a question about his pitching plans for the season's final days:

> Plans? After tomorrow when we have only three games and you want to know my pitching plans? Look, brother! I've got 11 pitchers, and my plans include all of 'em. First we gotta win tomorrow's game, then I'll decide when we get to the next game and the next one.

Meanwhile in St. Louis, the Cardinals were electrifying their fans with yet another come-from-behind victory. Trailing 1–0 in the bottom of the ninth after being held to two singles by Johnny VanderMeer during the first eight innings, St. Louis parlayed a walk, a sacrifice, and a single by Stan Musial into a tie game. In the 10th, with thousands of Cardinal fans screaming his name, Erv Dusak ripped a home run into the left-field bleachers for the win. More heroics from a club that refused to quit.

On Wednesday, Brooklyn was three outs away from nailing down a crucial victory against the Phillies when the Dodger bullpen flamed out, surrendering five runs and sending the club down to a crushing 11–9 loss. Following the game, the only sound in the tomb-like dressing room was a portable radio in the corner carrying updates from the Cardinals-Reds game in St. Louis. There was a collective sigh of relief when the final score — Cincinnati 6, St. Louis 0 — was announced, but the afternoon's devastating defeat had prevented the Dodgers from gaining ground on the Cardinals. The St. Louis lead remained at one game over Brooklyn.

Thursday, September 26, was an off day for the Cardinals. Eddie Dyer, wanting to keep his team sharp, had initially announced a mandatory workout for that afternoon at Sportsman's Park, but after conferring with his coaches he reconsidered, telling his team to "stay home and relax tomorrow." Easy to say, not so easy to accomplish; the Cardinal manager knew that Thursday would prove to be a restless day for his players.

In Brooklyn, the Dodgers prepared to square off against the Phillies. While the St. Louis radio stations carried no play-by-play broadcasts of the game, many stations were providing fans with regular updates every 15 minutes. Back in Brooklyn, Pete Reiser was approached by Durocher prior to his club's game against the Phillies. "How's it feel?" Durocher asked Reiser, referring to the outfielder's injured hamstring. "I can play, but I can't run" was the reply. For Durocher, that was good enough; Reiser at 50 percent was still better than most players at 100 percent.

Unfortunately, Durocher's decision to start Reiser would backfire with tragic results. In the first inning, Reiser reached first on a walk, then was amazed to see Durocher flash the steal sign for the next play. Nursing his wounded leg, Reiser took a cautious lead, then was driven back to the bag when Philly starter Charlie Schanz attempted a pickoff. Straining to reach the base with his right leg, Reiser's spike snagged the hard clay of the infield dirt, and his ankle snapped. Durocher ran onto the field to check on his star. "Get up," Durocher said. "You're all right." "Not this time, Skip," Reiser replied. "It's broke." It wasn't until Reiser was back in the dressing room and his uniform was removed that the severity of the injury was evident. The outfielder's fibula was shattered, and the splintered bone was protruding through the skin.

When play resumed, Brooklyn exploded for eight runs, and Kirby Higbe, pitching with a detached coolness, shut down the Philly bats to win his 17th game. It was the Dodgers' biggest win of the year and lifted the club to within a half game of the idle Cards. Now, with just three games left in the season, the tally sheet showed both clubs dead even with 95 victories, with St. Louis one game up in the loss column.

On Friday, September 27, a dog-tired Howie Pollet was ambushed by the Cubs at Sportsman's Park. The Redbirds, who'd held first place since August 28, suddenly found themselves in a flat-footed tie with the idle Dodgers with two games left to play.

On the season's penultimate day, 31,699 fans squeezed themselves into Ebbets Field for an afternoon game against the Braves. Planting themselves wherever they could find space, the overflow crowd was on hand to watch the Dodgers edge closer to what once seemed unattainable: the 1946 National League pennant. The locals wasted little time against 20-game winner Johnny Sain, parlaying three walks, a wild pitch, and a double into three first-inning runs. Before they were done, they added four more runs, and Joe Hatten, who went the distance for his 14th win, made them stand up. Following the game, Durocher was ebullient: "We've caught 'em. In fact, after today's game, we've passed 'em! Let 'em catch us tonight if they can!"

That night, behind the four-hit pitching of Harry Brecheen, the Cardinals did just that. Powered by the bats of Stan Musial and Terry Moore, St. Louis overcame Chicago, 4–1, to remain deadlocked with Brooklyn. "Hey, we're not done with this thing yet," Eddie Dyer told the press following the game. "It's going down to the wire. Brecheen saw to that tonight. What a great game he pitched. It'll be Munger tomorrow and maybe Murry Dickson too," Dyer said, responding to questions regarding who would start for the team on Sunday. "I'll use whoever I need to nail this thing down."

On September 29, 153 games of hard-fought baseball all boiled down to this for the Dodgers: zero runs, four hits, one error. In a masterful performance, Mort Cooper of the Braves thoroughly handcuffed the Brooklyn hitters as his teammates tallied four runs against Vic Lombardi. The gloom shrouding Ebbets Field over the day's events lifted only when word filtered in that the Cubs, who'd fallen behind early, were rallying against the Cardinals.

Back in the Brooklyn clubhouse, a tired group of Dodgers waited for updates from St. Louis. "What's the inning?" Pee Wee Reese shouted to anyone within earshot. When told it was the eighth and the score stood 8–3 in favor of the Cubs, Reese said, "Good, I've got time to shave," and disappeared into the shower. Then the announcement came; it was all over in St. Louis. The Cubs had defeated the Cardinals.

When the final out was recorded, Durocher slumped into a chair to speak with reporters. Because his team had backed into a tie for the pennant, Durocher displayed the relief of one who'd felt the trapdoor give way beneath his feet only to have the rope around his neck snap a second later. "We could have gone up there the rest of the night and not scored off of Cooper," Leo told the writers. "He showed the mark of a champion. Now we take tomorrow off, then we're in St. Louis for the playoff. Then we'll see what happens." For the first time in baseball history, two teams would battle beyond the season's final day for the right to represent their league in the World Series.

GAME ONE—TUESDAY, OCTOBER 1, 1946

On Monday, Leo Durocher surprised virtually everyone when he announced that Ralph Branca would start game one against St. Louis. In truth, Durocher had little choice in the matter. Lombardi and Higbe had pitched on Sunday, and Branca, the most rested member of the Brooklyn staff, had looked sharp in his previous two outings. Durocher was banking on the big right-hander holding his own against Pollet in game one; then he'd have Higbe, Lombardi, and Hatten ready when the club returned to Brooklyn.

Pitting the young, inexperienced Branca against the seasoned Pollet wasn't the fool's game that it might appear to be at first glance. Pollet had been the Cardinal workhorse all season, and by late summer, he was beginning to show signs of wearing out. Durocher knew that Pollet's pitches lacked the zip they'd had earlier in the season and was betting that his Dodgers would be able to break through against the veteran.

As he ascended the mound to face Brooklyn, Pollet twisted his torso first left, then right, testing the pain in his back. A few days earlier, Pollet had pulled a muscle in his lower back, and initial reports from the

Cardinal trainer had suggested that he might be done for the season. But the big left-hander had approached Eddie Dyer following the team's loss on Sunday and told him he was ready to go. "He told me he could go," Dyer said later, "so I said OK." Nonetheless, Dyer had his entire pitching staff on call, just in case. With the exception of Murry Dickson, who was scheduled to start game two in Brooklyn, no one would be spared today.

Pollet, fighting back pain and working with subpar stuff, managed to hold the Dodgers scoreless through the first two innings. In the bottom of the first, Branca, also working with below-average stuff, struck out Schoendienst, then yielded a single to Terry Moore. Ralph then fanned Musial looking, but Slaughter was able to roll a single past Stanky at second, which sent Moore to third. Striving to be too fine, Branca then walked Kurowski to load the bases. The next hitter was Garagiola, who chopped a bounder over the head of Branca that Reese gloved too late to cut down Moore at the plate. Branca retired the side without further damage, but the Cardinals were on the scoreboard with a run.

In the Brooklyn half of the third inning, Pollet was desperately trying to protect the Cardinals' slim lead when Howie Schultz belted his first offering into the left-field bleachers for a home run. "I remember it very well," says Schultz. "That was the first home run ever hit in a playoff game, and I hit it off of Pollet." The score was now deadlocked, 1–1. In the bottom of the third, St. Louis drove Branca to cover when three hits and a walk accounted for two runs, making the score 3–1.

In the fifth, Pollet, fighting his control, surrendered a pair of singles and then yielded a walk to load the bases. But with one out, he induced Stanky to hit into a double play, killing the Brooklyn rally. In the top of the seventh, the Dodgers threatened again when Reese and Edwards singled. Coming to the plate was Howie Schultz, who promptly lined a base hit to right field, scoring Reese. Following the path of the ball from the third-base coaching box was Charlie Dressen. Aware of Slaughter's rifle arm, but liking the odds anyway, Dressen waved Edwards toward third. Fielding the ball cleanly was Slaughter, who promptly gunned a strike to Kurowski to cut down Edwards and snuff out the Brooklyn rally. "That was probably the key play in the ballgame," says Schultz. "It took us out of a possible really big inning. That day was a big highlight in my career, but you lose the game and it kind of gets watered down a little bit." Now, instead of having men on second and third with one out, Brooklyn had a man on second with two out. When Pollet retired Bob Ramazzotti, the threat was erased.

In the seventh, Stan Musial, facing Vic Lombardi, who was pitching in relief, tripled. With two outs and Melton now on the mound for Brooklyn, Joe Garagiola singled to bring Musial home with a key insurance run for St. Louis. In the eighth, the Dodgers again tried to rally against a shaky Pollet when Stanky led off with a walk. With one out, Medwick singled to right, with Stanky holding at first rather than challenging Slaughter's arm. But Pollet settled down, retiring Dixie Walker and Carl Furillo. The Cardinals then shut down the Dodgers the rest of the way. Pollet's victory, all the more impressive given the circumstances, was his 21st of the season.

Back in the clubhouse, Eddie Dyer was touting his big left-hander's performance to anyone within earshot. "The boy's heart is bigger and better than his arm's been all season," he shouted above the clubhouse din:

> He didn't have a whole lot of stuff, and he was in trouble a lot of times, but he came through and the boys behind him came through. Now I'll throw Murry Dickson or Harry Brecheen at them Thursday. I can't say right now who it will be. I want to talk to the boys first and decide which one is ready, because we're after two straight now. It's not over yet, it's still a tough fight. But we have the jump and that means a lot.

Pollet sat in front of his locker, his arm wrapped in ice. "I was bothered a bit by the muscles in my back," he told the writers gathered around him. "I didn't have too much stuff to start with, and it seemed every time I looked up there were men on base to make it tougher."

At 4:45 PM on Wednesday, the Dodgers arrived back in Brooklyn after detraining at Penn Station. Observers, recalling the surging, pushing, shouting throng that had greeted the club following their pennant-clinching victory of five years earlier, were surprised at the small crowd of well-wishers on hand to greet the team. "It looks like the borough has thrown in the towel," one Dodger veteran was overheard to remark, as he left the train and greeted his wife. One of the first off the train was Leo Durocher, resplendent in suit, handkerchief, and spotted tie. To the fans gathered to greet the team, Durocher was every inch the optimist. "We'll get 'em tomorrow," Leo said, moving through the crowd to his car. "Watch and see."

Meanwhile, in Boston, Joe Cronin, manager of the American League champion Red Sox, was fuming over the delay of the World Series triggered by the pennant deadlock in the National League. Cronin, angered by an injury suffered by Ted Williams in an exhibition game with a group of American League All-Stars on Wednesday, suggested that any future pennant playoffs be decided by just one game.

"If Brooklyn and St. Louis were not going through this best-of-three playoff this week, we wouldn't have had to play any exhibition games to keep in trim," Cronin said. "And if there had been no exhibition games,

Ted would not have been hurt needlessly." Cronin suggested that it was time to implement a uniform playoff system and suggested that a single-game format be adopted.

GAME TWO—THURSDAY, OCTOBER 3, 1946

By Thursday, a World Series atmosphere had settled over Ebbets Field. Eyeing the crowd of sportswriters that was swarming the field, Eddie Dyer said, "By the time all this is over, I'll either blow my top, go completely crazy, or else I'll become a better manager." Standing beside him in the Cardinal dugout, sporting a broad, white cowboy hat was Dizzy Dean. Now a broadcaster for St. Louis, Dean was badgering Cardinal players for interviews and, during commercial breaks, announcing to everyone within earshot that the Cardinals were a cinch for the National League pennant.

In the Dodger dugout, Bruce Edwards was going over the signs with Brooklyn starter Joe Hatten. Behind them, Pee Wee Reese was moving among his teammates, emphasizing the importance of getting to Cardinal starter Murry Dickson early. Reese, a man whose maturity and character belied his 28 years, had over the past three years emerged as Brooklyn's undisputed team leader. "Pee Wee was a class act and a critical component of our club," recalls Howie Schultz. "A pretty darn good hitter. You know, everybody thought Marty Marion was the better shortstop, but I would tend to compare them very favorably. Just a class guy. Everybody loved him, he was that kind of a guy."

Under a cloudless fall sky in Brooklyn, Joe Hatten set the Cardinals down without incident in the first inning. In the bottom of the first, Murry Dickson retired Stanky and Whitman on routine outs but Augie Galan beat out an infield hit. After issuing a base on balls to Walker, Dickson surrendered a single to Ed Stevens, which scored Galan. Dickson retired the next hitter without incident, but the admonitions of Reese to his teammates just minutes earlier appeared to have paid off. Brooklyn had drawn first blood.

Unfortunately for the Dodgers, the Cardinals would prove to have Joe Hatten's number on this day. With one out in the second inning, Erv Dusak hammered a Hatten fastball to left field that Whitman appeared to catch but dropped when he collided with the left-field wall. On the play, Dusak steamed all the way to third. The next hitter was Marty Marion, who lifted a fly ball to Furillo in right that was deep enough to score Dusak with the tying run. Clyde Kluttz then raked a single to center field to keep the inning alive. The next hitter was the pitcher, Murry Dickson, who promptly laced a Hatten offering into right center for a triple, scoring

Kluttz on the play. Hatten was able to snuff out the Cardinal rally, but the score now stood at 2–1 in favor of St. Louis.

Dickson, so shaky in the first inning, settled down in the second and after walking Edwards, proceeded to retire the next eight Dodgers to face him. Dickson and Hatten dueled until the fifth, when Hatten, who had retired the first two Cardinal batters, surrendered a double to Stan Musial. With the dangerous Kurowski on deck, Edwards and Hatten glanced over to the Brooklyn dugout to see Leo Durocher holding up four fingers. After intentionally walking Kurowski, Hatten prepared to face Enos Slaughter. "I'll never forget what happened next," Slaughter remembers. "Musial's on third, and they walk Kurowski to pitch to me. And I got a pitch I could handle, and I tripled to right center and we scored two runs." A single by Dusak scored Slaughter, and the rout was on. Durocher yanked Hatten for Hank Behrman, who finally retired the Redbirds. The score was now 5–1.

In the seventh, the onslaught continued. Lombardi, now pitching for Brooklyn, walked Kurowski and Slaughter. After Dusak sacrificed the runners to second and third, Durocher lifted Lombardi and waved Kirby Higbe in from the bullpen. After completing his warmups, Higbe toed the rubber to face Marion. When Kurowski bolted from third, steaming full-tilt for the plate, the Dodgers realized that the squeeze was on. Marion deftly bunted Higbe's pitch between the mound and first base, making any attempt at cutting down Whitey at the plate impossible. After Higbe retired the side, the St. Louis lead stood at 6–1.

Meanwhile, Dickson continued to mow down Dodger hitters with impunity. Facing a mixture of off-speed pitches and the occasional fastball, Brooklyn hitters were a picture of futility. The spectacle was so distressing for Brooklyn fans that a mass exodus from Ebbets Field took place following the bottom of the seventh inning. In the eighth, the Cardinals pushed across two more runs on hits by Schoendienst, Moore, and Kurowski, raising their run total to eight.

In the bottom of the ninth, Brooklyn, which had been bucking the odds all year long, attempted another miracle. After Galan doubled to right, Ed Stevens tripled to center, scoring Galan. After Furillo singled, Dickson walked Reese. Eddie Dyer, realizing that Dickson was rapidly losing steam, signaled for Brecheen from the bullpen. Edwards greeted the pitcher with a single to left, driving in Furillo with the Dodgers' third run of the inning. The next hitter was Lavagetto, who drew a base on balls. With the bases loaded and one out, the Dodgers had the tying run at the plate in the person of Eddie Stanky. But Brooklyn's charge tapped out just short of its goal; Stanky, after battling Brecheen on every pitch, took a called third strike. When Schultz struck out on a letup, the 1946 pennant at long last belonged to the Cardinals.

At home in St. Louis, pandemonium reigned. Fans whose hopes had cascaded, then ebbed when Dickson faltered in the ninth, celebrated with relief all over the city. Downtown, department store public address systems carried the news to shoppers, and in the streets outside, cabbies sounded their horns. In the office of Cardinal president Sam Breadon, the portable radio that had carried the news of the Cardinals' victory was drowned out by shouts of "Bring on the Red Sox!"

Following the final out in Brooklyn, the Cardinals celebrated at midfield, then broke for their dressing room. Amid the tumult of the winning clubhouse, Eddie Dyer spoke of Brooklyn's gutsy campaign for the pennant. "No one club has a monopoly on courage, and the Dodgers certainly proved that today in the ninth inning," Dyer said. Behind him, less charitable sentiments were heard above the din of the clubhouse. "There will be no joy in Flatbush tonight!" screamed Joe Garagiola, who was waltzing from locker to locker, dousing his teammates with champagne.

"It was a terrible loss for us," Brooklyn first baseman Ed Stevens says today. "We felt we had a good shot at the pennant. But the Cardinals were a good, everyday, consistent ballclub."

When reporters and writers were granted admittance to the Dodger clubhouse, Leo Durocher was there to greet them. "I'm proud of every one of my boys," Durocher said. The funereal silence of the room provided a marked contrast to the wild celebration unfolding in the Cardinal clubhouse. "They hustled and gave everything they had from the first day," the Dodgers' skipper continued. "I'm proud of every guy on this club." Durocher then excused himself and took the long walk next door to congratulate Eddie Dyer and the Cardinals and wish them well against the Boston Red Sox in the World Series.

OCTOBER 1, 1946

BROOKLYN	AB	R	H	BI
Stanky 2b	3	0	1	0
Lavagetto 3b	3	0	0	0
Medwick lf	4	0	1	0
ªTepsic	0	0	0	0
Whitman lf	0	0	0	0
Walker rf	4	0	0	0
Furillo cf	4	0	0	0
Reese ss	4	1	2	0
Edwards c	4	0	2	0
Shultz 1b	3	1	2	2

BROOKLYN	AB	R	H	BI
Branca p	1	0	0	0
Higbe p	0	0	0	0
[b]Rojek	0	0	0	0
Gregg p	0	0	0	0
[c]Ramazzotti	1	0	0	0
Lombardi p	0	0	0	0
Melton p	0	0	0	0
Totals	31	2	8	2

[a]Ran for Medwick in 8th
[b]Batted for Higbe in 5th
[c]Batted for Gregg in 7th

ST. LOUIS	AB	R	H	BI
Schoendienst 2b	5	0	2	0
Moore cf	5	1	3	0
Musial 1b	4	2	1	0
Slaughter rf	4	0	2	0
Kurowski 3b	2	1	0	1
Garagiola c	4	0	3	2
Walker lf	3	0	1	1
Marion ss	4	0	0	0
Pollet p	4	0	0	0
Totals	35	4	12	4

Brooklyn	0 0 1	0 0 0	1 0 0	2
St. Louis	1 0 2	0 0 0	1 0 –	4

Triple: Musial
Home Run: Schultz

Brooklyn	IP	H	R	BB	SO
Branca (L)	2⅔	6	3	2	3
Higbe	1⅓	1	0	0	0
Gregg	2	1	0	1	1
Lombardi	⅓	1	1	0	0
Melton	1⅔	3	0	1	0

St. Louis	IP	H	R	BB	SO
Pollet (W)	9	8	2	3	3

OCTOBER 3, 1946

ST. LOUIS	AB	R	H	BI
Schoendienst 2b	5	1	1	0
Moore cf	5	1	2	0
Musial 1b	4	1	1	0

ST. LOUIS	AB	R	H	BI
Kurowski 3b	2	2	1	2
Slaughter rf	3	1	1	2
Dusak lf	3	1	2	1
Walker lf	1	0	0	0
Marion ss	3	0	1	2
Kluttz c	5	1	2	0
Dickson p	5	0	2	1
Brecheen p	0	0	0	0
Totals	36	8	13	8

BROOKLYN	AB	R	H	BI
Stanky 2b	5	0	0	0
Whitman lf	4	0	0	0
dShultz	1	0	0	0
Galan 3b	4	2	2	0
Walker rf	3	0	0	0
Stevens 1b	4	1	2	2
Furillo cf	4	1	1	1
Reese ss	2	0	0	0
Edwards c	2	0	1	1
Hatten p	1	1	0	0
Behrman p	0	0	0	0
aHermanski	1	0	0	0
Lombardi p	0	0	0	0
Higbe p	0	0	0	0
Melton p	0	0	0	0
bMedwick	1	0	0	0
Taylor p	0	0	0	0
cLavagetto	0	0	0	0
Totals	32	5	6	4

aBatted for Behrman in 5th
bBatted for Melton in 8th
cBatted for Taylor in 9th
dBatted for Whitman in 9th

St. Louis	0 2 0	0 3 0	1 2 0	8
Brooklyn	1 0 0	0 0 0	0 0 3	4

Doubles: Musial, Moore, Galan
Triples: Dusak, Dickson, Slaughter, Stevens

St. Louis	IP	H	R	BB	SO
Dickson (W)	8⅓	5	3	5	5
Brecheen	⅔	1	1	2	2

Brooklyn	IP	H	R	BB	SO
Hatten (L4)	⅔	7	5	3	0

Brooklyn	IP	H	R	BB	SO
Behrman	⅓	1	0	0	0
Lombardi	1⅓	1	1	2	0
Higbe	1	3	2	2	1
Melton	⅔	0	0	1	0
Taylor	1	1	0	1	1

2

1948: Cleveland Indians
vs. Boston Red Sox

If, as Emerson once noted, valor consists of the power of self-recovery, then the 1948 Cleveland Indians stand as one of the most valiant teams in baseball history. Written off for dead after a late-season swoon seemingly torpedoed their pennant hopes, the Indians bounced back to win the American League title in what many still regard as the most exciting pennant race in baseball history. From the first pitch of opening day to the moment of truth six months later in only the second sudden-death playoff in baseball history, the saga of the 1948 Cleveland Indians encompasses all the elements of a great story: suspense, tragedy, comedy, and even a dash of old-fashioned sleight of hand. Stir in a baseball visionary with the instincts of P. T. Barnum and a determined rival with dreams of its first world championship in over a quarter century, and the stage was set for one of baseball's most glorious seasons, the spring, summer, and fall of 1948.

In the quarter century prior to the 1948 season, not much had gone right for the Cleveland Indians. Between 1922 and 1948, the Tribe had seriously contended for the American League pennant just twice: in 1926, when it finished three games back of the first-place Yankees, and 14 years later, when a late season slump handed the pennant to Detroit. Hope quickened when 24-year-old *wunderkind* Lou Boudreau was named player-manager in 1942, but the wartime Indians continued to run in place, hovering around the .500 mark between 1942 and 1945.

Determined to change all this was Bill Veeck, Jr. As the owner of the Triple A Milwaukee Brewers of the American Association, Veeck had garnered a reputation as a promotional whiz kid. Veeck's approach to running a ballclub stemmed from a personal epiphany he experienced as a boy. As president of the Chicago Cubs, William Veeck, Sr., often had his son accompany him to work. One day during the summer of 1928, 11-year-old Bill Jr. watched as ticket sellers carted the day's receipts in and dumped them on the club secretary's desk. "You know, Bill," his father said to the young boy eyeing the pile of money in front of him. "It's a very interesting thing. You look at that money and it all looks exactly the same, doesn't it? You can't tell who put it into your box office. It's all exactly the same color, the same size, and the same shape. You remember that."

Veeck never forgot it. As a young man, Veeck served an apprenticeship with the Chicago Cubs, taking tickets and staffing the concession stands until he gradually worked his way up to the promotion department. In 1941, Veeck took his first step toward owning his own major league team when he purchased the minor league Brewers. The Brewers, probably the worst professional baseball team in America, continually lost money and played in a ramshackle ballpark that hadn't seen a fresh coat of paint in decades.

Veeck, armed with nothing more than youthful idealism and a stubborn belief that hard work could overcome any obstacle, was determined to transform the Brewers into winners and make money doing it. Veeck and a group of volunteers worked night and day to scrub the ballpark clean and then, with the season underway, launched a series of promotions designed to lure the local community back to the ballpark. Whether he was giving away live squabs to paying customers or sending his ballplayers into the stands playing musical instruments, nothing was too over the top for the Brewers' new owner. Soon, his efforts began to pay dividends as the once-recalcitrant Milwaukee fans packed the stands to see what outrageous new promotion Veeck would cook up next.

As a serviceman during World War II, Veeck sustained a serious injury to his leg and was forced to spend months recuperating in a military hospital. After being discharged in 1946, Veeck, in an effort to salvage his marriage, sold the Brewers and bought a dude ranch in Arizona. But it didn't take long for Veeck to realize that running a guest ranch wasn't his cup of tea; the solitude drove him crazy and horseback riding further inflamed his right leg, which was held together by bone grafts. Determined to return to baseball, Veeck ditched the dude ranch late in 1946 and entered into negotiations to buy the Cleveland Indians.

On June 22, 1946, Bill Veeck realized a lifetime dream when his offer to buy the Indians was accepted. Veeck's first task as owner was devising a way to somehow increase attendance at cavernous Municipal Stadium, which at 78,000, was by far the largest ballpark in the major leagues. Veeck knew that he had his work cut out for him; the Tribe was languishing in the standings and huge expanses of empty seats were the rule and not the exception at Indian home games.

Drawing on his experience with the Brewers, Veeck decided that a little old-fashioned, face-to-face politicking might help return the Indians to profitability. Shortly after taking over the club, Veeck visited towns throughout the state, trumpeting his new team to any civic or social group that would let him speak. At night, he carried his campaign into the bars and restaurants of Ohio, buying beers and talking baseball with anyone who would listen. Before his campaign was completed, Veeck had spoken in virtually every city in Ohio, averaging better than a speech a night. At times, Veeck became so emotionally charged from his travels and engagements that he'd be unable to sleep; often, he'd simply shower before heading off to the next city on his itinerary.

Huckster, visionary, and Renaissance man Bill Veeck fulfilled a lifelong dream when he entered the offices of the Cleveland Indians for the first time as the club's new owner. (*The Sporting News.*)

So active was Veeck during this period in his life that he occasionally found himself able to push worries regarding his diseased leg from his mind. Throughout 1946, the appendage had continued to decline and soon, a series of small amputations was required. "They'd take a piece off," a friend recalled later, "and the next day, he'd be at the game." Much of the time, Veeck's leg was openly infected and produced a nauseating smell. As Veeck himself put it, "The odor of decay seeping out of that cast would get so bad that I could have hired myself out to clear any room within 15 seconds." Always a people person, Veeck fretted about offending those around him and soon took to carrying small bottles of cologne in the pocket of his pants, which he applied to his leg whenever it became too pungent.

Veeck was a fighter, and bad leg or no bad leg, he would not be deterred from his goal of making the Indians profitable. Armed with his natural gift for promotion and with the proving ground of Milwaukee to guide him, Veeck pulled out all the stops in Cleveland. If he wasn't passing out orchids or giving away nylon stockings (in those days, orchids and stockings were considered luxuries), he was hiring a circus performer to hang by his heels and hit baseballs. One day, following a rainout at Municipal Stadium, Veeck spied a group of disconsolate fans at the Pennsylvania Railroad depot waiting for a ride home. Making a quick call to the Indians' clubhouse, Veeck arranged for Bob Feller and Lou Boudreau to meet and chat with the group until their train arrived. To placate residents who might be disturbed by the fireworks shows that were becoming commonplace at Municipal Stadium, Veeck initiated Good Neighbor Nights, admitting local home owners to the ballpark free of charge.

In his ongoing quest to increase attendance, Veeck also enlisted the aid of fireballing right-hander Bob Feller. Correctly figuring that a run at the all-time single-season strikeout record by Feller would trigger fan interest in 1946, Veeck asked the great pitcher if he would start every fourth day and remain in the game even if he were being hammered by the opposition. Feller agreed and broke the record on the season's final day, pitching with just two days' rest. During the same year, Feller racked up an amazing 26 victories for a club that won only 68 games all year. By season's end, Veeck's dog-and-pony show was yielding results. In 1946, the Indians drew a million fans for the first time in their history despite posting their worst record in 18 years.

When he wasn't devising clever ways to promote the Indians, Veeck worked on improving the product on the field. Disdaining the long view, the Cleveland owner was constantly on the lookout for players who would help his team contend in the shortest amount of time. Shortly after taking over the club, Veeck initiated a series of deals that proved critical to transforming the Indians into winners. Key among these was the trade he engineered in late 1946. While in New York to attend the World Series, Veeck bumped into Larry McPhail of the Yankees. During a short chat, Veeck discovered that McPhail was unhappy with Joe Gordon, the current Yankee second baseman. McPhail was so unhappy, in fact, that he was reported to have come to blows with the second sacker in the Yankee clubhouse late in the season. With Snuffy Stirnweiss waiting in the wings, McPhail was ready to unload Gordon for some pitching. Veeck, who had always liked Gordon, quickly engineered a deal that sent pitcher Allie Reynolds to the Yankees for the second baseman.

A year later, Veeck became the first American League owner to sign an African American when he brought Larry Doby up from the minor leagues. Veeck, whose plan of buying the Philadelphia Phillies and stocking it with black players in 1944 had run afoul of baseball commissioner Judge

Landis, was inundated with more than 20,000 letters protesting his actions. Like Jackie Robinson before him, Doby would encounter numerous episodes of racial prejudice once he arrived in the big leagues, but he would ultimately have the last laugh. While he didn't do much during his first year, he would soon blossom into one of the American League's premier power hitters.

With new players in the field and a newly energized fan base in the stands, the Tribe rebounded to an 80–74 record in 1947, a 12-game improvement over the year before. Equally impressive was the jump in attendance, up to 1,521,978, a dazzling figure for a fourth-place team. Things were looking up in Cleveland, but the Indians' owner had his sights set on a grander prize: the American League pennant. To Veeck, it was clear that the difference between pennant winners and also-rans was pitching. A year earlier, he had acquired knuckleballer Gene Bearden in a deal with the Yankees. As the throw-in on a trade with New York, Bearden hadn't attracted much attention in 1947, but Veeck believed the rookie was now ready to win at the big league level. Then, in a move to shore up his bullpen, Veeck engineered a deal with Connie Mack of the Philadelphia As for lanky relief pitcher Russ Christopher.

With his new pitchers on board, Veeck took stock of his club. The pitching staff was strong, with Feller and Lemon leading the way, Bearden showing improvement, and Christopher promising to bolster the bullpen. Veeck knew that the Indians lacked speed, but he believed that the club's strong defense could offset that handicap. Veeck was also confident that he had the game's best shortstop; what he didn't have, he believed, was the game's best manager. Unfortunately, both positions were being held by the same man, Lou Boudreau.

In 1941, 24-year-old Lou Boudreau had walked into the Cleveland front office and asked if he could manage the team. To the amazement of almost everyone, the Indians said yes. But in the war years of 1942 through 1945, the Indians languished under their youthful skipper. By the time he took over the club, Bill Veeck was determined to fire Boudreau and replace him with Casey Stengel, then managing the Oakland Oaks, a minor league franchise. In his first official act as Cleveland's owner, Veeck called Stengel and told him, "You can be vice president, or you can stay in the wings ready to take over as manager, or maybe we can work something out with Boudreau and you'll be able to take over as manager right away."

Stengel told Veeck that he had no stomach for standing over Boudreau's shoulder waiting for the young manager to fail. However, he would be interested in assuming the manager's job if it became available immediately. "If you can work it out so I come in as manager right away,"

Stengel told Veeck, "well, you know, there's still nothing like the big leagues.

Almost immediately, Veeck arranged to meet with Boudreau for dinner at his suite in the Cleveland Hotel. In the 24 hours since he'd assumed control over the club, Veeck had taken a couple of his friends in the press corps into his confidence, telling them of his plans for a managerial change. Newsmen being newsmen, it wasn't long before Veeck's plans were leaked, and the story hit Cleveland like a thunderbolt. In short order, the switchboard at Municipal Stadium was swamped with irate callers demanding that Veeck, not Boudreau, be fired. Realizing that he'd badly underestimated Boudreau's popularity with the Cleveland fans, Veeck immediately went to his fallback plan: he'd try to get Boudreau to step down voluntarily. Veeck understood the delicate nature of this new course of action. If he pushed his case too hard, the Cleveland owner was convinced that Boudreau would not only quit as manager but would also demand a trade.

By the time he arrived for his dinner with Veeck, Boudreau, buoyed by the overwhelming support of the Cleveland fans, was holding all the cards. During dinner, Veeck managed to guide the conversation toward a general discussion of how difficult it was for a ballplayer to also simultaneously manage. Players, Veeck told Boudreau, were at their best in the field when not distracted with thoughts of pitching changes or strategy, especially at so key a position as shortstop. "And you're the greatest shortstop I've ever seen," Veeck told Boudreau, piling it on. "It would be a shame, you know, if your duties as a manager diminished that."

Listening with cool detachment, Boudreau waited for Veeck to say his piece. When the Cleveland owner finally finished speaking, Boudreau played his hand. Sure, he agreed, managing and playing were difficult tasks to juggle. But only for some people. In his case, he found the challenge stimulating and didn't feel that it affected his play in the field at all. Outfoxed, Veeck relented, saying not another word on the subject through the rest of the meal. Finally, as dessert was being served, Veeck said to Boudreau, "Well, I want you to know that we certainly want you to stay on as manager. We've got all the confidence in the world in you, Louie, old boy."

But confidence was certainly one thing that Veeck did not have in Boudreau, and nothing he saw during the 1947 season did anything to change his mind. Particularly galling to the Cleveland owner was Boudreau's habit of relying on personal hunches and not on proven baseball strategy to guide his on-field actions. Often, when Veeck questioned Boudreau about a particular managerial move, Lou would reply, "The way we were going, we had to do something." Anger over the attempted firing of Boudreau may have subsided in Cleveland, but Veeck was not ready to challenge the Boudreau marching-and-chowder society again. He'd bide his time and wait for the right moment to rid himself of Boudreau.

As it turned out, Veeck didn't have long to wait. The club's fourth-place finish in 1947 had been an improvement over the year before, but given the club's talent, it was viewed by many as a disappointment. To Veeck's way of thinking, if finishing 17 games out of first place wasn't enough to convince the good people of Cleveland that Boudreau had to go, what would?

While in New York for the 1947 World Series between Brooklyn and New York, Veeck made his move. He decided to package Boudreau with outfielders George Metkovich and Dick Kokos plus $100,000 in cash and offer it to the Browns for shortstop Vern Stephens, pitchers Jack Kramer and Ellis Kinder, and outfielder Don Lehner. When St. Louis agreed in principle to the trade, Veeck called Al Lopez, Cleveland's backup catcher during the 1947 season, and instructed Lopez to meet him in one hour at the Savoy Plaza hotel, where he would be introduced to the press as the Indians' new manager.

As they often do, however, the proposed trade unraveled at the last moment when the Browns, balking over the cash amount, backed out of the deal. The press, which had already been alerted by Veeck that a deal was imminent, proceeded to break the story in Cleveland newspapers. In just hours, headlines appeared in dailies throughout Ohio, trumpeting Veeck's latest attempt to unload Boudreau.

The response of Cleveland fans to the news was rapid and vehement. Throughout Cleveland, petitions were circulated calling on Veeck to sell the team. One major daily printed a ballot on its front page for readers to fill out and return by mail. Before the newspaper stopped counting, more than 100,000 had been returned, most demanding Veeck's head on a platter. At the height of the maelstrom, a telegram was delivered to Veeck's room in New York. It read:

IF BOUDREAU DOESN'T RETURN TO CLEVELAND, DON'T YOU BOTHER TO RETURN EITHER.

The missive was signed by a local minister.

Following the debacle from New York, Veeck realized that his latest dump-Boudreau campaign had failed miserably. Shifting into damage control mode, the owner saw that the only recourse left to him was to accept his defeat graciously. Reluctantly departing New York before the end of the World Series, Veeck hopped a flight back to Ohio intent on throwing himself on the mercy of the Indians' fans. When word of Veeck's return hit Cleveland, a cadre of Boudreau supporters were on hand to meet him when his plane touched down. Unsure of how to handle the demonstration, Veeck finally climbed on top of a car and motioned the crowd to silence. "If I find that the people of this city are against trading Lou Boudreau, then you can be certain he won't be traded."

After placating the crowd at the airport, Veeck then detoured through downtown Cleveland. At Euclid and Ninth streets, he saw a throng of 3–4,000 people congregated in the street. Wading into the mob, Veeck yelled, "Was I wrong in trying to trade Boudreau?" The volume and vehemence of the reply left no doubt as to the crowd's loyalties. "I'm not going to trade him," Veeck told the crowd. "Because of his importance, as demonstrated here tonight, and because the fans in the last analysis run the ballclub, I am bowing to their will. I was stupid to even think about it."

Today, more than 50 years later, Bob Feller looks back at the controversy surrounding Boudreau and offers his own opinion:

> Veeck was wrong. Boudreau was a good manager. A much better player-manager than he was as a bench manager. Most bench managers make too many moves. The old saying goes, "If it works, don't fix it." Managers get paid to manage, and they're always fiddling. But all the players liked Boudreau. He was a loyal friend, a loyal manager. He stuck with me when I was struggling, saying, "We'll sink or swim with Feller," and that naturally made me feel good. Boudreau was a very fine manager.

In Cleveland, the latest Boudreau brouhaha finally blew over. Having bested Veeck for a second time in less than two years, Lou played his trump card prior to the start of the 1948 season. When Veeck offered Boudreau a one-year contract as player-manager of the Indians, the shortstop demurred, suggesting with feigned nonchalance that a two-year deal might be better. Over a barrel, Veeck acquiesced. On one issue, however, the Indians' owner held firm: the right to name Boudreau's coaches. If a plebiscite would force him to retain what he considered to be an inferior manager, Veeck at least wanted the right to pack Boudreau's coaching staff with the most experienced men available. After enlisting Boudreau's support, Veeck hired former Pirates manager Bill McKechnie and former great Indians center fielder Tris Speaker as coaches. With the highly regarded McKechnie on board as Boudreau's right-hand man, Veeck felt he'd done everything he could to ready his Indians for a run at the 1948 American League pennant.

As hard as it may be to believe today, there was a time in baseball history when world championships came with ridiculous ease to the Boston Red Sox. Between 1912 and 1918, the club won four, establishing a dominance over professional baseball that wouldn't be equaled for more than 20 years. The purchase of the club in 1916 by theatrical entrepreneur Harry

Frazee was viewed as a positive development at first, but when losses from failed theatrical ventures started piling up, Frazee began selling key Red Sox players for cash. For the team's fans, the final straw came in 1921 when Frazee peddled Babe Ruth to the New York Yankees. As a Yankee, Ruth would emerge as the game's premier slugger and gate attraction and, more than anyone else, be responsible for the Yankees' emergence as the American League's new powerhouse.

As New York's fortunes waxed, Boston's waned; between 1922 and 1932, the Yankees claimed four world championships while the Red Sox took a nose dive into the second division, finishing above last place only twice. The nadir came in 1932 when they lost an astonishing 111 games and finished 64 games behind the league-leading Yankees.

Riding to the rescue in 1933 was Tom Yawkey. With his family's wealth at his disposal, the new Red Sox owner was determined to restore the Sox to their former glory. An early attempt at reenergizing his club with fading stars fell flat, but a renewed focus on the club's farm system began to pay dividends almost immediately. Shortly, the arrival of players like Ted Williams, Bobby Doerr, and Tex Hughson signaled a new beginning for the long-struggling franchise. In 1938, the club increased its win total by eight games over the year before and jumped to second place. That's the way it stayed for the next four years as the improved Sox challenged for the pennant but always fell short of the dominant Yankees.

With most of Boston's young stars in the military between 1943 and 1945, Yawkey's campaign to rejuvenate his club was put on hold. In 1946, however, the Red Sox made Yawkey's dream a reality when the team nailed down its first pennant in more than a quarter century. During the year, the Sox put on an awesome offensive display as Williams, Doerr, and Dom DiMaggio pounded American League pitching. No less impressive was the pitching staff, which featured four starters in double figures, including rookie phenom Dave "Boo" Ferriss and Tex Hughson with 25 and 20, respectively. With a nucleus of young, exciting players and the deep pockets of the Yawkey family at the ready, a new Red Sox dynasty was in the offing.

But thoughts of domination would have to wait as the club fell victim to the injury bug in 1947. "See," Hall of Fame second baseman Bobby Doerr said,

> in '46 we had good pitching. Tex Hughson and Boo Ferriss were both 20-game winners. Along with Mickey Harris and Joe Dobson, we had pretty good pitching. And then Ferriss, Hughson, and Harris all got sore arms in 1947, so in '48, they practically had to build a new pitching staff. They got Jack Kramer, Ellis Kinder in a trade, [Mel] Parnell came up from the minors. But we didn't have the pitching we'd had in '46. If we'd had Hughson or

Ferriss, we'd have won in '48, '49, and '50. We'd have won three pennants, I'm sure.

Kramer and Kinder had come over in a deal with the Browns. In return, Yawkey offered nine inessential players and the then-princely sum of $400,000. Kramer had been the staff ace for the lowly St. Louis Browns and specialized in moving the ball around and changing speeds. Kinder was the throw-in on the deal; at 34 and with only 11 major league victories to his credit, he was better known around the league for his prodigious alcohol consumption than for his ability to retire opposing hitters. Also coming to the Red Sox as part of the deal with the Browns was Vern "Junior" Stephens, a slow-footed but power-hitting shortstop.

"Junior was a big man," Boo Ferriss remembers. "He was a power hitter that was made for Fenway. We had had a lot of respect for him when he played for the Browns."

Yawkey's attempts at bolstering his club didn't stop with the acquisition of Kramer and Kinder. Following the 1947 season, the owner announced that popular manager Joe Cronin, who had guided the Sox for the previous 11 years, was moving from the dugout to the front office. The new Red Sox manager would be the man who led the New York Yankees to eight pennants between 1931 and 1946, Joe McCarthy. Reserved and aloof, McCarthy was about as different from Joe Cronin as night was from day. Gruff, taciturn, and militant, McCarthy was a man who lived by rules and expected his players to do the same. Curfew violators, sloppiness, and card games ("a waste of time," according to McCarthy) were among his intense dislikes. As the manager of the Yankees, McCarthy once dressed down a player who had the temerity to have his hat on askew. "You're a Yankee," McCarthy told the player. "Act like one." McCarthy, a cigar smoker, also exhibited a strange antipathy toward pipe smokers.

"That's true," remembers Red Sox infielder Billy Hitchcock:

> I was a pipe smoker, unfortunately. I've told the story many times. We were on the Pullman, and I was in the men's room smoking a pipe. And this particular time, he stopped by for some reason and stuck his head in the men's room and said, "Hello, fellows, how you doing?" and I've got a pipe in my hand, just red-hot, burning a blister in my hand, but I was afraid to let go for fear of what he'd say. McCarthy did not like pipe smokers.

What McCarthy did like was a team that demonstrated grit and hustle, two traits that he found sorely lacking in the Red Sox. During spring training in 1948, McCarthy rode his players hard, drilling them hour after hour on fundamentals. Standing at his favorite spot at the foot of the dugout steps, working overtime on the ever-present chewing gum in his mouth, McCarthy would berate his players to a degree never experienced by the

Sox under Cronin. Some, like shortstop Vern Stephens, became particular targets of the manager's ire and grew resentful.

"I think McCarthy was probably a little tough on Vern because of the great ability and talent that he had," remembers Billy Hitchcock. "He wanted to get 100 percent out of him all the time. Stephens was a hard-nosed guy, and McCarthy wanted him to give his best all the time."

It's also likely that McCarthy disapproved of Stephens' extracurricular activities. One of the game's true carousers, Stephens was constantly on the town following Red Sox games in search of female companionship. "I roomed mostly with his suitcase," a former teammate once observed. As a member of the Browns in 1945, Stephens' prodigious appetite for female company had caught the eye of the team's owner. Concerned that Stephens' nocturnal sojourns were affecting his performance, he asked the shortstop to stay in at night and take better care of himself. Stephens did as he was asked, and over the next three weeks, his batting average nose dived. Alarmed, the owner again approached Stephens. "Go out and stay out," he told him. Stephens complied, and in short order, his average improved.

Stephens wasn't the only Red Sox player to incur McCarthy's enmity. His handling of Tex Hughson also illustrates how difficult it must have been to play under the Red Sox manager. Hughson was a country boy who, between the years of 1942 and 1946, was one of the American League's top pitchers, winning 72 and losing only 37. In 1947 he began suffering from acute pain in his right arm; a series of medical exams showed that an overdeveloped muscle was cutting off the circulation to the appendage. After undergoing surgery to remove a portion of the muscle, Hughson rejoined the team in 1948. "Tex," McCarthy said to the pitcher when he arrived, "can you help the team?" "Yes, if I'm used right," was Hughson's reply.

Suspicious by nature of pitchers and of Hughson in particular, McCarthy immediately pegged Tex as just another coddled Red Sox player. Finding himself unable to communicate with McCarthy, Hughson took his case to Boston pitching coach Larry Weddell. "You can't get me up, let me throw, sit me down for a few innings, and then get me up again. I'm not a troublemaker, but I can't do it," he told Weddell. Carrying the gist of his conversation with Hughson back to McCarthy, the manager exploded, "Fuck him. He's not going to help anyway."

Equally unnerving to the Red Sox was McCarthy's pattern of withholding approval from his players. No matter how well a player performed, the pat on the back so needed by some players from their manager was never forthcoming. "When McCarthy came over to manage our ballclub, I think he thought that we were just a bit too easily led," remembers Bobby Doerr:

Joe Cronin had been a real fine guy to play for. He was firm, but he'd still pat you on the back every once in a while to relax you if you were uptight. And when McCarthy came in, I didn't quite understand him. In my case, he never would come up, my God, I don't think he ever patted anyone on the back. He just was more of a firmer makeup guy. But he got a lot out of his ballplayers. I had my three best years with him.

"McCarthy was a different type fella than Joe Cronin," remembers Boo Ferriss:

Of course, everybody's different, and they manage in different ways. He was a great manager, and his record speaks for itself, with all of those great years with the Yankees and everything. But he was a little more aloof from the fellas than Joe [Cronin] was and I think it took awhile for our fellas to get adapted to Joe [McCarthy] during the first part of 1948.

THE RACE

"Opening day," Lou Boudreau once observed, "is all future and no past." During the early part of the 1948 season, the future was looking bright for the Cleveland Indians. Opening the season on a roll, the Tribe, behind a two-hitter from Feller, defeated the St. Louis Browns. His colleagues in the Indians' infield were also doing their part; by early summer, Lou Boudreau was batting .368 and was among the league's RBI leaders with 51. At second base, Joe Gordon was turning plays that other second sackers only dreamed about and was also having a banner year at the plate.

"Gordon was a great second baseman," remembers Bob Feller:

He was a good backup leader behind Boudreau. He was a good teammate, he gave you confidence. He was a good clutch hitter and everybody liked him. He didn't have an enemy in the world. He and Ken Keltner and Boudreau were the best second baseman, third baseman, and shortstop in the business.

Prior to the start of the 1948 season, the consensus around the league was that Ken Keltner was finished. He'd had an awful year for the Tribe in 1946, managing just 13 homers and 46 RBIs. He improved a bit during 1947, but by the time contract discussions for the '48 season rolled around, Keltner felt sure that Veeck would cut his salary. To the third sacker's surprise, Veeck offered him an incentive; if the third baseman had a good year, he would receive a $5,000 bonus. "What do you consider a good year?" Keltner asked Veeck. "Oh, if you hit .280 and drive in 80 runs, that's a good year," responded Veeck. Energized by Veeck's offer, Keltner emerged as the Tribe's hottest hitter in the early weeks of 1948, hammering ten home runs in less than three weeks.

On the mound, Bob Lemon, who had pitched in the shadow of Feller in 1947, was suddenly starting to eclipse the fireballing Indian ace. By early July, Lemon, with a 12–6 record, was the hottest pitcher in the American League. Meanwhile, Feller was having nothing but problems, posting no better than a .500 record by early July. So poor were some of Feller's performances that voices were being heard around the league that he was finished. Luckily for the Indians, Feller's travails were offset by the performance of rookie Gene Bearden, who was confounding American League hitters with a dancing knuckleball that enabled him to compile a 7–3 record by late June.

The Indians' quick start in 1948 stood in marked contrast to the lackadaisical Red Sox. From opening day, McCarthy had constantly tinkered with his pitching staff, using nine different starters over the season's first three weeks. McCarthy also initiated a major change to the Sox lineup when he shifted shortstop Johnny Pesky to third base to make room for Vern Stephens. While McCarthy continued to shuffle his deck in search of a combination that would work, his players struggled to adjust.

"We had to get accustomed to Joe's way of managing, and we had a lot of new players on the team. Things were different," says Billy Hitchcock:

> Pesky had been a shortstop, and he was moved to third base. We had new pitchers like Kramer and [Denny] Galehouse. Additionally, the right field situation was uncertain. He [McCarthy] had tried to make Stan Spence work in right field. Now Stan was a fine ballplayer, a good hitter, but he was sick. He had bad teeth, and he never was able to play that year. Those things, when taken together, caused us to get off to a poor start.

"In the early going, we just weren't quite putting it together," agrees Boo Ferriss:

> We'd had that trade with Cleveland that brought over Vern Stephens and Ellis Kinder and Billy Hitchcock. You know, baseball's a crazy game and no matter how great you are, things don't always fall together. Hughson, Harris, and I had been pitching so much the previous couple of years that we were having trouble with our arms and that was part of the negative stuff, you might say.

By late May, rumors were swirling around New England that McCarthy's job was in jeopardy. Contributing to the unrest was the awful play of the Sox when away from Fenway; in a road trip that ended June 1, the team hit bottom, dropping 12 of 16 to fall 8½ games behind first-place Cleveland. Today, Billy Hitchcock believes that the rumors regarding McCarthy's handling of the club were unfounded:

> Actually, he was a fine manager with a fine baseball mind. He was a great observer. He just didn't miss anything. He handled pitchers well. We had

good pitching in '48. Parnell was a good pitcher. Kramer, Galehouse. A lot of people say McCarthy couldn't handle pitchers because of his decision on that playoff game, but I felt that he handled pitchers pretty well.

Mel Parnell echoes Hitchcock's assessment of the Red Sox manager:

I liked McCarthy. I thought he was a very good manager. He more or less made a study of each and every ballclub and tried to work the pitching staff against various ballclubs, depending on our success against them. His wife told me at night that he'd sit up in his room and go over the whole lineup of the opposition ballclub, trying to figure out different ways that we could have success against them.

By late spring, the hard work of McCarthy and his players finally began to show results. Between Memorial Day and the All-Star break, the Sox were the hottest club in the major leagues, going 26–13. During the streak, they averaged more than 5½ runs per game, providing a tremendous boost to a pitching staff that was still searching for a reliable fourth starter. "It was around midseason when we really started to gel," remembers Mel Parnell. "We were way behind, I think it was something like 12 games, but we came on with a late rush.

With the trade deadline approaching, pitching was also on the mind of Bill Veeck. In June, Veeck played a hunch and handed $100,000 to the St. Louis Browns for journeyman lefty Sam Zoldak. Veeck's gamble paid off; Zoldak won his first two starts for the club and soon thereafter won a key game against the Yankees to prevent them from sweeping a series at Municipal Stadium. Chubby and good-natured, Zoldak drew laughs from his teammates whenever he referred to himself as "the $100,000 pitcher."

Bill Veeck's next effort at shoring up his pitching staff would stun the baseball world. On July 7, Veeck purchased the contract of Leroy "Satchel" Paige from the Kansas City Monarchs and announced that the legendary pitcher would join the club the following day. Paige, whose age varied depending on which day you asked him, was at least 48 years old. Long an admirer of Paige, Veeck was convinced that the old warhorse could still pitch. The Cleveland owner, knowing that the signing of Paige would stir controversy, had been waiting for the right moment to offer him a big league contract. Paige, itching for an opportunity to showcase his stuff in the majors, had sent Veeck a telegram a year earlier, following Veeck's signing of Larry Doby: "IS IT TIME FOR ME TO COME?"

"ALL THINGS IN DUE TIME, Veeck had wired back. Now, with Feller struggling, Veeck felt sure the time was right.

Veeck may have believed that Paige could still pitch, but others weren't so sure. Among them was Lou Boudreau. Knowing of Boudreau's feelings, Veeck sat down with his manager and told him of his plans to sign Paige.

Boudreau told the owner that he'd heard that Paige had very little left. Determined to prove Boudreau wrong, Veeck arranged to fly Paige into Cleveland on July 4 to meet with his manager. Paige, displaying his usual casualness about punctuality, arrived a day late. When he did show, Veeck had the old pitcher transported directly to the ballpark from the airport.

With Paige finally on hand, Veeck reached Boudreau by phone. Veeck asked him how he'd like to take some extra batting practice against a new pitcher he was thinking of signing. Boudreau, unaware that the new pitcher was Paige, readily agreed. A couple of hours later, Veeck met with Paige in the dugout. "Satch, it's important to me that you look good against this guy. I've been telling everybody for lo these many years that you're the greatest pitcher in baseball. Now's here your chance to prove it."

"Man, I'm not ready for this," Paige told Veeck, shaking his head. "But you know old Satch. He don't need anything extra. Don't worry, Mr. Will, I've been there before."

At that moment, Lou Boudreau walked into the dugout. "Where's the kid?" he asked Veeck. Veeck pointed to Paige. Surprised, but willing to find out for himself if Paige's well-traveled right arm had any miles left in it, Boudreau prepared to take some swings in the cage. Stiff from his plane ride, Paige announced that he'd jog around the park "a few times" before facing Boudreau. After one lap, Paige reconsidered this plan and opted instead to warm up with Boudreau on the sidelines. Once he felt his arm was loose, Paige walked to the mound to face the American League's batting leader. Over the next five minutes, Paige threw 20 pitches to Boudreau, 19 of which were strikes. Unable to connect solidly with any of the old pitcher's offerings, Boudreau left the box and sidled over to Bill Veeck. "Don't let him get away, Will," he told the owner. "We can use him."

One of baseball's true originals, Satchel Paige had vagabonded around the country for more than 20 years, baffling hitters with his repertoire of dancing deliveries. Seemingly oblivious to, or perhaps above, the prejudice he invariably encountered in his travels, he charmed those he met with a mixture of country philosophy and wicked wit. "I've majored," he often said, "in geography, transportation, and people. I been a travelin' man."

Elusive to the core, Paige dodged efforts to pin him down regarding his personal life. When pressed as to his marital status, Paige would respond, "Yes" or "No," depending on his mood. In virtually every park he pitched in, the old pitcher left a ticket for "Mrs. Paige" at the box office. Each day, the ticket was picked up by a different woman. "Well, it's like this," he responded when questioned on the practice. "I'm not married, but I'm in great demand."

Blessed with a blazing fastball in his youth, Paige increasingly turned

to off-speed stuff to retire batters as he aged. On the mound, he was a hitter's worst nightmare; he'd flinch his shoulders, wiggle the fingers of his
glove, or even wind up multiple times before finally delivering the ball.
Always blessed with pinpoint control, Paige used to amaze spectators during his barnstorming days by sticking tenpenny nails into a plank behind
home plate, then driving the nails into the board with pitches thrown from
the mound.

However good Paige might still have been, his signing by the Indians
was deemed by many to be just the latest in a long line of Bill Veeck publicity stunts. Even the *Sporting News*, long a supporter of the Indians'
owner, found his motives questionable:

> To bring in a pitching "rookie" of Paige's age casts a reflection on the entire
> scheme of operation in the major leagues. To sign a hurler at Paige's age is
> to demean the standards of baseball in the big circuits. Further complicat-
> ing the situation is the suspicion that if Satchel were white, he would not have
> drawn a second thought from Veeck.

As an admirer of the *Sporting News*, Veeck was dismayed by the edi-
torial. But he stood his ground, defending his belief that Paige was a major
league–caliber pitcher to anyone who would listen. To the claim that Paige
was only signed because he was black, Veeck responded that if Paige were
white, he would have been in the major leagues 25 years earlier. As the
controversy raged, Paige remained unruffled, and on July 10, he made his
major league debut against the St. Louis Browns, yielding two hits and no
runs in relief.

With the All-Star break imminent, the attention of the baseball world
was increasingly focused on the plight of Bob Feller. Through the first half
of the 1948 season, the perennial All Star had struggled with control problems, and his mediocre 9–9 record was the worst midseason mark of his
career. Despite his poor record, the Feller mystique was still a force to be
reckoned with, and the fireballing right-hander was named to the All-Star
team. The only question that remained was whether he would play.

"I turned down the All-Star game," Feller recalls today:

> I was on the All-Star team and I turned it down. I didn't feel I deserved it.
> Others deserved it; send Lemon instead. I didn't want to go because I couldn't
> get anybody out. I wasn't all that bad, but I didn't deserve All-Star game sta-
> tus. I told Veeck that I wouldn't play in the All-Star game. He said, "You can't
> do that. Pretend you cut your finger with a razor and wrap your hand up
> and put it in a sling and tell them you cut your finger." I said, "I'm not gonna
> lie to them." Who'd he think I was, Bill Clinton? I wasn't going to go because
> I didn't deserve it. I wasn't going to go for old times' sake. Then he [Veeck]
> came out with some statement that was put out by the PR director, Marge
> Samuel, that said, "Bob Feller withdraws from the All-Star team for some

reason unknown to us." But they knew exactly what the reason was: I couldn't get anybody out.

Throughout the season's first half, speculation as to what was ailing Feller grew. One physician who examined the pitcher's right arm said a "hardened muscle" was the source of the pitcher's woes. Some players

As the game's greatest pitcher, Bob Feller was accustomed to success. But a series of uneven performances during 1948 left him searching for answers. (National Baseball Hall of Fame Library, Cooperstown, N.Y.)

around the league felt that Feller's mechanics were to blame. Through it all, Feller himself remained unsure of what was plaguing him. "I don't know what it was," Feller says. "I was doing everything the same. Working out the same, eating the same food, getting the same rest. Doing everything the same.

"I don't remember him being any different," Bobby Doerr said:

> It always seemed to be that every time you saw Feller, he'd have good stuff for nine innings. On some days he was just outstanding, and on most days, he was in the upper 90s. Just a shade on the wild side, not that he was trying to knock you down. He was just tough every time you faced him. When I broke in in 1937, I was about to face Feller for the first time, and I remember Cronin telling me, "Just cut the plate in half. Don't worry about the outside part of the plate. Don't be worrying about a perfect strike. If you think that you can get your bat on it, be swinging." And that was the best advice I had. I remember hitting three or four home runs off of Feller that were probably up around my eyes. So the advice that Cronin gave me on hitting Feller was a lot of help.

At least two players in the American League felt that Feller's struggles during 1948 were due to inadvertent telegraphing of his pitches. Watching Feller working during spring training in 1948, Eddie Joost and teammate Rudy York, who fancied himself a student of pitching, noticed that when Feller began his windup, his right hand would be straight when he swung it behind his back to throw a curve and cupped if he were delivering a fastball. Armed with this insight, Joost hit Feller hard throughout the year. Whenever Feller would pass Joost on the field, he would ask, "Hey, where do you get off hitting me like you do?" and Joost would laugh. Then, during the final series between the As and the Indians in mid-September, Joost was at the plate facing Feller when Bob unleashed a fastball that whizzed within inches of Joost's head. "We found out," Feller yelled at Joost.

"Who told you?" Joost yelled back.

Never mind, but it's going to be tougher from now on," Feller retorted.

Ted Williams always said that Boston was a hot weather ballclub, and following the All-Star break, it proved to be just that. On July 20, Jack Kramer won his ninth consecutive game, and the Sox completed a four-game sweep of the Browns. "Kramer was a fine competitor," Boo Ferriss says today. "He was a real pitcher, a finesse guy. He spotted his fastball, he wasn't very fast. He didn't have great velocity by any means. He had a fine curve ball and mixed up his pitches well. He knew the hitters. I thought he was a real pitcher."

It wasn't just Kramer who was doing the job for the Red Sox. Mel Parnell and Joe Dobson were also consistently providing McCarthy with quality starts. Parnell was the curiosity of the bunch. The conventional wisdom had always been that Fenway Park ate up left-handers, but Parnell pitched well at home, fashioning a 2.29 earned run average in Fenway, compared to 4.13 on the road. Blessed with the grace of a natural athlete, Parnell had entered the major leagues as a power pitcher, but after a couple of rough outings in Boston he consulted with his friend Howie Pollet of the Cardinals for advice on how to pitch in Fenway. "Mel, you can't do it with the fastball," Pollet told him "You'll go up in big games against the best hitters in baseball, and they'll just sit on it and kill you."

Recognizing the truth in Pollet's words, Parnell developed a slider and also worked with teammate Joe Dobson on improving his curve ball. Equipped with his new arsenal, Parnell began to do what was once seen as madness: pitch inside to right-handed power hitters at Fenway.

"I guess I pitched different than every other left-hander," Parnell says today:

> Left-handers more or less tried to keep the ball away from the hitters. I pitched inside; I wanted to keep the ball in on the hitter. I felt like if the hitter swung with his elbows closer to his body, he was sacrificing strength, therefore losing power. When you tried to hit the outside corner, but missed it, now you're down the middle of the plate and the hitter's swinging with his arms extended and gets full power that way. I think, by pitching inside, the hitter was always thinking about that short left-field fence and was always trying to hit the ball outta the ballpark. And in doing that, he's doing the unnatural, so he's helping me rather than himself.

By the third week of July, the Sox were riding a nine-game winning streak, and record crowds were expected in Fenway for their pending three-game series against the Indians. On Saturday, July 24, Cleveland climbed all over Jack Kramer, but strong relief pitching by Boo Ferriss and timely hitting by Ted Williams provided the edge in game one of a doubleheader. In game two, Mel Parnell was working without his best stuff but held on for a 2-1 win. The victory, the Sox's 11th straight, boosted Boston over Cleveland into second place, just a half game behind the Philadelphia As. On Sunday the Sox did it again as Dobson shut out Cleveland for the club's 12th straight win. The amazing Boston winning streak would reach 13 before finally being snapped by the Detroit Tigers on July 28.

At month's end, the stumbling Indians regained their footing. On July 31, they swept the Red Sox in a doubleheader before more than 70,000 fans at Municipal Stadium. So tightly bunched were Philadelphia, Cleveland, New York, and Boston at the top of the American League that the sweep dropped the Sox from first to fourth place. During the contest,

McCarthy began showing the first signs of pennant pressure when he publicly tongue-lashed pitcher Mickey Harris and catcher Matt Batts at home plate for a mental lapse that enabled Cleveland to score its first run.

Following their sweep of the Sox, the Tribe kept it rolling, winning eight straight between August 14 and August 22. Throughout the streak, the booming bats of Lou Boudreau, Ken Keltner, and Joe Gordon pulverized opposing pitching while Gene Bearden, Bob Lemon, and a newly effective Bob Feller provided a terrific one, two, three punch from the mound. When the starters faltered, left-handed relief artist Russ Christopher was ready in the bullpen.

The story of Russ Christopher is one of the oddest in baseball history. Throughout his career, Christopher had been plagued by a recurring medical condition that sapped his strength and threatened his livelihood. Born with a defective heart valve that allowed used blood to course back into his bloodstream instead of into his lungs, Christopher sometimes became so winded after pitching that he had to be helped from the field. In spite of his affliction, Christopher had carved out a successful career for himself as a short reliever. Tall and rail thin, Christopher utilized a submarine delivery that frequently tied up opposing batters.

Throughout 1947, Veeck had watched with interest as Christopher preserved late-inning leads for the Athletics. Convinced that the pitcher would be a valuable addition to the Cleveland bullpen, Veeck approached Connie Mack in the spring of 1948 and inquired about a trade for Christopher. Mack told Veeck to forget it. In addition to his heart problem, Mack told Veeck that Christopher had new woes: he'd recently contracted pneumonia while pitching against the Senators in a spring game. Mack told Veeck that it was possible that the left-hander would never pitch again. Undeterred, Veeck said he was willing to take a chance. After offering Mack $25,000 for the ailing pitcher, Veeck next went to see Christopher in the hospital. Lying in bed with just his head protruding over a mountain of blankets, the pitcher's long, pale face looked even more cadaverous than usual.

"Hey Russ," Veeck said to the stricken pitcher, "do you think you can pitch?"

"I don't know" was the weak reply.

"Do you want to?"

"Sure I want to. I'm a pitcher and I want to pitch. But I don't know. Look at me."

"I'm going to go down and buy your contract," Veeck said. "I'll take a gamble on you."

"Bill, I think you're crazy," the hollow-eyed pitcher responded. "But you have my word on one thing. I'll do the best I can for you."

Christopher recovered from the pneumonia and took his place in the Indians' bullpen. At times during the 1948 season, he would become so exhausted from just warming up that he'd be forced to sit down. Often, when he was required to throw more than a dozen pitches from the mound, his lips would turn purple. Because of his limitations, Boudreau seldom used Christopher for more than one or two batters and never for more than an inning at a time. In 1948, Christopher appeared in 45 games, pitching only 59 innings. The lefty was very effective in the early part of the season, preserving wins for the starting staff with regularity. But as summer wore on, Christopher began to fade, and Veeck knew that he could do no more. "Look Russ," Veeck said to the ailing pitcher in September. "You've done your part. You can go home if you want to."

"No," Christopher replied. "The doctors know what's wrong with me, and they say it doesn't matter. I told you the first time you asked me. I'm a pitcher. If I die, I might as well die pitching." After providing a solid boost to the pennant hopes of the 1948 Cleveland Indians, Russ Christopher never pitched again in the big leagues. Soon after the season ended, he returned to his home in San Diego, where he died six years later at the age of 37.

With the pennant race in a near-deadlock, Cleveland rolled into Boston on August 24 for a three-game showdown with the second-place Red Sox. In game one, Vern Stephens' two-run homer in the ninth provided the winning edge as the Sox took over first place. During the game, an overflow crowd of 34,172 was horrified when a fan, standing on the rooftop of a nearby building to watch the game, fell and was critically injured. On Wednesday, the Tribe, behind the shutout pitching of Bob Lemon, won handily, 9–0. On Thursday, with record heat baking New England, a towering three-run homer by Bobby Doerr provided the winning margin as the Sox regained sole possession of first place. As he had done all season, Doerr had helped lead his club over the opposition in a crucial game.

"Bobby Doerr wasn't a talkative sort of fella," remembers Billy Hitchcock, "but he demonstrated leadership by the way he played. Granted, Ted [Williams] was the number one man and he didn't like to lose and he'd get on somebody if they didn't hustle. But Bobby was the leader of that ballclub."

On Friday, a record-breaking heat wave continued to smother the East Coast as the Red Sox prepared to face the Yankees in New York. In game one of a doubleheader, Bob Feller turned in yet another fine outing, scattering six hits to win his 13th in game one. In game two, the Yankees bounced back behind the sterling pitching of Allie Reynolds, 7–2. The same day at Comiskey, Boston hammered the White Sox behind a Ted Williams three-run homer.

By month's end, the airtight American League race was a four-team affair, with Boston, Cleveland, New York, and Philadelphia all within three games of first place. An early September swoon by the As would spell the end of their pennant hopes, but the remaining three teams would battle virtually to the finish line. In late August, it was the Yankees' turn to get hot as strong pitching performances by Vic Raschi and Eddie Lopat and torrid hitting from Joe DiMaggio powered the club to its 20th win in 24 games, including nine straight between August 29 and September 6. The Yankee surge boosted them over Cleveland and into second place behind the Red Sox.

While the Yankees prospered, Lou Boudreau fretted. Uneven play by the Indians on their recent road trip had dropped his team 4½ games behind the first-place Red Sox. Concerned that his team was about to follow Philadelphia's example and drop from contention, Boudreau searched for a way to ensure that his club would continue to win.

Within two days, Boudreau had his answer. On Thursday, September 8, in a series against Detroit, Boudreau stationed the son of the Indians' head groundskeeper inside the Cleveland scoreboard for the express purpose of hijacking signs from the opposing catcher. Convinced that the use of binoculars for such a task signaled a lack of imagination, Boudreau armed his spy with a spotting scope, a type of portable telescope used in rifle ranges. When he picked off a sign, the scoreboard sleuth would relay it to the hitter at the plate by dropping a white or black card into an open slot in the scoreboard.

Interestingly, not every Indians batter was eager to know what pitch was coming his way. Among them was Boudreau himself, who found that the practice impaired his concentration at the plate. Larry Doby's receptiveness to the practice varied, depending upon his success with any given pitcher. Eddie Robinson, Kevin Keltner, and Joe Gordon never balked, welcoming any and all information on what pitch was headed their way.

Almost immediately, Boudreau's cunning began to pay off for Cleveland. On September 8, the Tribe kicked off a seven-game winning streak during which they picked up a game and a half in the standings. But on September 14 the plan nearly backfired. In game one of a crucial doubleheader against New York, Joe Gordon was at the plate against Joe Page. Picking off the sign from the Yankee catcher, the spy in the scoreboard signaled to Gordon that the next pitch would be a curve ball. Practically leaping out of his spikes with eagerness, Gordon deposited Page's next pitch 15 rows up into the left-field bleachers. But a player in the Yankee dugout spotted the shenanigans and before Gordon's ball could rattle into the seats, half the Yankee bench was on the field screaming and pointing at the scoreboard.

In truth, gamesmanship was nothing new to the Cleveland Indians. Shortly after taking over as owner, Veeck had been dismayed at how fly balls from the bats of Gordon, Keltner, and Doby constantly fell short of the distant Municipal Stadium fences. Determined to do something about it, Veeck instructed his grounds crew to install a temporary wire fence in the stadium outfield. The fence, which measured 320 feet down the lines and 410 feet to dead center, violated no league rules, so far as anyone knew. What did violate league rules was what Veeck did with the fence once it was in place.

To all appearances, Veeck's fence appeared permanent. When it was installed, sleeves were driven into the ground and fence poles were placed into them at regular intervals. What wasn't evident was that Veeck had directed his crew to install a number of additional sleeves in front and behind where the fence would actually stand. This enabled the Cleveland grounds crew to move the fence closer or further from home plate by as much as 15 feet. If the Yankees and their cast of home-run hitters were in town, the fence went back. When the lowly Browns visited, the fence came in. Wishing not to trouble the league office over issues related to his new fence, Veeck instructed his workers to move the standard in or out only under the cover of darkness.

Veeck's subterfuge didn't end with his outfield fence. The owner also felt that his infield needed alteration. Disconcerted by the random, indiscriminate manner in which ground balls from opposing bats reached his infielders, Veeck decided to tailor his infield to more satisfy the individual needs of his players. To reduce pressure on Lou Boudreau's bad ankles, Veeck told his grounds crew to keep the grass in front of the shortstop's position high and well watered to slow balls down. For the fleet and sure-handed Joe Gordon, the grass was trimmed to a nub. Third baseman Ken Keltner's aging knees were a constant problem to the Indians, so Veeck mandated that his crew keep the dirt around the bag heavily watered.

As the pennant race ground on, Boston began turning the heat up on the opposition in early September. Clinging to a sparse 1½–game lead over New York on September 8, the Sox fashioned a stirring come-from-behind victory. The next day, an eight-run third-inning rally and first-rate pitching by Ellis Kinder enabled the Sox to humble the Yanks again. The win, the club's ninth straight, also increased the team's first-place cushion to 3½ games, its largest margin of the year. The win, the Sox's seventh straight over New York at Fenway, seemed to signal to the doubters in New England that the Sox could do battle with the mighty Yankees and hold their own.

"You know, the Yankees were somewhat of a different type of ball-club than we were," remembers Boo Ferriss:

> The Red Sox were such a good offensive club, with so much of the lineup hitting over .300. And the Yankees were a good defensive ballclub, a lot better than the Red Sox. And of course, their pitching was probably a little better than ours. You know we had Williams, and they had DiMaggio, and they were the key players on both of our clubs. You always knew you had your work cut out for you when you faced them.

On September 10, darkness was settling over Fenway when a tenth-inning Joe DiMaggio grand slam lifted New York over the Sox. The win allowed New York to move within 2½ games of first place. In Detroit, the Tribe continued its winning ways behind Gene Bearden, shellacking the Tigers 10–1.

On Tuesday, September 15, Ted Williams continued his hot hitting against the White Sox, leading his club to a 3–1 victory in game one of a doubleheader in Chicago. With the season heading into its final days, excitement was being stirred by the neck-and-neck batting race between Williams and Lou Boudreau. In the clubhouse prior to game one, catcher Birdie Tebbetts was needling his teammate. "Looks like the Frenchman's got you beat this year, Ted," he said to Williams. "The hell he has," responded Williams, who promptly went seven for eight in the two games.

"He was something, boy," Billy Hitchcock says today of Ted Williams:

> He made himself a great hitter. Even after he came to the Red Sox, he continued to make himself a better hitter. If he went one or two days without hitting the ball good, he'd be at the ballpark at ten o'clock in the morning to get somebody to throw to him. I'd throw to him many times early in the morning. He wanted to get that stroke back.

"Ted was a great hitter, the greatest I've ever seen," says Mel Parnell:

> Everybody said it was natural ability, and to a certain extent, it was. But Ted also worked very hard. I pitched a lot of batting practice to him, along with Marty McDermott. Because we played at Fenway Park, he saw very little left-handed pitching, and for that reason, we pitched a lot of batting practice to him. And of course, I benefited from it as much as he did. I figured if I could make a study of Ted Williams, the rest of it would come much easier for me.

"He was the greatest I've seen," says Bobby Doerr. "I didn't see Joe Jackson or Ruth. I saw Gehrig, I saw DiMaggio, I saw Foxx. I played with Foxx and Greenberg. For just pure hitting the ball, Ted, I would think, would have to be the best of all of them."

"Well, you can talk all day about Ted," says Boo Ferriss today with a chuckle:

> It was just a tremendous thrill to be a teammate of Ted Williams'. Just watching him go to the plate everyday, watching him work those pitchers. His great mind, his great work habits, I just had so much admiration for him. He's just one of the all-time greatest hitters, if not the all-time greatest hitter that's ever put on a uniform.

On Sunday, September 19, Boston sent the pennant race into a scramble by dropping both ends of a doubleheader to the Tigers in Detroit. Adding injury to insult, second baseman Bobby Doerr aggravated a leg ailment that had kept him out of the lineup earlier in the season. Initial reports from the club's trainer following the game suggested that Doerr might be out for the season.

In Cleveland, the Tribe continued to roll, sweeping a doubleheader from the Athletics. In St. Louis, the Yankees blew a chance to tie for first by splitting a twin bill against the Browns. With its losses, Boston's first-place lead over the Indians was now a paltry half game, and the team was just one game ahead of the Yankees. On Monday, September 20, the Sox, Indians, and Yankees all won, each seemingly waiting for one of the others to yield. Tuesday was an off day for Cleveland and New York, while in Detroit, Mel Parnell shut down the Tigers for his 14th win. With the victory, Boston picked up one half game in the standings.

Wednesday, September 22, was Don Black Day at Cleveland's Municipal Stadium. Black, an Indians pitcher, had suffered a cerebral hemorrhage while batting in a game against the Browns on September 13. For more than a week, the pitcher's life hung in the balance before he slowly began to improve. Shortly after the incident, Bill Veeck declared that Wednesday's game between the Red Sox and Indians, originally scheduled for daytime, would become a night game and would be played as a benefit for Black.

On Wednesday, more than 76,000 fans watched as a resurgent Bob Feller pitched the Indians into a flat-footed first-place tie with the Red Sox. Throughout the contest, Feller was in full command, using a snapping curve ball to keep the Sox hitters off balance. Keltner's first-inning, three-run homer off of Dobson set the tone for the afternoon. It was the Tribe's seventh straight victory and Feller's fifth consecutive win.

"I've got it back," Feller told reporters following the game:

> Control is the answer. There was a hitch in my pitching motion. My arm was a bit sore. But I've got it back now. Before, I couldn't get the ball over. I'd get into a hole, ease up on my pitches, and they would tee off. Can't tell how

I got it back. All I know is that I'm free and loose out there once more. I'm throwing more overhand, and the hitch is gone.

Today, Feller views his club's victory over the Red Sox that Wednesday as a turning point for himself and his team. "The Don Black game, that was the game that turned it around, in my opinion. Before that, the Red Sox had us. The score was 5–2, and I had a good night. I felt good and then went on and won a few more games."

If the Red Sox were despondent over the tough loss to Feller on Wednesday, they were doing their utmost to hide it. "Back on May 31, we were 11½ games out of first place," Birdie Tebbetts had told the press Wednesday night. "If anyone told us at that time that we'd be tied for the league lead with only eight games left to play, we'd have felt content. So why should we be alarmed now? Besides, we've got Bobby Doerr back and ready to play, so I like our chances."

On Thursday, September 23, the Red Sox boarded a train bound for New York. On Friday, they would kick off a crucial three-game showdown with the Yankees. "That was a big series," remembers Mel Parnell:

> The Yankees had better team speed than we had. But the basic difference between the two teams was the guy in the bullpen, Joe Page. We didn't have a Joe Page. And he was very instrumental in a lot of their wins. At the time, he was the best relief pitcher in the league. Our defense was probably capable with the Yankees. They might have been a shade quicker than we were. But we had good defense too. We knew it was a big series.

It seems unlikely that one of the most exciting pennant races in American League history could become even tighter, but on Friday, that's just what happened. In New York, the Red Sox pitching collapsed as the Yankees cuffed around Kinder, Johnson, and Ferriss for nine runs. In Cleveland, the streaking Indians won handily over the White Sox. At day's end, the resulting combination of loss and victories left the American League standings looking like this:

Team	Games Behind	Record
Cleveland	—	91–56
Boston	—	91–56
New York	—	91–56

"They wanted a close race," Yankees manager Bucky Harris told the press later that evening. "Well, they've got it. It can't be any closer. But somebody has to drop tomorrow. Maybe two of us will be off the roof."

On Saturday, September 25, Jack Kramer tossed a seven-hitter against the Yankees to secure his club's hold on first place. "It wasn't the best game I ever pitched," Kramer said following the game. "I did a lot of throwing. But it was the most important for the team." In Detroit, Gene Bearden's knuckleball was dancing, and he hit the Tigers, 9–3. With just six games left in the season, the Yankees were one game off the pace of Boston and Cleveland.

On Sunday, September 26, the snapping, snarling curve ball of Tommy Byrne put the Red Sox bats in the deep freeze as the Yankees prevailed, 6–2. The Sox's dismal six-win, eight-loss road trip was finally over and appeared to signal the end of the club's pennant hopes. In Detroit, Feller notched his 18th win of the season when he beat the Tigers 4–1. Cleveland now had sole possession of first place, with Boston and New York each a full game back.

After an off day on Monday, the three combatants resumed the pennant race on Tuesday, September 28. In Boston, the Red Sox's two-week old funk continued as the Senators chased Joe Dobson in the second inning and went on to a 4–2 win before a tiny crowd of just 10,000 fans at Fenway. In Cleveland, a pennant-crazed crowd of more than 60,000 saw the Tribe rout the White Sox, 11–0. Gene Bearden went the distance on three days' rest and allowed just four hits as he won his 18th. In Philadelphia, the Yankees continued to fade with a loss to the Athletics. Armed with a full two-game lead over their rivals, the Indians now appeared to be in the driver's seat.

On Wednesday, the Sox finally shook themselves. Paced by strong mound work from Ellis Kinder and timely hitting from Doerr and Billy Goodman, Boston prevailed over the Washington Senators, 5–1. In Cleveland, the hot bats of Joe Gordon and Ken Keltner made the difference as the Indians beat the White Sox 5–2. In Philadelphia, the Yankees, fighting elimination, parlayed Hank Bauer's sixth-inning, three-run homer into a 4–2 win over the As. With just four games remaining in the season, Cleveland remained atop the standings by two games.

By Thursday, it was apparent that no one in Boston gave the Red Sox much of a chance at overtaking Cleveland. A paltry crowd of just 4,998 was on hand to watch the Sox beat the Senators 7–3. In Philadelphia, Eddie Lopat picked up the win as the Yankees beat the As, 9–7. With Cleveland idle, the Sox and Yankees inched to within 1½ games of the Indians.

On Friday, October 1, the Indians, playing to clinch a tie for the American League pennant, were facing the Tigers in Cleveland. With mist shrouding Municipal Stadium, Bob Lemon was clinging to a 3–2 lead in the ninth when he slipped while trying to field a bunt from the bat of Eddie Mayo. After finding his balance, Lemon threw the ball to first, but the ball hit Mayo in the back. With Mayo now at second and the game in doubt, the crowd in Cleveland fell silent.

After Lemon fanned Frank Bero, he ran the count to 3–2 on Johnny Groth before walking him. Fighting his nerves, Lemon then walked Joe Ginsberg. With the bases loaded, Lou Boudreau called for time from his perch at shortstop, then brought in Russ Christopher from the bullpen. Christopher couldn't find the plate and ended up walking Johnny Lipon on four pitches to force in the tying run. Now, with the infield in, Christopher induced Neil Berry to rap a grounder to Keltner, who rifled the ball home in time to cut down the potential winning run. After making the out, Jim Hegan then gunned it to first in an attempt to complete the double play. But Cleveland first baseman Walt Judnich's view was partially obscured on the play, and he dropped the ball. With two out, Jimmy Outlaw lined Christopher's next pitch to right for a base hit that scored Ginsberg and Lipon to make it 3–2. In the bottom of the inning, Cleveland went quietly. With the crushing loss, the idle Red Sox and Yankees inched to within a single game of the Indians with just two days left in the season.

"The outlook is brighter," Joe McCarthy told the press Friday evening upon hearing of the Tribe's loss. "Make no mistake about it. This thing is going down to the last putout." As the Red Sox manager was speaking to the press, a train carrying the archrival New York Yankees for a season-ending showdown pulled into Boston.

On Saturday, October 2, the Red Sox, in a desperate attempt to eliminate the Yankees, were threatening against Tommy Byrne in the first inning. After Pesky walked, Ted Williams picked a fastball and jacked his 25th homer into the stands to give the Sox a 2–0 lead. In the fifth, another walk by Pesky, a double by Williams, and a walk for Doerr loaded the bases. Stan Spence then singled to right, with Pesky scoring. Williams scored when Billy Goodman lined a fly to Bauer in left. The Red Sox added another run and that was all Jack Kramer needed. The final score was 5–1, and with the loss, the Yankees were eliminated.

"Kramer pitched a great game that day for us," remembers Bobby Doerr. "When he was with the Browns, we never thought he was the competitor that he turned out to be. A tough competitor with good control. He just was a better pitcher with us than he'd been with the Browns."

In Cleveland, the Indians rebounded from Friday's devastating loss with a victory over the Tigers. The win, Gene Bearden's 19th of the season, assured the Tribe of at least a tie for the pennant.

With the race for the American League pennant now a two-team affair, Bill Veeck had an ace up his sleeve. Following his club's victory over Detroit on Saturday, Veeck was sitting in his office thumbing through a well-worn copy of the major league baseball official rule book. Finding the section he was looking for, Veeck read the words carefully: "The manager of the home team shall be the sole judge as to whether a game shall not be started because of unsuitable weather conditions or the unfit conditions of the playing field."

Veeck knew that the term *manager* meant the Indians' front office. Veeck also knew that throughout baseball history, clubs had called off games for the most trivial of weather-related reasons. In deference to fans who might be in the stands staring up at a sunny sky while hearing that a game was cancelled, excuses such as "threatening weather" or "wet field" were usually trotted out as justification. Weighing his club's circumstances, Veeck could see absolutely no advantage to having his Indians take the field the next day against Detroit. First of all, with Tiger ace Hal Newhouser on the mound, runs would be very hard to come by. Second, if Boston beat the Yankees on Sunday, the Indians would be forced to square off against the Sox in Fenway Park on Monday, where Boston was almost unbeatable. However, if the Indians did not play, they would remain atop the league standings no matter what Boston did, and the pennant would be assured.

Considering his options, Veeck reached for the phone and called the weather service. The forecast was "possible showers." Wrestling with his conscience, Veeck next put in a call to American League president Will Harridge. "Under the rules," Veeck told Harridge, "I can determine what the weather is and how the field looks. I can call off the game without giving any reason."

"You wouldn't do that," Harridge responded.

"Will," Veeck said, "I have a strange feeling that if a cloud crosses the sun tomorrow, I am going to call off the game. I am willing to surrender my prerogative to your office. You'd better come down here or send a representative from your office."

"Come on, Bill," Harridge said, taking another tack. "You wouldn't throw 80,000 people away."

"We've already drawn all the people anybody could want," Veeck responded. "What's another 80,000? Especially when I'm sure of at least two World Series games if I don't play."

Unsure if Veeck were kidding or not, Harridge dispatched two representatives to Cleveland to rule on the weather, which turned out to be beautiful.

Following Saturday's bitter contest between the Yankees and the Red Sox, Joe and Dom DiMaggio were together, driving to a family dinner to celebrate Dom's impending marriage. During the ride, Joe, never much of a conversationalist under the best of circumstances, was even more sullen than usual. Still smarting over the Yankees' loss earlier in the day, Joe finally told his brother, "You knocked us out today. But we'll get back at you tomorrow. We'll knock you out. I'll take care of it personally."

Sunday, he almost did. With the pennant on the line, the Red Sox battled the Yanks' Bob Porterfield through two innings with no success. In the third inning, a tremendous roar went up from the capacity crowd at Fenway Park. Portable radios in the stands told the story. In Cleveland, Detroit had knocked Feller from the box and jumped to a 3–0 lead. Energized by the news, the Red Sox jumped all over Porterfield in the third for five runs. Out to avenge Saturday's loss, the Yankees, led by the torrid bat of Joe DiMaggio, pecked away until it was 5–4. In the sixth, Dom DiMaggio hit a home run into the screen in left, and by the time the inning ended, the Sox had increased their lead to 9–4. In the top of the seventh, the Yankees loaded the bases, and the Fenway crowd fell silent. Summoned from the bullpen, Boo Ferriss entered the game and over the final two innings shut down the Yankees.

"It was one of the thrills of my lifetime," remembers Ferriss,

> because I got the save in that game. I came in with the bases full to face Bauer and DiMaggio. Fortunately, I got Bauer on a sacrifice fly, and I think DiMaggio on a ground out. We went on to win the game, and the place was going wild. Everybody was watching the scoreboard to see what Cleveland was doing. And, of course, Detroit was beating them. It got nearer the ninth inning and all the scoreboard had to do was show Cleveland getting beat and Fenway was really jumping.

The final score was Sox 10, Yankees 5. In just four days, the given-up-for-dead Red Sox had won four straight and battled their way back into contention.

"Hey, those guys were real competitors," Billy Hitchcock says today of his Boston teammates:

> I mean, Williams was tough in the clutch, and McCarthy was a great leader. The feeling was always "we're gonna win." Even before that last week of the season, so many times I'd be sitting in the dugout going into the sixth, seventh, or eighth inning, we'd be three, four, five runs behind and Joe would say, "We're gonna get 'em, fellows, we're gonna win this game." We'd always find a way to come up with the runs we needed in the late innings to win a game. Joe was a leader. He never gave up.

Back in Cleveland, Hal Newhouser was continuing his mastery over the Indians. In complete command all afternoon, Newhouser held the

Indians scoreless until the ninth inning. When the game ended, he had limited the powerhouse Indians to just five hits. The final score was 7–1. Now, with two first-place teams sharing identical 96–58 records, the stage was set for baseball's second sudden-death playoff and unlike the National League playoff of 1946, this one would be decided by a single game, as mandated by American League Rules.

In Cleveland a downcast Boudreau told the press, "I don't know who'll pitch against the Red Sox tomorrow. It could be any one of three men. I can't tell you because I don't know. It could be among Lemon, Feller, and Bearden. Yes, Feller's a possibility. All I know is it doesn't make any difference to us. We're going up there to win."

From the pandemonium in the Red Sox clubhouse, it wasn't evident that the club had to win another game. A crowd of reporters, well-wishers, and players mingled, and confidence among the players was at an all-time high. When told that Lemon might start for Cleveland the next day, a boisterous Ted Williams said, "We'll knock his brains out." Standing nearby, Bobby Doerr was talking to reporters regarding his club's chances. "You bet we're in a great spot," he said. "But we've got to bear down all the way. It won't be easy."

In his office, a visibly tired McCarthy met the press. Twirling a cigar in his fingers, the manager was providing reporters with a history lesson:

> We were counted out in the spring. We were counted out as late as last Wednesday night. But those players never gave up. You've got to take your hat off to them for coming from behind the way they did. This is the greatest piece of work ever done. They wouldn't give up. Never gave up. First they made a great comeback, fell out and came back again.

Regarding his pitcher for Monday's sudden-death contest, McCarthy said, "I can't name my pitcher for tomorrow's game. I haven't had a chance to get my thoughts together."

In the Boston clubhouse, the guessing game over who would start the next day had begun. "Did he name him yet?" Mel Parnell asked a reporter. Told that he hadn't, Parnell nodded. It made no difference. To most of his teammates, Parnell was the obvious choice. His 2.29 ERA at Fenway, his fearless pitching style, and his three victories over the Indians in 1948 made him so. In fact, Parnell was so sure that he'd start Monday that he'd made arrangements for his family to travel from New Orleans to Boston for the game.

At nine PM that evening, a tired but determined band of Cleveland Indians was boarding a train that would carry them through the night to Boston. At that same moment, Mel Parnell was returning home from dinner with his family and preparing to hit the rack. Tomorrow would be a big day for the rookie pitcher. Lou Boudreau, Ken Keltner, Joe Gordon, and the rest of the Cleveland Indians were headed east, ready to claim the American League pennant. And when they got there, Mel Parnell would be ready.

MONDAY, OCTOBER 4, 1948

On the morning of October 4, Mel Parnell arrived at Fenway Park. As he entered the stadium, he noticed that the flag atop the pole in dead center field was facing away from home plate, indicating that the wind was blowing out. Entering the clubhouse, Parnell headed for his locker and began to change into his uniform.

"While I'm dressing," Parnell recalls,

> McCarthy comes up behind me and puts his hand on my shoulder and says, "Kid, I've changed my mind. I'm going with the right-hander today. The elements are against us with a left-hander today, with the wind blowing out." With that, he called Don Fitzpatrick, our clubhouse boy, and told Don to go out on the field and call Denny Galehouse in. So Galehouse comes in, and McCarthy tells him that he's the pitcher. Galehouse turned white.

Denny Galehouse, a veteran right-hander, had been mainly used in relief during the 1948 season. To McCarthy's way of thinking, Galehouse's experience and success in an extended outing against Cleveland earlier in the season made him the natural choice to start against the Indians. McCarthy also wanted to have a right-hander on the mound to counter the Indians' power at the plate.

"After I got the word on Galehouse," Parnell continues,

> I went out on the field for batting practice and all the fellows asked, "What are you doing out here?" I said, "I'm not pitching," and they said, "You gotta be kidding" and I said "Nope, I'm dead serious. Galehouse is going to be pitching today." I think our ballclub was more or less demoralized.

"I do remember the club before that game being let down that Parnell didn't start," remembers Billy Hitchcock:

> At the time, he was our best pitcher. This is no criticism of Denny Galehouse, because he was a fine pitcher. In those days, left-handers weren't too successful in Fenway Park. Now that's not always true; they do win there. Parnell would win there, as well as on the road. But that was the thinking that McCarthy had.

"Of course, we thought Parnell was going to be our pitcher," recalls Boo Ferriss:

Galehouse had pitched a good game against Cleveland in Cleveland. He was probably in the twilight of his career but still was a fine pitcher. I don't know whether McCarthy just had a hunch or whatever, but we were shocked when we saw the lineup. Nothing against Denny, because he'd been a fine pitcher, but Parnell had had a fine season for us. So Parnell was "it" as far as we were concerned.

"Parnell was ready, and he was the best pitcher we had," says Bobby Doerr. "Just put him in there and let him go as long as he can go. Not taking anything away from Galehouse, but he hadn't pitched all that much the last month of the season. It was kind of a letdown to the club I think."

For catcher Matt Batts, the selection of Galehouse made no sense. Throughout Sunday's tough 10–5 win over the Yankees, Batts had watched as Galehouse repeatedly warmed up, then sat down again in the bullpen. How fresh, Batts remembers wondering, can a guy be who pitched the equivalent of six innings in the bullpen the day before?

From his vantage point in the visitors' dugout, Lou Boudreau was convinced that Joe McCarthy was up to some sort of trick. From the final out of Sunday's game, the Indians' manager had fully expected that his club would be facing Mel Parnell.

"Lou Boudreau told me later that Cleveland thought McCarthy was trying to play a trick on them," remembers Mel Parnell:

> He thought we were trying to get a left-handed lineup in there so McCarthy could bring me in the second inning. They thought maybe that I was warming up underneath the stands. They actually sent the team trainer or someone connected with the ballclub to see if I was warming up underneath the stands.

Finally convinced that McCarthy was serious about starting Galehouse, Lou Boudreau called Bill Veeck and asked him to stop by the Cleveland dugout. As Veeck made his way through the stands and crossed the field to meet with Boudreau, he encountered an aide with the Indians organization. Veeck, never flagging in his belief that his Indians would win the American League pennant, instructed the assistant to make arrangements for a postgame victory party at Boston's Kenmore Hotel.

When Veeck arrived at the Cleveland dugout, he sat down on the bench next to his manager. Wasting no time, Boudreau told the Cleveland owner that he was thinking of forgoing the left-right percentage and loading his lineup with right-handed hitters to take advantage of Fenway's inviting left field wall. Boudreau wanted Veeck's opinion. "Louie," Veeck said, "You've managed the ballclub without aid all year. I'm certainly not

going to be looking over your shoulder in the most important game of all."
Veeck knew that his manager was taking a calculated risk but, feeling
confident to the end, elected to let Boudreau do things his way.

To face Galehouse, Boudreau had chosen 28-year-old rookie Gene
Bearden. Bearden didn't possess overpowering stuff, but a formidable
knuckle curve ball had kept American League hitters off balance throughout the season. His 2.43 ERA had led the league, and his 19 wins were second only to Bob Lemon on the Indians' staff.

With a boisterous overflow crowd on hand, Denny Galehouse went
to work in the first inning against the Indians. Things started ominously
for the Red Sox when lead-off man Dale Mitchell hammered Galehouse's
second pitch almost to the scoreboard before it was hauled in by Williams.
After Clark grounded out, Lou Boudreau took two balls and then a strike
from Galehouse before homering to left field. Galehouse then retired Gordon to end the inning.

The Sox answered back in the bottom of the first when Pesky doubled to right center. Only a fine play by Kennedy prevented the ball from
hitting the gap and rolling to the wall. After Ted Williams, battling against
Boudreau's "Williams shift" defense, grounded to short, Stephens singled
on Bearden's third pitch to score Pesky with the Sox's first run.

In the second, Galehouse continued to struggle. After Keltner hit his
first pitch for a single, Doby hammered a drive to center that required a
spectacular catch from DiMaggio to prevent it from going for extra bases.
Galehouse was then able to retire the side without further damage. In the
third, Galehouse showed signs of faltering again when he walked Bearden
to start the inning, but he escaped danger when he induced Mitchell to hit
into a double play.

With the game deadlocked 1–1 in the fourth inning, Galehouse finally
tapped out. Struggling with his control, the pitcher walked Boudreau, then
surrendered a single to Joe Gordon. The next hitter was Keltner, who hammered his 31st homer of the season to make the score 4–1. With that turn
of events, McCarthy had seen enough. After lifting Galehouse from the
game, he summoned Ellis Kinder from the bullpen.

Wasting no time, Larry Doby greeted Kinder with a double off the
left-field wall. After Kennedy bunted Doby to third, Hegan rolled a slow
grounder to Stephens, which allowed Doby to score. The score was now
5–1 in favor of Cleveland. In the fifth, Boudreau did it again; with two out
and nobody on, he belted his second homer of the day to make the score
6–1.

In the bottom of the sixth, the Sox tried desperately to rally back
against Bearden. After Gordon booted Williams' high pop fly, Stephens

struck out swinging. But Doerr jumped on Bearden's second pitch and rode it high over the left-field wall for a two-run homer. The Red Sox were now within three runs of the Indians, 6–3.

That's the way it stayed until the top of the eighth when Doby doubled to left. After Kennedy sacrificed Doby to third, Kinder walked Hegan intentionally. With Bearden at the plate, Boudreau signaled for a suicide squeeze, but catcher Birdie Tebbetts, playing a hunch, called for a pitchout, and Doby was hung out attempting to score. Bearden then lifted a fly ball to left that Williams misplayed, allowing Hegan to score. At the end of the eighth, the score stood 7–3. In the ninth, the Tribe parlayed singles by Robinson and Boudreau and a walk to Gordon for the team's eighth run. When Bearden shut the Sox down in the ninth, it was over. With his 20th win of the season, Bearden had propelled his team into a World Series berth against the Boston Braves. Bearden's win was all the more remarkable considering that he had pitched a complete game 8–0 shutout over the Tigers just two days earlier.

In the Cleveland clubhouse, pandemonium reigned. A handful of players grabbed Lou Boudreau, hoisted him on their shoulders, and carried him around the room chanting, "Lou, Lou, Lou!" "There has never been a thrill for me like this," Boudreau told the press. "The boys really should get the credit for winning it the hard way on the other fellows' field."

"Boudreau had a big day," remembers Boo Ferriss. "And Gene Bearden had the year of his life with that knuckle curve ball of his. He was uncanny that day, we just couldn't handle him. It was a sad day. So much had happened the day before, then the next one was a sad one. But that's the game, you know."

The following day, second-guessing McCarthy's selection of Galehouse had become Boston's favorite pastime. "In all fairness to Denny Galehouse," says Mel Parnell,

> he was a helluva pitcher in his time. But his time had passed. He was at the end of his career at that point. And he'd been up and down in the bullpen the day before. I think McCarthy was relying on the fact that Galehouse had pitched well in relief in a game in Cleveland and was probably hoping that the same thing would happen in this ballgame But it didn't.

"The question always comes up about the last day," says Billy Hitchcock:

> Why did he use Galehouse instead of Parnell? He [McCarthy] thought that Galehouse, with his little quick slider, would keep Cleveland's right-handed

hitters away from the left-field wall in Boston. Galehouse was a fine pitcher and a great competitor. He just didn't have a good day.

Later that night at the Kenmore Hotel in Boston, the American League champion Indians celebrated. When the party broke up in the wee hours, Veeck and Joe Gordon, still too excited over the day's events to sleep, toured downtown Boston, talking and walking until dawn. Returning to his hotel for a few hours' sleep, Veeck was awakened when someone from the Indians' front office called to tell him that Gene Bearden, who apparently had carried his personal celebration into the following day, was lost somewhere in Boston. Veeck organized a search party and finally found the wayward pitcher.

It's interesting to trace the future paths of the two men who started the playoff game. Denny Galehouse, Monday's surprise choice to start over Mel Parnell, never started another big league game and pitched only two more innings in his career. Unlike Galehouse, the fates would grant Gene Bearden one more moment in the sun. Three days following his victory over the Red Sox, the knuckleballer hurled a shutout over the Braves in the World Series. The win would conclude Bearden's only successful year in the major leagues.

In 1949, Casey Stengel was finally back in the big leagues as manager of the New York Yankees. Throughout the 1948 season, Stengel had watched Bearden with interest. After a few starts, Stengel realized that Bearden's dancing knuckler, which had tied up so many hitters during the 1948 season, rarely crossed the strike zone but dipped instead toward the dirt just as it approached the plate. As manager of the Yankees in 1949, Stengel instructed his hitters to take two strikes before swinging at any of Bearden's pitches. Invariably, Bearden would fall behind hitters, then be forced to come over the plate with his modest fastball. In a

Three of the men most responsible for the Indians' success during 1948 celebrate the team's win over the Boston Red Sox in baseball's second sudden-death playoff. *From left:* Gene Bearden, Lou Boudreau, Ken Keltner. (National Baseball Hall of Fame Library, Cooperstown, N.Y.)

flash, this information was relayed around the league, and Bearden, unable to adjust to this challenge, never had another successful big league season.

OCTOBER 4, 1948

CLEVELAND	AB	R	H	BI
Mitchell lf	5	0	1	0
Clark 1b	2	0	0	0
Robinson 1b	2	1	1	0
Boudreau ss	4	3	4	2
Gordon 2b	4	1	1	0
Keltner 3b	5	1	3	3
Doby cf	5	1	2	0
Kennedy rf	2	0	0	0
Hegan c	3	1	0	1
Bearden p	3	0	1	0
Totals	35	8	13	6

BOSTON	AB	R	H	BI
DiMaggio cf	4	0	0	0
Pesky 3b	4	1	1	0
Williams lf	4	1	1	0
Stephens ss	4	0	1	1
Doerr 2b	4	1	1	2
Spence rf	1	0	0	0
ªHitchcock	0	0	0	0
ᵇWright	0	0	0	0
Goodman 1b	3	0	0	0
Tebbetts c	4	0	1	0
Galehouse p	0	0	0	0
Kinder p	2	0	0	0
Totals	30	3	5	3

ªWalked for Spence in 9th
ᵇRan for Hitchcock in 9th

Cleveland	1 0 0	4 1 0	0 1 1	8
Boston	1 0 0	0 0 2	0 0 0	3

Doubles: Doby, Keltner, Pesky
Home Runs: Boudreau, Keltner, Doerr

Cleveland	IP	H	R	BB	SO
Bearden (W)	9	0	3	5	4

Boston	IP	H	R	BB	SO
Galehouse (L)	3	4	4	1	1
Kinder	6	9	4	3	2

3

1951: New York Giants vs. Brooklyn Dodgers

Word association and baseball go together. Say "1927" to a baseball fan, and he will think of Babe Ruth's 60–home run season. Say "1941," and images of DiMaggio's 56-game hitting streak, Ted Williams, and .400 flood to mind. Say "1951," and it's the New York Giants and the Brooklyn Dodgers.

By the start of the 1951 season, the Giants and the Dodgers—baseball's version of the Hatfields and the McCoys—had been bitter rivals for more than 30 years. Not many residents of Brooklyn or New York could remember just how the enmity had begun, but depending on who you asked, the names of Wilbert Robinson, John McGraw, and Bill Terry were sometimes brought forth as explanation. One thing was sure: by 1951, the rivalry was about Leo Durocher and Charlie Dressen.

If singularity of vision is a component of greatness, then Leo Durocher was the greatest manager who ever lived. Nobody wanted or needed to win more. During the 1920s and 1930s, Durocher was a light-hitting infielder of little renown, but by 1939, he'd managed to parlay a keen baseball mind and a pathological competitiveness into a position as player-manager of the Brooklyn Dodgers. In 1941, Durocher led the Dodgers to their first World Series in 19 years and, overnight, became the toast of Brooklyn. Off the field, things weren't as smooth. Durocher had an unquenchable thirst for bright lights and fast living and was often spotted in the company of card sharks and con men. In time, Durocher's high living, which had increased exponentially with his baseball success, would catch up with him. Baseball commissioner Happy Chandler, citing the Dodger manager's association with "known and notorious gamblers," suspended Durocher for the duration of the 1947 season.

In Durocher's absence, the Dodgers won the 1947 National League pennant. By the time Leo returned to the team in the spring of '48, Dodger owner Walter O'Malley had come to feel that Durocher's shady dealings were hurting the club's image. When the Dodgers fell into last place in midsummer 1948, O'Malley had the excuse he needed and promptly fired Durocher. Watching the developments with interest from across the Hudson River was Giants owner Horace Stoneham. Just hours after Durocher was cut loose by Brooklyn, Stoneham fired his current manager, Mel Ott, and hired Leo to lead the New York Giants.

As Leo Durocher's second-in-command in Brooklyn, Charlie Dressen had often dreamed of managing the Dodgers. Dressen's first and only managerial stint with the Cincinnati Reds in the mid-1930s had ended in failure, and in 1939, he signed on as Leo Durocher's third-base coach. While he enjoyed the work, Charlie chafed under Durocher's leadership and secretly yearned for another chance to prove himself as a major league manager.

"Dressen had been the first lieutenant of Durocher," remembers Brooklyn Dodger right-hander Carl Erskine. "Dressen was always chided by the fact that Leo got all the headlines. He [Durocher] was the smart guy, he was the manager, he was the flamboyant guy. And Dressen was always second fiddle."

For Dressen, Durocher's departure from Brooklyn hadn't solved the Dodgers' managerial problems. Burt Shotten, who succeeded Durocher, led the Dodgers to the pennant in 1949 and then nearly did it again a year later. But Walter O'Malley thought Shotten too old for the job and, following the 1950 season, fired him. The same day, O'Malley announced that the new manager of the Brooklyn Dodgers would be Charlie Dressen. At long last, Dressen would have a shot at proving that he, not Leo Durocher, possessed the superior baseball mind. "Now, as manager of the Dodgers, he was competing against Leo," recalls Erskine. "He wanted to bury Leo. He had a passion. He was neurotic about it. He wanted to kill Durocher. And now he had a chance to do it."

"Durocher and Dressen used to bait each other just to stir up a lot of stuff," remembers Giants right fielder Don Mueller. "If they could get their ballclubs fired up, they'd have a winning advantage. So everything you've heard about the rivalry between the Dodgers and Giants is pretty much true."

The bad blood between the Dodgers and the Giants didn't stop with the managers. The players felt it too. "There was a rivalry between those two teams that you will never ever see again in baseball," Tommy Lasorda once told a reporter. "You'll never hear a Dodger saying anything good about a Giant. And you'll never hear a Giant say anything good about a Dodger."

Throughout the 1950s, contests between New York and Brooklyn were punctuated by bean-ball wars and on-field brawls that, often as not, involved Jackie Robinson. Robinson's hatred of Durocher can be traced back to the spring of 1948. Durocher, having just returned from his year-long banishment and eager to prove himself again as Dodger manager, was dismayed to see team catalyst Robinson report to spring training 20 pounds overweight. Knowing of only one way to motivate a player, Durocher went on the attack and in short order began addressing Robinson as "Fatso." Robinson never forgot the humiliation and vowed his revenge on the field. With tensions between the Brooklyn Dodgers and the New York Giants at an all-time high in 1951, the stage was set for one of baseball's most exciting seasons.

THE RACE

With a lineup that included Jackie Robinson, Carl Furillo, Roy Campanella, Gil Hodges, and Duke Snider, it's no surprise that the Brooklyn Dodgers began 1951 as odds-on favorites to win the National League pennant. An awesome combination of power and aggression, they opened the 1951 season like a house afire, steamrolling opponent after opponent.

In contrast to the Dodgers, the 1951 season began disastrously for the Giants. After splitting its first two games of the season with Brooklyn, the team swooned, and lost its next 11 straight. Things improved after that, but with the Dodgers threatening to run away with the league,

"The Lip" and his former lieutenant. Leo Durocher (left) and Charley Dressen, competitors first, last, and always. (National Baseball Hall of Fame Library, Cooperstown, N.Y.)

Durocher knew that he'd have to make changes if his team was to contend. On May 24, the Giants purchased the contract of a 20-year-old center fielder from their Minneapolis farm team and announced that he would start for the Giants the next day against the Phillies in Shibe Park. Leo Durocher had seen Willie Mays play only once, but it was enough to convince him that Mays, who'd been hitting a tidy .477 for the Millers, would be the Giants' center fielder for years to come.

To make room for Mays, Durocher moved Bobby Thomson from center to left field and announced that henceforth, Mays would bat third. "I was playing center field when a man by the name of Willie Mays showed up," Bobby Thomson recalled years later. "This guy immediately caught your attention. He could swing the bat, he was young, he was full of life, and he looked like a gazelle in the outfield. I remember that he had all these bats with him and I thought, 'This guy must be Babe Ruth and Lou Gehrig combined.'"

If Mays had anything in common with Ruth and Gehrig, it would take him awhile to prove it with the Giants. Initially overwhelmed by big league pitching, the young rookie struggled at the plate and, before long, began to doubt his ability to help his team. Years later, Alvin Dark remembered how tough it had been on Mays:

> The first thing I remember about Willie is that he got off to a real bad start. One day, he was sitting over in the corner of the clubhouse actually crying because he felt that he was letting the ballclub down. He'd gotten a chance to come to the big leagues, and he wasn't doing well.

"Willie really got down when he first came up, because he wasn't hitting," remembers Don Mueller. "He was really tore up about not hitting the ball the way he did in the minor leagues. And Leo really had to be a dad to him to keep his head on right."

Durocher saw that Mays wasn't hitting but knew it would just be a matter of time before he would. Doing his best to calm the young player's doubts, Leo told Mays in no uncertain terms that he considered him to be the Giants' center fielder for years to come. Durocher's words helped; Mays began to relax and, shortly thereafter, found his timing at the plate.

Back in Brooklyn, the Dodger juggernaut continued at full throttle. In addition to cannonading their opponents with power, the team's pitching — long considered its Achilles heel — was superb. By mid-July, Don Newcombe had 13 wins, Preacher Roe and Ralph Branca 12, and Clyde King 10. On July 13, the Dodgers beat the Cubs for their eighth straight win and opened up a 9½–game lead over the second-place Giants. By the time Durocher's club arrived at Ebbets Field on August 7 for a three-game series, the New York press was treating a Brooklyn pennant as a *fait accompli*.

A midsummer rainstorm had dampened Brooklyn on Tuesday, so the two teams squared off in a doubleheader on Wednesday. Both games were punctuated by knockdown pitches and near-brawls. After Giants pitcher Sheldon Jones sent both Pee Wee Reese and Roy Campanella sprawling with chin-high fastballs in the seventh inning, the benches emptied. Somehow the umpires were able to restore order, although an unsettling edginess hung over the remainder of the afternoon.

The Dodgers took game one, 7–2, then pieced together four straight singles in the 10th inning of the second game to sweep the doubleheader. In game three of the series, Roy Campanella blasted two home runs as the Dodgers bested the Giants again, 6–5. With the sweep, Brooklyn's lead over the second-place Giants swelled to a gaudy 12½ games.

A baseball team chasing a miracle often looks for something to believe in. Following game three of their series against the Dodgers, an event took place that would transform the Giants from a somnolent gaggle of also-rans into the most ferocious band of pennant contenders in baseball history.

"When we swept that last game against the Giants," Carl Erskine recalls,

> we go into the Ebbets Field clubhouse and in the back of the clubhouse was this door which opened into the visitors' clubhouse. Now, that door was always respected, but there were guys traded or whatever, and they'd come back with another team, say hello, then go back and shut the door. That day, Dressen came in and he's going down the locker row and saying, "Come on, come on, you guys, come on back here! We're gonna sing through the door, we're gonna sing the Giants are dead." Well, Erv Palica and Ralph Branca and Erskine were side by side in the row of lockers, and he [Dressen] knew Branca was always singing. Branca used to sing, he still does. He just asked the three of us pitchers to come on back and sing through the door to Leo, "Leo, the Giants are dead." Well, I didn't have any appetite for that, and neither did Palica, so we didn't do it. Somehow, Ralph did do it. Ralph kind of had a burr in his tail, too, for Leo. In the emotion of the moment, Ralph went back with Charlie, and I guess they sang through the door.

Clem Labine confirms Erskine's account of the day's events. "We had a lot of people on our club, including Robinson and Branca. Well, Ralph could tell you, although Jackie's not around to tell you, that they were singing, 'The Giants are dead, the Giants are dead.'"

"This is a true story," Ralph Branca said later. "The clubhouses adjoined with just a door between them, and Chuck Dressen was the instigator of it."

Did the Giants hear the taunts? Outfielder Bobby Thomson leaves little doubt that they did. "We always felt the Dodgers rubbed it in a little bit," remembered the Giants' left fielder years later, "but you have to remember, it was just this fantastic rivalry."

"It was like going to war in those days," umpire Al Barlick would recall later. "It was just like going to war. There was so much rivalry there, it was hard to believe. I'm not saying you don't have rivalries today, but I don't think baseball will ever have the rivalries they had back then with those ballclubs."

"It was like going to war. You've said it all," remembered Giants infielder Bill Rigney. "You went to Ebbets Field, you were going to war. It was two good teams with a lot of good players. Maybe 'hate' isn't the exact word, but no holds were barred, everything went. And it usually did."

"I remember disliking some of the Dodgers, both on and off the field," says Monty Irvin. "None of the Dodgers had ever done anything to me personally, but on the field, you wanted to beat their brains out. And they felt the same way about us. And this carried on for year after year, and the fans expected it to be that way."

The incident over the clubhouse door was the final straw for Leo Durocher. Irate over what he termed "the unprofessionalism of the Dodgers," Durocher and the Giants lodged a formal protest with the league office over the matter. A few days later, in response to the complaint, workmen were dispatched to brick up the door.

Still smarting over the clubhouse incident, the Giants hosted the Dodgers at the Polo Grounds the following Tuesday. Playing with grit and steely determination, the Giants swarmed all over Brooklyn, scoring three runs in the first inning of game one to win 4–2. The following day, led by Wes Westrum's bat and Jim Hearn's six-hit pitching, the Giants beat the Dodgers again, 3–1. Then, on Thursday, Sal Maglie four-hit the Dodgers to complete the sweep.

Fueled by their performance against Brooklyn, the Giants began tearing up the National League. Between August 12 and August 27, they won, they won again, and when they were done doing that, they won some more. The *way* they won was as amazing as how often they won. On August 21, Westrum, Eddie Stanky, and Whitey Lockman each hammered eighth-inning home runs to beat the Reds; on August 22, they rallied in the seventh and eighth to again top Cincinnati; on August 25, they rallied with two out in the ninth for their 14th win in a row; on the 27th, the Giants scored two in the 12th inning to win their 16th straight. When the amazing run was finally halted by the Pirates on August 28, the Dodgers' once-splashy lead had been whittled to a paltry five games.

In light of the impact that it had on the Giants, Dressen's behavior at the clubhouse door seems amazingly foolhardy. Charlie, the self-styled baseball mastermind, had allowed his obsession with Leo Durocher to cloud his judgment. "The old saying is 'Let the sleeping dog lie,'" says Clem Labine. "We didn't ... and it didn't lie." Now with the Dodgers' huge lead gone and the Giants closing, Dressen would have to demonstrate his superiority over Durocher where it counted: in a real head-to-head pennant race. But as the clubhouse door incident demonstrated, Dressen would first have to find a way to prevent his emotions from overwhelming his good sense.

Over the next three days, Brooklyn regrouped, and by the time the two teams met again on Saturday, September 1, the club's lead had been rebuilt to seven games. In a contest marred by cold, windy weather and a bean-ball incident between Sal Maglie and Jackie Robinson, Don Mueller hit three home runs in game one of the series as the Giants humiliated the Dodgers 8–1. On Sunday, Mueller hit two more round-trippers as New York battered three Dodgers pitchers for 11 runs. Following the series, the Polo Grounds looked more like a crime scene than a ballpark; the Giants had now beaten the Dodgers six straight times. In Brooklyn, Dodger fans began to wonder how such a great team could fall so flat on its face so quickly.

Actually, Brooklyn's slump had more to do with the law of averages than lack of ability. In baseball, teams get hot together, then teams cool off together; fewer things are more certain. While the clubhouse door incident was instrumental in altering the character of the 1951 pennant race, fate also played a hand. In the early going, it had been almost too easy for Brooklyn; they'd cranked out wins like a foundry stamping out metal parts. But then, the dynamic shifted. Mr. Yin, may I present Mr. Yang? Hitters slumped, grounders stopped finding infield holes. And when a team's luck turns, the psychological buffer between success and failure starts to erode. If $E=MC^2$ is the key to understanding relativity, then

Confidence + Success = Achievement

is the key to fathoming baseball. Remove one component from the equation's left side, and the sum automatically becomes 0. "If you look at the starting lineup of the Dodgers and the Giants, you'll be able to figure out that they had a better ballclub than we did," remembers Don Mueller. "Man for man, they had the power. Everyone of those guys in their lineup could hit the ball out of the park. But as the season wore on, we had the feeling that they were pressing."

"Sure, we were pressing. There's no doubt about that," says Clem Labine. "Every time we won, they won, and every time we lost, they won. And before long, we started looking over our shoulder."

With his team struggling, Charlie Dressen soon began to fret about the state of his pitching staff. Recently, Branca, Erskine, Palica, and King had developed injuries, and the Dodger manager knew that if his team were to stave off the Giants, he'd need some fresh arms. On August 28, Charlie started 25-year-old rookie Clem Labine against the Reds. Labine had actually been summoned from the minors a month earlier, but an ankle injury suffered during his last minor-league game had kept him out of action. The Dodgers—basking at the time in the glow of a 12-game lead — never bothered shipping Labine back to the minors. "My God, they just let me stay there," he recalls. "They taped my ankle every day. I'd go out and pitch batting practice and take outfield."

Now, with their lead at just five games and the pitching staff in shambles, Dressen turned to Labine. It was a brilliant move. In a dazzling outing, Labine pitched a complete game, seven-hit victory over Cincinnati. Then, between September 4 and September 21, Labine won his next three starts and was well on his way to becoming the National League's newest pitching nova.

On September 13, the Giants were beaten by the Cardinals in game one of an oddball, three-team doubleheader that saw St. Louis lose the nightcap to the Boston Braves. It was the first time a National League team had met two rivals on the same day since 1883. With the loss, the Giants fell six games behind the idle Dodgers, and the relief felt by Dodger fans was palpable. With just over two weeks left in the season, the feeling in the borough of Brooklyn was that the Dodgers might just be able to hold on.

On September 26, with its lead hovering at three games, Brooklyn was in Boston on a rainy fall afternoon to face the Braves in a doubleheader. With seemingly no one else to turn to (more on this later), Charlie Dressen marched a dog-tired Ralph Branca to the mound. Branca was hammered for six runs in the first inning, and Brooklyn lost 6–3. In game two, the Dodgers, now clearly a team looking over its shoulder, were pounded 14–2. That same day in Philadelphia, the Giants continued their amazing pace, beating the Phillies at Connie Mack Stadium. The once-yawning chasm between the two teams now stood at just a single game. Following the contest, the Giants announced to the press that they would start accepting ticket requests for the 1951 World Series, an action that would have been greeted with guffaws just two weeks earlier.

Players in a pennant race often look back and agonize at the games that got away, the "sure thing" that somehow slips through a team's fingers. Such a game for the Dodgers took place on Thursday, September 27. With the score deadlocked at 3–3 in the eighth inning, Bob Addis of the Phillies singled. Sam Jethro followed with a base hit, which advanced Addis to third. The next hitter, Specs Torgenson, rolled a grounder to Jackie Robinson, who gloved the ball and fired to Roy Campanella in an attempt to cut down Addis at the plate. Campanella tagged Addis, then spun around to see umpire Frank Dascoli, arms wide, palms face down, signaling "safe." The Dodgers howled in protest.

"Now, our team, believe me, including Jackie [Robinson], were rabble-rousers," remembers Carl Erskine:

> And Jackie was no shrinking violet. Spike Lee wanted to do a movie about Jackie's life, and we tried to tell him that you can't depict Jackie as a victim always, because he had fire in his veins. I mean, he was on Dascoli like a shot, along with everybody else. Campy, as soon as the call was made, threw his mask about 30 feet in the air, and Dascoli threw him out before the mask even came down. Campy never showed that kind of outburst over a call. He'd make his case, but he would never demonstrate like that. It was such an obvious bad call to us.

Play continued, but by now, invective was in full flow from the Dodger dugout toward the plate umpire. Suddenly, Dascoli halted play, ripped off his mask, stalked over to the Dodger dugout, and ordered the entire bench cleared. After play resumed, the Braves clinched the victory, reducing the Dodgers' lead over the idle Giants to a paltry half game. The loss to the Phillies would prove to be one of the most crushing regular-season defeats in Brooklyn history.

Following the game, a number of enraged Dodgers congregated around the umpires' dressing room to settle accounts. In the tumult, somebody kicked in the door. Press reports the following day suggested that the guilty party was Jackie Robinson. Robinson denied it. "I know who did it," Robinson told reporters later, "and it wasn't me. But I won't tell who did it." Carl Erskine corroborates Robinson's story: "Somebody kicked the door, it was a panel door, and somebody kicked a panel out of it. Jackie got blamed for it, but it was not Jackie. It didn't really matter who, because whoever did it really spoke for everyone. This was the lousiest break. It was a crucial game."

With just three days left in the season, the Dodgers carried their half-game lead into Connie Mack Stadium to again battle the Phillies on Friday, September 28. Playing with extraordinary care, the Dodgers were holding a 3–1 lead in the bottom of the eighth when Philly catcher Andy

Seminick homered to left field off of Carl Erskine with a man on base to deadlock the game. Then, in the bottom of the ninth, a slashing single by Puddin' Head Jones scored Ritchie Ashburn with the winning run. Another devastating loss for Brooklyn.

The Giants who, in a scheduling quirk, were idle for a second day had gathered at Boston's Bay Hotel to await the outcome of the Dodgers-Phillies game. When the final score was announced, they celebrated loudly and joyously. They'd finally caught the Dodgers. Leo Durocher jumped up on a chair, signaled for quiet, and told his players: "This is the greatest team I've ever managed. It will be the biggest thrill of my life when we clinch this pennant here Sunday."

The next day, both teams waited for the other to blink. In Boston, Sal Maglie outdueled Warren Spahn for his 23rd win of the season as the Giants won their sixth straight. In Philadelphia, Don Newcombe, in just one of his many gallant performances during 1951, shut out the Phillies 5–0. In a flat footed tie atop the National League standings, the two teams would now carry their fight for the pennant into the season's final day.

Unlike the Dodgers, the Giants would have it relatively easy on Sunday. In a game that started an hour earlier than normal due to the end of daylight savings time, Larry Jansen went the distance to beat the Braves 3–2. A home run by Bobby Thomson and a clutch single by Monte Irvin accounted for the Giants' runs. Following the game, the team boarded a train back to New York, awaiting word on the outcome of the Dodgers game in Philadelphia.

In Philadelphia, Brooklyn and the home team were locked in one for the ages. With nothing at stake and playing loosely, the Phillies drew first blood and, by the third inning, had staked themselves to a 6–1 advantage. Trailing 6–2 in the fifth inning, the Dodgers rallied when Jackie Robinson tripled and Andy Pafko singled to narrow the gap to 6–5. But the Phillies pushed across two more runs in the bottom of the fifth to make it 8–5.

In the sixth inning, at exactly 3:35 PM a huge roar went up from the crowd. Sensing what the commotion was, Jackie Robinson glanced over his shoulder at the Philadelphia scoreboard and saw the numbers settling into place: Giants 3, Braves 2. Final. The Dodgers, now on the brink of elimination, would somehow have to score four runs just to tie for a pennant that all season had appeared destined to fly over Ebbets Field.

As proof that people who are scared to death sometimes do the best work, the Dodgers rallied. In the eighth inning, Hodges beat out a slow roller to Granny Hamner. After Billy Cox singled to right, Rube Walker promptly lined a double to left center, which scored Hodges and Cox.

Furillo, in one of many clutch performances by a Dodger this day, then lined a single to left center, which tied the score. Don Newcombe, on the heels of his complete game victory just the day before and battling exhaustion, was now pitching in relief for Brooklyn.

With the score still tied at 8–8 in the 12th inning, darkness began to settle over Connie Mack Stadium. The so-called Pennsylvania Rule, which proscribed the use of stadium lights on Sundays, was in force, mandating that the National League pennant would be decided in an eerie early evening gloom. In the top of the inning, the Phillies loaded the bases against Newcombe with two out. The Dodgers were now a hair's breadth from the most ignominious pennant collapse in baseball history.

In Brooklyn, they still talk about what happened next. On the mound, Newcombe picked off a signal, kicked, and delivered to left-handed hitter Eddie Waitkus. Unleashing a vicious swing, Waitkus ripped a line smash up the middle that appeared destined for center field. Jackie Robinson, playing Waitkus to pull and shifted around toward first base, suddenly reversed field, dove, and backhanded the ball a split second before it hit the ground. The umpire, after ensuring that Robinson had clearly caught, not trapped, the ball, raised his right arm to signal Waitkus out. "It was the most heroic play I ever saw," Dodger first baseman Gil Hodges said later. "Jackie saved us in the 12th."

In a setting of almost unimaginable tension, neither team scored in the 13th. Then, in the top of the 14th, Jackie Robinson completed the final act of what surely must be baseball's greatest clutch performance. With two out, Robinson hammered a Robin Roberts fastball into the upper left-field stands for a home run. Somehow, they'd done it. They might not be in the catbird seat, but somehow Brooklyn had staved off elimination and would face the Giants in a three-game playoff for the pennant the following day. Any suggestion that the Dodgers were dismayed at not winning the pennant outright is dismissed by Carl Erskine. "We were celebrating," Erskine says today. "Listen, the noose was tight and we slipped out of it. We were celebrating because we were still alive."

GAME ONE—MONDAY, OCTOBER 1, 1951

It was Baseball Week in New York. As officially proclaimed by the acting New York mayor, Joseph T. Starkey, the period of September 30th through October 6th was designated by the city as a time to honor New York's baseball teams. In addition to the Giants and the Dodgers, who were carrying their battle for the National League pennant into a sudden-death playoff, the Yankees, who'd clinched their third straight American League pennant just three days earlier, were also feted.

In Brooklyn, any talk of a Yankee-Dodger World Series rematch had faded with the summer light. In the past six weeks, Dodger fans had watched with amazement as the Giants played like they were channeling the '27

Willard Mullin's classic "Brooklyn Bum" feigns indifference, but the empty aspirin bottles at his feet speak volumes. (Shirley Mullin Rhodes and the Estate of Willard Mullin.)

Yankees. The Flatbush Faithful knew it would take everything the Dodgers had just to get by Durocher and his Giants. A full-page ad in the *New York Times* captured Brooklyn's mood perfectly: it depicted Mullin's classic "Brooklyn Bum" imperiously proclaiming, "Dem Gints Don't Have Me Worried fer a Minute," while scattered at his feet were newly emptied aspirin bottles.

Because the Dodgers had won the coin toss earlier in the week, the third sudden-death playoff in baseball history would begin in Brooklyn. On the field before the game, Giants captain Alvin Dark passed Pee Wee Reese. "Fancy meeting you here," Dark said to Reese in a teasing reference to the Dodgers' near-elimination of the day before. "I thought you'd be back home in Louisville today."

"There ain't no money there," Reese shot back before ducking into the Brooklyn dugout to go over pregame strategy with Dodger starter Ralph Branca.

For the first two innings, Branca was sharp, and he set the Giants down without incident. In the bottom of the second, Andy Pafko homered off Giants starter Jim Hearn, and the Dodgers led 1–0. Then the Giants struck. In the top of the fourth inning, Branca hit Monte Irvin with a pitch, then surrendered a home run to Bobby Thomson. It was Thomson's 31st homer of the season, a career best, and it would stand for exactly two days as the biggest hit of his career. It was now Giants 2, Dodgers 1.

In the bottom of the fourth, hearts quickened in Ebbets Field when Duke Snider and Jackie Robinson singled. But Jim Hearn, who was pitching the game of his life, induced Campanella to roll into a double play, which ended the rally. In the eighth, the Giants struck again when Monte Irvin hammered a Branca slider over the fence. That made it Giants 3, Dodgers 1.

It was more than enough for Hearn, who went the distance for the win. When it was all over, Hearn told reporters, "It's just like a dream to me. You wait so long and then suddenly you're in the big game of your life. I'm about the happiest fellow in the world."

In the Dodger clubhouse, Branca was stoic: "I pitched well. We just didn't score enough runs." Actually, there was more to the story than that. The Dodger team that took the field Monday was no more than a pale imitation of the powerhouse that had dominated the National League for so much of 1951. The team's high-wire act against Philadelphia the day before had taken its toll and left the entire Dodger squad emotionally drained. With less than 24 hours remaining before game two, the Dodgers would have to somehow regroup, or the tortured lament of "wait 'til next year" would once again resonate throughout Brooklyn.

GAME TWO—TUESDAY, OCTOBER 2, 1951

Roy Campanella was going nuts. Nursing a charley horse sustained Sunday in Philadelphia, he'd been barely able to run the bases on Monday. But playing in pain was nothing new to Campy, and he fully intended to catch today. Now all he had to do was convince Charlie Dressen. Dressen, who had winced noticeably as he watched Campanella limp through Monday's game, told the press that he might be forced to start backup catcher Rube Walker on Tuesday.

Before the game, Campy approached Charlie Dressen. "I'm healthy," he said. "I want to play."

"If you're so healthy," countered Dressen, "let me see you run." Campanella broke into a lame hobble that fooled no one. Dressen shook his head. "If you can't run any better than that," he said, "I'll have to use Rube Walker."

Following Monday's loss to the Giants, Dressen hedged when he was asked to name his starting pitcher for Tuesday's second game. "I'll tell you tomorrow," was his reply. Dressen wasn't being coy; he didn't know himself. The following morning, he still hadn't made up his mind. During the team's bus ride from Brooklyn to the Polo Grounds Tuesday morning, the Dodger manager motioned for Clem Labine and Carl Erskine to come sit beside him. "One of you is going to start today," he said. "But I'm not sure who. I want you both ready."

Since his last start on September 21, Clem Labine hadn't pitched an inning. After winning his first four outings, Labine had suddenly disappeared from Dressen's radar, spending the season's crucial final days riding the Brooklyn bench. All the while, Charlie trotted the arm-weary triumvirate of Newcombe, Branca, and Roe to the mound time and again. Around Brooklyn, fans were puzzled. Was Labine injured? With the season on the line and the pitching staff resembling an emergency ward, why wasn't Labine pitching?

To understand Labine's sudden anonymity, a brief detour through the psyche of Charlie Dressen is necessary. Widely regarded as a shrewd strategist, there's no question that Dressen possessed one of baseball's best minds. However, Dressen's mind also played host to a formidable ego. Now, few would dispute the importance of ego to achievement; managed carefully, a degree of egoism can serve as a necessary buffer between dreams and reality. For example, nobody much cared when Dressen would strut the length of the dugout during tight games and proclaim, "Keep 'em close boys, I'll think of something," because often as not, he did think of something. It was only when Dressen gave his ego free rein that it turned counterproductive and clouded his judgment. That had happened on August 9, when, fueled by illusions of invincibility, he had allowed his taunts to transform the moribund Giants into fierce pennant rivals. And it had happened again in September; that time, Dressen allowed his ego to destroy everything that he and his team had worked so hard for all year.

It was September 21. In his fifth start since being summoned from the minors, Clem Labine was pitching against the Phillies in Connie Mack Stadium. With the bases loaded in the bottom of the first inning, Labine toed the rubber and started to pitch to the Phillies' Puddin' Head Jones from a stretch position. Bolting from the dugout, Dressen screamed, "Time out," and ran to the mound. "I don't want you to go into a stretch," the manager told his young pitcher.

Labine, not confident of his control when pitching from a full windup, responded, "I can't get my curve ball over from a windup."

Dressen wouldn't yield. "You take a full windup," he ordered before running back to the dugout.

Royally ticked off by the whole affair, Labine disregarded Dressen's edict and delivered to Jones from a stretch. In a flash, Jones lined Labine's delivery over the outfield wall for a grand slam, which cost the Dodgers the game. Nearly 50 years later, the memory of what happened next remains crystal clear in Labine's mind.

> He came out and got the ball and then for four days he never talked to me. I was, at that time, probably as good as I could be. But he thought he had enough to win without me, but, let me tell you, the pitching staff was very thin. There were a lot of tired arms. But he was teaching me a lesson as a rookie.

A costly lesson, to be sure. While the exhausted Dodger pitching staff ran on fumes during the crucial final days, Labine rode the pine. Eleven days would elapse before Dressen would finally relent and announce to the press that Labine would start game two of the playoff series against the Giants.

Against New York, Labine was brilliant. Serving up a baffling combination of sliders, curves, and the occasional fastball, Clem completely dominated the Giants. He scattered just six hits and was in trouble only in the third inning, when the Giants loaded the bases. But Labine struck out Bobby Thomson to kill the rally. Meanwhile, Dodgers hitters, shaking off the lethargy that had shrouded them in game one, came alive. In the first, Jackie Robinson hammered a Sheldon Jones curve ball into the lower left-field bleachers with Reese aboard to make it 2–0. In the fifth, Snider doubled off the left-field wall, and Robinson lined a shot to center, which made it 3–0.

An act of youthful rebellion landed Clem Labine in Charley Dressen's doghouse, and the Dodger manager's prodigious ego kept him there, possibly costing the Dodgers the 1951 pennant. (National Baseball Hall of Fame Library, Cooperstown, N.Y.)

In the sixth, with the lights on and the sky threatening, Hodges homered into the upper left-field tier. After Cox reached base on an error, the skies opened and the game was delayed. Following a 41-minute rain delay, Snider and Furillo singled to account for another run. In the seventh, Brooklyn added two more runs, and it was now a laugher at 8–0. Then, for good measure, Rube Walker homered to right field with Cox aboard in the ninth. Final score: Brooklyn 10, New York 0.

After the game, Labine was gracious in victory. Perched on a trunk in the clubhouse, still perspiring from his efforts, he resisted the temptation to wax bitter over his manager's vindictive actions. When asked about the game, he simply said, "I was lucky. You have to be lucky when you pitch a shutout anywhere."

In his office in the Dodger clubhouse, Charlie Dressen dodged questions about where Labine had been the previous 11 days. Second-guesses could wait; right now, the sounds of his celebrating players resonated in his ears. There was still tomorrow.

Because 1951 was, is, and always will be about Leo Durocher and Charlie Dressen, it's interesting to ponder how Durocher might've handled the Labine situation had he, and not Dressen, been managing the Dodgers. Would he have allowed his anger at Labine's insubordination to hurt the team, as Dressen had? Clem Labine himself provides a clue: "You see, you had one fellow, Leo, who could use his anger and turn it into a plus factor, and you had Charlie Dressen, who could not."

Shortly following the 1951 season, the Baseball Writers Association held their annual dinner. During an amateurish but entertaining portion of the show, a song composed by a number of Brooklyn sportswriters was performed for the assembled crowd. It included these lines:

Turn back the hands of time,
Where, oh where, was Clem Labine?
Give me the lead that once was mine,
And let's do it all over again.

GAME THREE—WEDNESDAY, OCTOBER 3, 1951

All season long, the Giants had pushed, edged, and shoved against the Dodgers. Finally, on October 3, in the shadow of Coogan's Bluff, they engaged in the final act of their quixotic quest to become the champions of the National League.

New York had gone baseball crazy, and the evidence was everywhere. For Wednesday's game, stock market tickers in the financial district were rigged to add game updates to the usual stock reports. At the Brooklyn City Prison, inmates were issued transistor radios, which enabled them to stay in touch with game developments. In Manhattan's upscale restaurants, programmed dining music gave way to game updates every ten minutes. For those unfortunate few out of reach of radio or television, updates were available by phone, courtesy of the New York Telephone Company.

When asked late Tuesday who would start for the Giants on Wednesday, Durocher, in a statement that included no reference to Sal Maglie's ability with a safety razor, announced, "The Barber will be shaving." Don Newcombe, who'd pitched so valiantly all season, would start for the Dodgers. Because Maglie was the better rested of the two men, odds makers made the Giants favorites to win.

In the first inning, Maglie, showing signs of big-game jitters, walked Reese and Snider. When Jackie Robinson lined a base hit that drove Reese home, the score was Dodgers 1, Giants 0. Then, for then next six innings, Maglie and Newcombe settled into a gritty battle of attrition, with each holding the opposing side scoreless. Finally, in the seventh inning, with the lights of the Polo Grounds cutting through the fall gloom, the Giants broke through against a tiring Newcombe. Monte Irvin doubled, then advanced to third on Whitey Lockman's attempted sacrifice. Bobby Thomson then lifted a fly ball to center, which scored Irvin. Newcombe quelled the rally before there was further damage, but the score now stood at 1–1.

In the top of the eighth inning, Maglie finally faltered. After yielding singles to Reese and Snider, he uncorked a wild pitch that allowed Reese to score. Then, after intentionally walking Robinson, Pafko singled Snider home. Brooklyn wasn't done yet, as the next hitter, Billy Cox, rifled a shot past third, which scored Robinson and made it 4–1. The inning finally ended, but when it did, Brooklyn had edged to within six outs of at last finishing off the Giants.

While the Dodgers rallied in the eighth inning, Don Newcombe was undergoing a crisis of confidence in the Dodger dugout. "The zip's off my fastball," he announced to his teammates. Maybe it was time to rattle the bullpen. From the far end of the Brooklyn dugout, a voice rang out: "Don't give me that shit." Newcombe immediately recognized the voice as belonging to Jackie Robinson. Robinson, who would rise from his deathbed to beat the Giants, found talk of fatigue at this stage of the game akin to treason. Eyeing Newcombe steadily from his place on the bench, Robinson said, "Go out there and pitch."

With Robinson's words ringing in his ears, Newcombe rallied in the bottom of the eighth. Throwing harder than he had all day, Big Newk struck out the side. Watching this development with dismay from the third-base coaching box was Leo Durocher. That the greatest stretch run in baseball history was about to tap out, here, now, just short of its goal was unthinkable to the Giants' manager. In a last, desperate attempt at rattling the big right-hander, Durocher veered toward the pitcher as he left the mound at the end of the inning. "You'll never finish," he screamed at Newcombe, appending a few choice epithets in an attempt to unnerve the pitcher. Sensing Leo's desperation, Newcombe wouldn't bite. Turning to Durocher with a wry half-smile, he winked and, without breaking stride, ducked into the Dodger dugout.

In the top of the ninth, Larry Jansen replaced Maglie on the mound and retired the Dodgers in order. Brooklyn then took the field for the bottom of the ninth, needing just three outs to claim the National League crown. At the same moment, it was announced in the press box that credentials for Thursday's first World Series game between the New York Yankees and the Brooklyn Dodgers were ready for distribution. At the other end of the Polo Grounds, the Brooklyn clubhouse was a swirl of activity as team personnel hurriedly ripped open cases of champagne amidst a swelling throng of newsmen and city officials, who were gathering to greet the victorious Dodgers.

Back on the field, the moment of truth was at hand for New York. "I remember the feeling as we went into the dugout for our last at-bat," Bobby Thomson would later recall. "I never felt worse in my life. Total dejection. I remember thinking, 'Well, we were just good enough to get this far, but we're not good enough to go all the way.'" Thomson had no way of knowing that the Giants—a team that had chased lightning all season—were finally about to catch it.

For Brooklyn, things began ominously in the ninth inning when lead-off hitter Alvin Dark lined a Newcombe fastball to center for a base hit. The next hitter, Don Mueller, then rolled a grounder past Hodges into right field, which advanced Dark to third.

"Dark had singled to right," remembers Mueller:

> And I knew what I was going to do. I was going to single to right too. That's where the biggest hole was in the infield. Later on, of course, the Dodgers and some of their writers said that Hodges should've been playing back instead of holding Dark at first, because we were still three runs down, and he didn't represent the winning run. Well, a sportswriter in New York once gave me the nickname "Mandrake the Magician" because of the way I could guide a ball between two infielders. And Hodges holding Dark at first just made the hole in the infield bigger. And I put it through there.

The next Giants hitter to dig in against the struggling Newcombe was Whitey Lockman. In a flash, Lockman ripped a double to left center, which scored Dark. It was now Dodgers 4, Giants 2. Mueller, running hard all the way, barreled into third and broke his foot: "I went into third base and I was looking over my shoulder to see if the Dodgers might miss the cut-off man and give me a chance to score. I overstepped the bag and broke my foot. They carried me right off the field to the trainers' table in the clubhouse."

Emerging from the Brooklyn dugout and slowly walking to the mound to talk to Newcombe was Charlie Dressen. Years later, Don Newcombe remembered the scene:

> I'd been in three ballgames in six days down the stretch, and I guess I'd got-

ten tired. Charlie came out to the mound. We called Pee Wee, Jackie and Billy over to discuss the situation. Dressen said, "How do you feel?" I said, "I'll do whatever the fellas decide to do." Then Pee Wee said, "Charlie, get a fresh man out here." He [Dressen] goes right to the dugout, if I recall right, calls the bullpen, and talks to [bullpen coach] Clyde Sukeforth and says, "Clyde, who's throwing the hardest down there?"

As this point, Carl Erskine, who was warming up in the bullpen with Ralph Branca, picks up the story:

Dressen had Branca or Erskine. We were both up in the bullpen, we'd been throwing, and we were ready. When the call came to the bullpen, here's what I recall: Dressen I couldn't hear of course, but he must have asked Sukeforth, "Are they ready?" and I recall Suke saying, "They're both ready. Erskine's bouncing his curve some."

Dressen told Sukeforth that he wanted Branca.

In the history of baseball, fewer managerial moves have been more second-guessed than Dressen's selection of Branca to pitch to Thomson. Thomson had always hit Branca hard; his home run off Ralph just two days earlier had helped the Giants win the series' opening game. During the 1951 season, Thomson connected seemingly at will off of Branca, hitting a total of six home runs off the right-hander. With the season on the line, why would Dressen call on Branca to face Thomson?

Carl Erskine has a theory, and it involves Roy Campanella and his own overhand curve ball:

Campanella used to tell me, "Now Carl, don't you worry about throwing that ball in the dirt. You give me that good hard curve down low, I'll get that sucker." Now Walker [playing in place of the injured Campanella on Wednesday] was a good receiver, but not real quick. Whether Dressen, hearing that I was bouncing my curve, thought to himself, "Well, I don't have Campy back there, I can't afford a wild pitch, let me have Branca." Now I'm speculating, because I don't know what went through his [Dressen's] head. And I don't really know what he asked Suke. Sukeforth has always contended that he always made his decision based on who had the best stuff.

Thus, on October 3, 1951, at 3:50 PM, Ralph Branca walked from the Ebbets Field bullpen to face Bobby Thomson with the National League pennant on the line. Halfway to the mound, Branca passed Newcombe, who was making his way across the playing field to the Dodger clubhouse in dead center field. After stopping to wish Branca well, Newcombe walked to within a few yards of Duke Snider in center field. "Keep it cold, Newk," Snider yelled, referring to the champagne on ice in the Dodger clubhouse. "We'll be right in."

With Ralph Branca still in his follow-through, Bobby Thomson hammers the most famous home run in baseball history. (National Baseball Hall of Fame Library, Cooperstown, N.Y.)

Then, just as Branca reached the mound, Dressen did something curious. Instead of waiting to discuss strategy with his new pitcher, he flipped the ball to Branca just before he reached the mound and, without saying a word, turned on his heel and ran from the field. Duke Snider, watching the scene from center field, remembers attributing Dressen's odd behavior to a bad case of nerves.

Branca and catcher Rube Walker met briefly at the mound. They agreed on a strategy they'd employ against Thomson: get ahead in the count, then waste a fastball inside in an effort to set Thomson up for a curve on the outside corner. The meeting broke up, and Walker settled into his crouch behind the plate. Branca's first pitch was a fastball that split the plate. "If I was a better hitter," Thomson would say later, "I would've swung at the first pitch." Then, with his back arm twitching in anticipation, Thomson dug in to await Branca's next offering. Walker signaled for an inside fastball. Branca nodded and delivered. Thomson swung and lifted a fly ball toward left field.

In centerfield, Duke Snider, who had seen the ball leave the bat, was off in pursuit. Years later, Snider would recall what happened next:

What you do in the Polo Grounds when the ball's hit to left field and you're the center fielder is you run at full speed to play the ball off the wall in case it gets by the left fielder. As the ball was hit, it was hit low and sinking a little bit, and I took off as fast as I could.

Standing in the third-base coaching box, Leo Durocher suddenly realized that the ball might have just enough lift to clear the lower tier in left field, and he started screaming, "Get up! Get up! Get up!" Dodger left fielder Andy Pafko, hurtling backward, reached the left-field fence just in time to watch the ball settle into the seats for a game-winning, three-run homer. Game, season, and pennant to the New York Giants.

In an instant, the Polo Grounds was transformed into a kaleidoscope of noise, delirium, and frenzy. In the Giants' broadcast booth, Russ Hodges was rejoicing, "The Giants win the pennant! The Giants win the pennant! The Giants win the pennant! The Giants win the pennant!" Down below, joyous fans bolted from the stands and engaged in a broken field ballet with Polo Grounds security in an effort to reach Bobby Thomson who, now released from all care, was dancing around the basepaths amidst a shower of confetti. Running like a shot from the New York dugout toward his manager, Eddie Stanky tackled Durocher and wrestled him to the ground. Just before he reached home plate, Thomson kangarooed into the air, landed with both feet on home plate, then fell joyously into the arms of his celebrating teammates.

In minutes, the chaotic display rippled from the Polo Grounds and washed over New York. All over the city, people poured out of taverns, homes, and workplaces and danced in the street with total strangers to the accompaniment of car horns and blaring factory whistles. The sound of shrieking horns was heard from ferries and tugboats moored at Staten Island wharfs, and within an hour, a crowd of hundreds would gather outside Bobby Thomson's home in Dongan Hills.

For Brooklyn resident and Dodger fan Bill Schlansky, the memories of that fateful afternoon remain vivid:

> I lived in a postwar housing project, and veterans of World War II were the only ones who could get into these buildings. It was veterans and their families, which meant a lot of kids about my age. In my building, which included 36 apartments, there were two common areas with TV sets where you could sit with other folks and watch TV or, of course, you could listen to a radio in your own apartment. Anyway, I remember coming home from first grade, and after changing my clothes, I went outside to play. Occasionally, someone would call down from one of the open windows with an update of the Dodgers-Giants playoff. "Snider just singled" or "Lockman doubled to left." In the bottom of the ninth, the reports started coming pretty regularly. I knew that the Giants had two men on and that we were ahead by two runs.

Then suddenly I heard this collective groan. It was like it came out of the earth. It was everybody, in front of every radio or every TV in that apartment suddenly going, "Aauugh!" And I remember this kid like it was yesterday, leaning out of one of the upper-level windows and yelling, "Thomson just took Branca over the wall!"

After Thomson's blast, a stunned squad of Dodgers stood fixed in disbelief on the field of the Polo Grounds for a few moments, then began the torturous trek to their clubhouse. Duke Snider, who'd been in a dead run toward left field when Thomson's homer cleared the fence, reversed field and ran full speed into the Dodger clubhouse to escape the frenzied throng pouring onto the field. By the time he got there, the stark reality of what had happened hit home. "It really didn't hit me that we'd lost the ballgame," he recalled later, "until I got in and saw all the champagne, newspapermen and cameramen running to the Giants' clubhouse."

"I was in the clubhouse early after that devastating home run by Thomson," recalls Carl Erskine:

> And they had the TV cameras set up on our side, and the champagne cases were stacked on our side, and when this thing happened, they moved all this stuff across to the Giants' side. It was like a tomb in our clubhouse, because all the bedlam was outside. Finally, our guys started coming in one at a time, with their heads down. Dressen never unbuttoned his shirt, he just ripped it off. Robinson fired his glove into the back of his locker with as much force as he had. Branca came in. There's this famous picture of Ralph sitting on the clubhouse steps, pitched forward, with his arms between his knees and his head down, big number 13 shining on his back. I looked at all that, man, and said, "This is some day. We're on the losing side, but this is a historic moment."

Already in the clubhouse when Thomson hit his historic home run was Don Mueller:

> I was on the trainers' table in the Giants' clubhouse, being treated for my foot. I was probably the only guy in the place who missed Thomson's home run. But that's the way it happens, I guess. When I heard the roar, you couldn't tell if we'd lost or we'd won. So I had to wait until I heard a lot of commotion to find out that we'd won.

By the time the jubilant Giants fought their way through the mob and reached their clubhouse, the crowd swarming on the field numbered in the thousands. Inside, Thomson was the man of the hour. Shouting to be heard above the din of reporters, club executives, league officials, newsreel cameramen, and celebrating players, Thomson exulted, "What a finish! I didn't run around the bases, I rode around them on a cloud!"

Following the game, Charlie Dressen made his way through the chaotic Giants dressing room to Leo Durocher's side. "Somebody had to win," he told Durocher. "And if it couldn't be us, I'm glad it was you. Now go out and beat the Yankees." Before leaving the scene, Dressen answered a few questions from the press, then turned and disappeared in the crowd. Losing the pennant was hard enough but losing to Durocher and the Giants was an especially bitter pill. For Charlie, it would be a winter of what-ifs. What if he hadn't yielded to hubris and taunted the Giants through the clubhouse door? What if he'd used Labine during the last crucial week when the pitching staff was so exhausted?

A year later, Dressen finally realized his dream of beating Leo Durocher. The Dodgers won the National League pennant, and Durocher's Giants finished a distant second. Then, in 1953, Dressen led the Dodgers to their second consecutive pennant, while Leo's Giants finished an embarrassing fifth. Yet, in spite of his success, Dressen was never able to shake his obsession with Leo Durocher. Ultimately, it would cost Dressen his most treasured possession: his position as a major league manager.

Following the 1953 season, the Giants awarded Leo Durocher a new two-year contract. Watching all this with great interest was Charlie Dressen. In what he believed would be his grandest stroke yet at besting Durocher, Dressen immediately contacted the Dodgers and demanded a three-year deal. The Dodgers countered with one year. Dressen wouldn't yield. The next day, the Dodgers scheduled a news conference. Charlie Dressen, the manager who'd led Brooklyn to two consecutive pennants, was fired. Two weeks later, after an unsuccessful attempt at finding work as a major league manager, Charlie Dressen swallowed his pride and signed a three-year contract to manage in the minor leagues.

OCTOBER 1, 1951

NEW YORK	AB	R	H	BI
Stanky 2b	5	0	2	0
Dark ss	4	0	1	0
Mueller rf	5	0	0	0
Irvin lf	4	2	1	1
Lockman 1b	4	0	1	0
Thomson 3b	2	1	1	2
Mays cf	3	0	0	0
Westrum c	2	0	0	0
Hearn p	3	0	0	0
Totals	32	3	6	3

BROOKLYN	AB	R	H	BI
Furillo rf	4	0	0	0
Reese ss	3	0	1	0
Snider cf	4	0	1	0
Robinson 2b	3	0	1	0
Campanella c	3	0	0	0
Pafko lf	3	1	1	1
Hodges 1b	2	0	0	0
Cox 3b	3	0	1	0
Branca p	2	0	0	0
aRussell	1	0	0	0
Podbielan p	0	0	0	0
Totals	28	1	5	1

aHit into double play for Branca in 8th

New York	0 0 0	2 0 0	0 1 0	3
Brooklyn	0 1 0	0 0 0	0 0 0	1

Doubles: Dark
Home Runs: Pafko, Thomson, Irvin

New York	IP	H	R	BB	SO
Hearn (W)	9	5	1	2	5

Brooklyn	IP	H	R	BB	SO
Branca (L)	8	5	3	5	5
Podbielan	1	0	0	0	0

OCTOBER 2, 1951

BROOKLYN	AB	R	H	BI
Furillo rf	5	0	0	0
Reese ss	5	1	2	0
Snider cf	4	1	2	1
Robinson 2b	5	1	3	3
Pafko lf	5	1	1	1
Hodges 1b	4	2	2	1
Cox 3b	3	2	0	0
Walker c	5	1	3	2
Labine p	4	1	0	0
Totals	40	10	13	8

NEW YORK	AB	R	H	BI
Stanky 2b	5	0	1	0
Dark ss	5	0	0	0
Mueller rf	4	0	1	0
Irvin lf	4	0	1	0

NEW YORK	AB	R	H	BI
Lockman 1b	3	0	0	0
Thomson 3b	4	0	1	0
Mays cf	4	0	1	0
Westrum c	3	0	0	0
cWilliams	0	0	0	0
Jones p	1	0	0	0
Spencer p	1	0	1	0
aRigney	0	0	0	0
Corwin p	0	0	0	0
bThompson	1	0	0	0
Totals	35	0	6	0

aWalked for Spencer in 6th
bFouled out for Corwin in 9th
cRan for Westrum in 9th

Brooklyn	2 0 0	0 1 3	2 0 2	10
New York	0 0 0	0 0 0	0 0 0	0

Doubles: Thomson, Snider
Home Runs: Robinson, Hodges, Pafko, Walker

Brooklyn	IP	H	R	BB	SO
Labine (W)	9	6	0	3	3

New York	IP	H	R	BB	SO
Jones (L)	2⅓	4	2	1	2
Spencer	3⅔	6	4	1	0
Corwin	3	3	4	5	2

OCTOBER 3, 1951

BROOKLYN	AB	R	H	BI
Furillo rf	5	0	0	0
Reese ss	4	2	1	0
Snider cf	3	1	2	1
Robinson 2b	2	1	1	3
Pafko lf	4	0	1	1
Hodges 1b	4	0	0	1
Cox 3b	4	0	2	0
Walker c	4	0	1	2
Newcombe p	4	0	0	0
Branca p	0	0	0	0
Totals	34	4	8	8

NEW YORK	AB	R	H	BI
Stanky 2b	4	0	0	0
Dark ss	4	1	1	0
Mueller rf	4	0	1	0

NEW YORK	AB	R	H	BI
cHartung	0	1	0	0
Irvin lf	4	1	1	0
Lockman 1b	3	1	2	0
Thomson 3b	4	1	3	0
Mays cf	3	0	0	0
Westrum c	0	0	0	0
aRigney	1	0	0	0
Noble c	0	0	0	0
Maglie p	2	0	0	0
bThompson	1	0	0	0
Jansen p	0	0	0	0
Totals	30	5	8	0

aHit for Westrum in 8th
bHit for Maglie in 8th
cRan for Mueller in 9th

Brooklyn	1 0 0	0 0 0	0 3 0	4
New York	0 0 0	0 0 0	1 0 4	5

Doubles: Irvin, Thomson, Lockman
Home Runs: Thomson

Brooklyn	IP	H	R	BB	SO
Newcombe	8½	7	4	2	2
Branca (L)	0	1	1	0	0

New York	IP	H	R	BB	SO
Maglie	8	8	4	4	6
Jansen (W)	1	0	0	0	0

4

1959: Los Angeles Dodgers vs. Milwaukee Braves

On April 18, 1958, Willie Mays left a darkened runway of the Los Angeles Coliseum and stepped into the spring sunshine of southern California. In just hours, the San Francisco Giants and the Los Angeles Dodgers would rekindle their historic rivalry on the West Coast, but for the moment, Mays had something else on his mind. He wanted a look at the Coliseum.

To be sure, the Los Angeles Memorial Coliseum looked like nothing that Mays had ever seen before. The left-field fence, shoehorned by necessity into an alcove just 250 feet from home plate, was topped by a gargantuan edifice resembling a drift net left to dry in the sun. And if left field were no more than a decent fungo shot from home plate, then what about center field and the expanse that resembled open prairie in right? The marker in dead center read "410"; to right center it was an incredible 440 feet. Down the line it measured a mind-boggling 390 feet. Bedford Avenue had just become an airport runway. Shaking his head in disbelief, Mays suddenly found himself facing Dodger slugger Duke Snider. "Look where the right field fence is, Duke!" Mays exclaimed, pointing to the distant standard. "You couldn't reach it with a cannon! You're done, man!"

"Done" is as good a word as any to describe the 1958 Los Angeles Dodgers. Just three years removed from its first world championship, time and events had diminished the fiercely proud team. Two years earlier, burned out from a grinding ten-year battle against the forces of ignorance and bigotry, Jackie Robinson had retired. In 1957, dispirited by rumors of a move to California, the defending National League champions had staggered to a third-place finish, 11 full games behind the Milwaukee Braves. Then there was the matter of Roy Campanella. For the past decade, the catcher had been the heart and soul of the Dodgers. A three-time MVP, Campy had played a pivotal role in helping the team win five National League pennants and a world championship. His bat, his savvy handling of the Dodger pitching staff, and his irrepressible clubhouse presence were vital components of the Dodger chemistry. Then, shortly before the opening of spring training in 1958, he was paralyzed when his car ran off the road on a rainy night in New York.

"The loss of Campy was a major downer because he was such a good man for the team," recalls catcher Johnny Roseboro. "Sure, he'd been injured in the latter part of 1957 and was having major trouble holding the bat, but he was still going to be the number one catcher in 1958."

Time was catching up with the rest of the club too. Team captain Pee Wee Reese was nearing 40 and was playing out the string. Star pitcher and team class act Carl Erskine was pitching in constant pain, paying the price for a career built upon a foundation of overhand curve balls. Duke Snider, dogged by a bum left knee since wrenching it in a game against the Cubs in 1955, often required pregame cortisone injections just to take the field.

Disoriented and demoralized, the Dodgers finished a dismal seventh in 1958, 21 games behind the dominant Milwaukee Braves. The team's collapse was complete and all-consuming. Just one pitcher, Johnny Podres, was able to win as many as 13 games. Only one hitter, Carl Furillo, managed to drive in as many as 65 runs. For a team that had relied on pitching and hitting to bludgeon National League opponents for more than a decade, it was a humiliating fall from grace.

Today, explanations for the team's collapse are as varied as the '58 Dodgers themselves. Danny McDevitt, the last Brooklyn Dodger pitcher to start a game at Ebbets Field, points to the city of Los Angeles itself. "I'd been trying all of my life either to get to the Yankees or the Dodgers and to play in New York," McDevitt remembers:

> They were the teams in those days. And then to finally get there, and then go to a minor league town, which Los Angeles had always been, wasn't a happy thought. And the city provided too many distractions. I'd be in the bullpen, and I'd turn around and some movie star's legs would be right in my eyes. In the clubhouse, Danny Kaye would always be there, Bing Crosby, Jerry Lewis, and people like that. I think it was mostly distractions in 1958.

"When everyone moved out to Los Angeles, it was hard," remembers first baseman and outfielder Norm Larker. "It was hard to get acclimated.

Everyone thought they'd have the same team in LA as they had in Brooklyn, but it didn't happen. And, of course, there were the new guys."

Fireballing pitcher Stan Williams points to the Los Angeles Coliseum for some of the team's difficulties in 1958:

> Whenever you're pitching in a ballpark where it's 251 feet to left field — that's 64 feet shorter than Fenway's Green Monster — you're talking about a small ballpark. I always jokingly say, "Well, pitching in the coliseum didn't bother me, because I was a line-drive pitcher." But what hurt me most is left-handed hitters. I'd throw the ball by them, and they'd kind of open up and check their swing, and the ball would hit and go over the fence. Or a guy would hit a pop up, and the pitcher would run over to back up third and you look back, and there's your left fielder, your third baseman, and your shortstop all standing side-by-side up against the fence waiting for the ball to come down. That's the way it was.

The Los Angeles Coliseum might well be the strangest ballpark in baseball history. Prior to the 1958 season, Dodger president Walter O'Malley had scouted a number of facilities around the Los Angeles area, searching for a suitable home for his Dodgers. City officials at first suggested Los Angeles's Wrigley Field, a traditional baseball facility that shared the beauty and simple elegance of its namesake in Chicago. O'Malley was impressed by the ballpark's character but was less thrilled with the stadium's limited seating capacity. The owner fully intended for his Dodgers to play before enormous crowds, and by process of elimination, the cavernous Coliseum seemed the logical choice. The Coliseum Commission balked at funding the work required to transform the facility into a suitable site for baseball, but when O'Malley threatened to move his team to the Rose Bowl in neighboring Pasadena, the city relented.

In their wildest dreams, the architects of the Los Angeles Coliseum never foresaw baseball being played in their stadium. Through much of 1957, efforts at converting the facility for baseball were being dubbed "O'Malley's Folly" by critics. Because of the Coliseum's oval shape, O'Malley had no choice but to suspend a screen that stood 42 feet high at its sides and 145 feet at its center over the left-field fence to prevent every Punch-and-Judy hitter from threatening Babe Ruth's single-season home run record. Once O'Malley's screen was in place, Commissioner Ford Frick took one look and shook his head, saying that home runs would still come too cheaply. The commissioner then ordered an additional screen be erected behind the original, 333 feet from home plate. According to Frick, only balls that cleared both structures would be considered home runs. However, the plan soon ran afoul of California earthquake laws, and Frick was forced to accept a single screen.

O'Malley's screen did circumvent an onslaught of cheap home runs, but it also engendered a bizarre on-field ballet whenever a ball would bounce off it and spring back toward the field, usually with the third baseman, shortstop, and left fielder in mad pursuit. During 1958, the Dodgers' pitching staff, who'd watched their earned run averages inflate like grandma's slacks following Christmas dinner, had come to hate the screen with a passion. "I gotta change my style of pitching," Don Drysdale said early in the 1958 season. "My knuckles drag against that fence every time I wind up to pitch."

The Coliseum wasn't just tough on pitchers; hitters suffered too. "It was tough being a hitter in that ballpark," remembers outfielder Don Demeter. "There was no background in the outfield, you'd hit the ball right out of the white shirts; everybody was wearing light-colored clothing. It was tough to see out there, and of course, there was all that room in right center."

"That ballpark was particularly tough on Gil Hodges," recalls Norm Larker,

> because he pulled everything anyway. Pitchers pitched him different there. They threw him a lot of breaking balls out of the strike zone; when they got ahead of him, they'd break it outside about six inches and he'd swing at it. I also think it hurt me. I was a line-drive hitter, and if I hit a ball to left, they usually caught it on me. It messed me up for the batting title the next year. The other thing that was so bad was the lights. All the lights were at second base. It was tough, real tough to see in that ballpark.

"If you hit a long ball to center or right center in the coliseum," says Roseboro,

> you were in deep crap. When I got to the major leagues, they wanted me to hit the ball on the ground because I ran so fast. So hitting there didn't bother me much at all. I didn't hit the ball to left field at all. But it affected the other guys. Wally Moon was the only one on the team who could hit the ball over that left field fence.

If the players despised the ballpark, there was one man who loved it: Walter O'Malley. In an amazing display of drawing power for a seventh-place team, the Dodgers lured 1,845,268 fans to the cavernous Coliseum in 1958, an increase, O'Malley noted often and loudly, of 817,000 over the club's final year in Brooklyn.

Elated as he was over the financial dividends afforded by his new home city, O'Malley fretted equally over the poor play of his team during 1958. Knowing that the novelty of major league baseball would pale quickly among Angelenos if the Dodgers didn't start winning, O'Malley was determined to make whatever changes were necessary to improve his team's level of play for the 1959 season.

For O'Malley's lieutenants, the first order of business was to find some relief for the team's contingent of aging stars. During the spring of 1959, promising talent from the team's farm system were carefully evaluated and offered every opportunity to make the club. When help wasn't available in the minors, the club traded for the personnel it needed. In a particularly savvy deal in December 1958, the Dodgers snookered the Cardinals into trading them outfielder Wally Moon for Gino Cimoli. Arriving in Los Angeles the following day to meet with the press, Moon waxed confident. "The Dodgers just made a helluva deal," he told the press. "A lot better deal than the Cardinals made." Moon's swagger raised eyebrows among the gathered reporters but was indicative of a new spirit about to infuse the Dodgers.

Moon wasn't the only player determined to restore viability to the once-proud franchise. Dodger veterans, now diminished by one with the retirement of Pee Wee Reese, were also smarting over the team's dismal performance during 1958. The first sign that things might be different became apparent in the spring of 1959 when Furillo, Snider, and first baseman Gil Hodges reported to training camp in better shape and more focused than anyone could remember.

Shortly before the team broke camp to open the 1959 season, Dodger manager Walter Alston sat down with newspaper reporters to discuss his team's prospects. "They've made me optimistic," he said. "Everybody has worked harder. The general attitude is by far much better than it was last year. There's been less moaning. That seventh-place finish undoubtedly hurt their pride last year. That's clear."

For the archrival Milwaukee Braves, resenting the Dodgers had always come easily. Between 1953 and 1956, the Dodgers had won three National League pennants and a world championship, while each year, the Braves finished a half step behind them in the standings. Finally, with new manager Fred Haney at the helm in 1957, the Braves broke through. Led by the deepest pitching staff in either league and two of baseball's most feared sluggers, Milwaukee manhandled National League opponents throughout the season and won the pennant by eight games. That October, any doubts about the Braves' mettle were laid to rest when they steamrolled the heavily favored Yankees in the World Series. In 1958, the Braves again dominated the National League, winning the pennant going away while the Dodgers floundered in the second division.

The 1959 Milwaukee Braves were a beautifully balanced team. Led by

Lew Burdette, Bob Buhl, and the seemingly ageless Warren Spahn, the team's pitching was superb. Spahn, a native of Buffalo, New York, was the staff ace. Consistency and endurance were his hallmarks; between 1949 and 1957, the left-hander failed to win at least 20 games only twice. In 1958, at an age (37) when most pitchers were weighing retirement options, Spahn led the National League in wins (21), innings pitched (290), and complete games (23).

Since coming to the Braves as the throw-in on a deal that sent Johnny Sain to the Yankees, number two starter Lew Burdette had baffled National League hitters with his array of sinkers and sliders, which he alternately delivered from overhand, side arm, or three-quarters delivery points. On the mound, Burdette resembled a man with a bad case of hives. He'd fidget, squirm, twitch, and tug at his uniform until opposing hitters wondered if he'd ever get around to throwing the ball. When pressured in game situations, Burdette was often charged with adding a spitball to his repertoire, an accusation he steadfastly denied. Artful or not, Burdette's act worked; between 1952 and 1958, he won 105 National League games.

At third base was Eddie Mathews, a power hitter who, at 28 years old,

Milwaukee power on display. *From left:* Henry Aaron, Eddie Mathews, Joe Adcock. (National Baseball Hall of Fame Library, Cooperstown, N.Y.)

had already racked up more home runs than any man his age. His quiet, relaxed demeanor — mistakenly labeled as "lackadaisical" during his first years in the majors — was now recognized as a fierce dedication to his craft. Through sheer will, Mathews had transformed himself into a complete player, taking as much pride in his sure-handedness around the hot corner as he did in his towering home runs. Mathews' quiet demeanor masked a simmering aggression that often erupted when he was challenged, on or off the field. Mathews — usually with teammate Bob Buhl in tow — had developed a reputation as someone more than willing to exchange insults or even blows with fans of opposing teams foolhardy enough to chide him about a bad day at the plate or in the field.

At age 25, right fielder Hank Aaron had already taken his place among the game's finest hitters. At 5'11" and 175 pounds, Aaron was not an imposing physical specimen, but his lightning-fast wrists and smooth powerful swing enabled him to spray the ball to all corners of the field. Aaron's relaxed, laconic manner was bred of an almost crystalline self-confidence. Even when digging in against the league's most feared pitchers, Aaron's faith never flagged. "I have a bat and all the pitcher has is a ball," Aaron often said. "I figure that gives me an advantage over him."

Strong behind the plate with Del Crandall, dubbed by teammates the "All-American boy" because he neither drank nor smoked, and up the middle with Johnny Logan, Red Schoendienst, and Bill Bruton, the Braves figured to be the team to beat. Not counting the occasional iconoclast, the general consensus among baseball pundits was that the Braves had the 1959 National League pennant in the bag. A few, looking at the talent assembled in Pittsburgh, picked Danny Murtaugh's Pirates. Others, eyeballing the addition of Sad Sam Jones and Jack Sanford to San Francisco's pitching staff, pegged the Giants for an outside shot at the title. Not one picked the Los Angeles Dodgers.

THE RACE

Inclement weather in the eastern and midwestern portions of the country provided a bone-chilling backdrop to the start of the 1959 season. In Chicago to face the Cubs on April 10, the Dodgers were ambushed by an early spring snowstorm, which postponed their opener. In Pittsburgh under threatening skies, the Braves fared better. Picking up where he'd left off a year earlier, Warren Spahn shut out the Pirates 8–0. The following day, fighting arctic conditions, the Cubs, behind Bob Anderson, beat the Dodgers 6–1.

In May, one of baseball's great spectacles took place in Los Angeles when more than 90,000 fans jammed the Coliseum to watch the Dodgers and the New York Yankees square off in an exhibition game to honor Roy Campanella. Prior to the game, Dodger coach Pee Wee Reese guided Campanella's wheelchair to home plate to thunderous applause. Then, with all lights inside the ballpark extinguished, fans raised candles aloft in silent tribute to the man who had represented his team with class and distinction for more than ten years. It was a poignant moment and just one more reminder of how much had changed for the Dodgers since they had left Brooklyn.

Throughout the early weeks of 1959, stellar pitching by Spahn, Burdette, and Buhl and hot hitting by Aaron and Mathews kept Milwaukee at or near the top of the National League standings. Also vying for the top slot were the surprising San Francisco Giants, whose quick start had captured the attention of the baseball world. With a pitching staff anchored by Sam Jones, Jack Sanford, and Johnny Antonelli and an offense that featured Willie Mays and Orlando Cepeda, San Francisco matched Milwaukee win-for-win in the season's early weeks.

In contrast to the hot play of the Braves and Giants, things had yet to gel for Los Angeles. During April and May, the club ran hot and cold, winning three or four in a row, then dropping an equal amount in succession. Thanks to torrid hitting by Don Demeter and some cagey relief work by Art Fowler, the team was able to enjoy brief stints atop the standings before falling back. "That's right," remembers Stan Williams. "Early in the year, we had an older guy that did a great job for us, Art Fowler. We just wore him out. By summer, we'd just worn him out."

"The big thing for us at the start of the season was Art Fowler," says Norm Larker. "And he was great, for his age. He'd come in and shut them down."

But Fowler couldn't do it alone. Throughout the early weeks of the season, Walter Alston juggled his lineup constantly, searching for the combination that might help his club mesh. The only sure bets, day in, day out, were Charlie Neal at second base, Jim Gilliam at third, and John Roseboro behind the plate. The rest of the time, Hodges, Furillo, Snider, and other veterans found themselves competing for playing time with youngsters like Bob Lillis, Ron Fairly, and Norm Larker.

By mid-June, the team's inconsistent play was threatening to become a habit, and the team tumbled to fifth place in the standings. The gloom in the Dodger clubhouse over the team's uneven play was matched only by the early summer marine layer that was shrouding the Los Angeles basin. To make matters worse, Carl Erskine, one of the team's best-liked players, was flirting openly with retirement after being bombed in game one of a doubleheader against the Pirates in mid-June. A winner of 122 major league games, Erskine had baffled hitters for more than 11 years with a wicked overhand curve ball that kicked viciously toward the dirt just as their bats rushed to meet it. However, the violent snapping motion required to deliver the pitch had exacted a tremendous toll on Erskine's right arm, and by 1959, he was pitching in constant pain.

Aboard the team's private jet bound for Los Angeles, Erskine weighed his options. Perhaps if he placed himself on the disabled list and gave his arm some time to rest. Maybe another start or two would prove to be more encouraging. He'd sleep on it, maybe he'd have his answer in time for the meeting he'd scheduled with team general manager Buzzie Bavasi the following day.

"When Buzzie and I sat down in June of 1959," Erskine recalls,

> I said, "Buzzie, I think I ought to pack it in." "No, no, Carl," Bavasi responded. "You gotta start one more time." But the club was in fifth place, we'd had a bad year in '58, and I knew they were gonna have to do something with me. So finally, after a poor start in Pittsburgh, I went in and said, "Buzzie, I gotta do something." He said, "Let me send you to Spokane, and I'll bring you back at the end of the year." I said, "Buzzie, if I could pitch, I gotta pitch here." I didn't want to go back to the minors and do that again. So he said, "Well, I won't release you. I'm not gonna do that." I said, "What other options do I have?" and he said, "You can voluntarily retire, that's the only way I'll accept it." I said, "You draw it up."
>
> While he was drawing it up, I'm sitting in this office by myself in Los Angeles in the coliseum, and I said to myself, "Carl, burn this in your mind real good, because you never thought you'd ask out of uniform." But I'd always heard it said that when you get to the point you don't want to put the uniform on, that's the time to leave. And that's the way I felt. I couldn't help anybody, so I said burn that in your mind, because two years from now, you're gonna be watching TV, you're gonna say, "You know, I could probably still be pitching."

Ironically, the loss of Erskine proved to be a catalytic event for the Dodgers. On June 17, behind the pitching of Sandy Koufax and Danny McDevitt, the Dodgers swept the Braves in a doubleheader to climb to within 2½ games of first place. The next day, right-handed pitcher Roger Craig arrived in Los Angeles following a 1,200-mile drive from Spokane to fill Carl Erskine's place on the roster.

A 6'4" right-hander, Craig had pitched for the Dodgers in Brooklyn, but shoulder inflammation had torpedoed his effectiveness in 1957. Finally, in 1958, after a series of ineffectual starts, the team gave up on him and shipped him to the minors. In Spokane, Craig hit rock bottom, finishing the season with a 5–17 record. Then, against all odds, his arm began to grow stronger. In the early weeks of 1959, Craig found his groove and began to pitch effectively again. Now, with Erskine's retirement creating an opening on the starting staff, he'd been summoned back to the big leagues. "I know I can help them if they let me pitch," Craig told reporters upon his arrival in LA. "I'm throwing the ball real good, and I'm ready to start."

Taking him at his word, Alston started Craig the following day against the Cincinnati Reds. Craig was brilliant, allowing just five hits and striking out six as the Dodgers coasted, 6–2. Since his last stint with the major league club, Craig had morphed from a "thrower," who tried to blow the ball past hitters, into a savvy pitcher. "Roger came up sharp, pitching well," remembers Stan Williams. "He'd learned to change speeds and pitch to spots. He was very valuable to the team at a time when we needed him."

The arrival of Craig also seemed to energize the Dodger offense. Suddenly, lead-off man Jim Gilliam's bat came alive, and he reached base in game after game. The bats of Hodges, Demeter, and Moon also took on new life, and between June 22 and June 28, the team rolled, winning seven straight to climb to within one game of the first-place Braves. Proud, self-reliant, and composed, veterans and green rookies were learning to play side-by-side, and slowly they began to mesh into a unit of uncommon closeness. Through it all, redemption from the team's embarrassing performance of 1958 was the drawstring that pulled them together.

"Every one of those guys, the young guys who came along after the Brooklyn days, were made to feel welcome by the veterans," remembers Don Demeter:

> They were just a great bunch of gentlemen. Pee Wee Reese was third-base coach that year; just a great guy. He and Hodges too. And of course, Campanella, who didn't play but was a great encouragement just to have around. Snider was very helpful to me, personally. You'd think that a guy that was trying to get your job might be a problem, but he was great to me. And we were loose. Whenever we'd win a game, our clubhouse guy, John Griffin, would play "Happy Days Are Here Again." He also had this hat he wore following our victories, and then he'd switch to another hat when we'd lose. It kept the guys loose, and it was a lot of fun.

"The 1959 Dodgers were a family affair," remembers Stan Williams. "We didn't need a manager or coaches. If you screwed up, by the time you got to the dugout, you had three or four guys ragging on you."

"There were two or three groups on that team," says McDevitt. "There were the old fellows like Duke and Pee Wee, and they didn't need anyone to lead them like maybe some of the kids might. But there were probably two or three leaders on that team, Gil and Pee Wee, for sure."

"Snider was one of the top guys on that club," remembers Norm Larker. "He was a veteran, you had Hodges, just a bunch of guys who'd been around and been on championship teams. You'd get down a little bit, and they'd pick you up."

From the start of the season, Walter Alston had a modest goal for 1959: to reestablish the credibility of his club among his team's National League opponents. Now, with July approaching and his team still in contention, he was allowing himself the luxury of grander designs. During a press briefing in late June, Alston was handicapping his team's chances. "For us to win the pennant, four things have to happen," he said, indulging in a waking dream. "Snider and Hodges need to keep on hitting, and the pitching has to hold up. Lastly, we need to avoid injuries. If we do, we've got a chance." His comments may have fallen short of the Four Ennobling Truths for profundity, but coming from the manager of a team that had finished in seventh place just one year earlier, they were heady words indeed.

While the Dodgers were prospering, signs were emerging that all was not well in Milwaukee. Sure, Burdette and Spahn were winning, and home runs continued to jump from the bats of Aaron and Mathews, but players around the league had detected a disturbing complacency about the Braves. The intense competitiveness and hunger to win that had been so evident in '57 and '58 seemed strangely absent. Perhaps the mere notion of being outplayed by the lowly Dodgers or the upstart Giants stretched the team's credulity. Whatever the explanation, it was clear to many that the Braves lacked fire. "Milwaukee just isn't the same team we've seen in the past," a puzzled Duke Snider told reporters in late June. "At this point, they certainly don't look like the team to beat."

The lackluster play of Milwaukee stood in stark contrast to the inspired baseball being showcased in San Francisco. Like the Dodgers, the Giants had migrated from New York to California in 1958, but the transition had proved less harsh than for their rivals from the south. "When we arrived in California from New York, it was pretty much a new ballclub," remembers Giants relief specialist Stu Miller. "We'd left the '57 club behind. I was looking forward to the move. I'd never been west of St. Louis, and I'd heard so much about sunny California. I was kind of anxious to get out here."

Led by the game's greatest player, Willie Mays, and slugging first baseman Orlando Cepeda, the team finished third in its first season in California. Recognizing that improved pitching was the key to future success, the Giants traded for Jack Sanford following the 1958 season and then, in a master stroke, stole Sam Jones from the St. Louis Cardinals shortly before the 1959 season. With manager Bill Rigney at the helm, most, if not all of the pieces seemed to be in place for a run at the National League pennant.

"Rigney was the best manager I ever played for," Stu Miller says today:

> You know, managing is handling players; anybody can go out and change a pitcher. It's getting a club united that counts, and he could do that. He was good with the players. He had 25 players, and some managers have eight, and that's all they care about. A good example is Jim Leyland with the Marlins in 1997. He pulled that club together and got them to play together. Rigney did the same.

In early July, the Dodgers hopped a bus from Chicago to Milwaukee's Country Stadium for a three-game showdown with the Braves. Hobbled by the absence of Johnny Logan and perennial Dodger-beater Bob Buhl, the Braves were swept by Los Angeles. Suddenly, things were looking up for the Dodgers. The one area of concern in a sea of optimism was the ongoing slump of center fielder Don Demeter. "I remember I'd lost a lot of weight by summertime, had gotten kind of weak," recalls Demeter. "I wasn't swinging the bat as good as I was earlier in the year. But that's the one thing I remember about that team; everybody just worked together as a unit. When somebody wasn't going so good, somebody else just picked them up."

In place of the slumping Demeter, Alston turned to his bench. He shifted Wally Moon from left field to right, Duke Snider from right to his natural position in center, and inserted Norm Larker, who'd been hitting over .300 as a pinch-hitter, into left field. When Snider's trick left knee prevented him from starting, Alston turned to 21-year-old rookie Ron Fairly. Throughout the summer, Larker's clutch hitting and steady glove work in the outfield and at first base provided a lift for the team. When Carl Furillo returned to the team in mid-July following a long stint on the disabled list, the Dodgers were finally at full strength.

Throughout the summer of 1959, the Dodgers' trump card was its pitching. During a 20-game stretch in midseason, the team's starting staff allowed just five home runs. During June and July, Don Drysdale was almost unhittable, posting consecutive wins over the Reds, Phillies, and Cubs. Left-hander Danny McDevitt, working in both starting and relief roles, also got hot and ran off a five-game winning streak. "You get in that zone," McDevitt recalls, "and it's like a hitter having a hot streak. The difference in major league pitchers is consistency. I would have streaks, where the great pitchers are consistent all year long usually. But I was definitely throwing the ball well during June and July."

"We had a great staff to work with," remembers Johnny Roseboro:

I had no knuckleballs, I had a few spitters, I had a staff with great control. We did have a few kids who just came in and threw BBs, and didn't know where they were going, but you couldn't ask for a better pitching staff. They weren't difficult to catch, they weren't difficult to work with. They were my good friends, and we worked together like a clock.

Following the sweep by the Dodgers in early July, the Braves were suddenly in free fall. After dropping out of first place on July 5, the team swooned, losing seven straight games. By the third week of July, the club had tumbled to fourth place, 4½ games behind San Francisco.

Alarmed at their sudden futility, the Braves gathered for a players-only meeting to discuss the situation. "I'll tell you what's held us back until now," Joe Adcock told his teammates. "Everybody on the club thought we would win this thing from the start — and everybody figured he'd let the other guy do it. Well, the other guy isn't going to do it, we're going to have to do it ourselves, if it's going to be done at all." Adcock's impassioned speech did the trick. After some soul searching, the Braves found themselves and got hot. By month's end, they'd won nine of ten and leapfrogged over the Dodgers into second place.

Meanwhile, the Dodgers' pennant hopes suffered a blow on July 23 when Gil Hodges pulled a muscle in his right leg during a game against the Cubs. The injury was severe enough to keep the big first baseman out of the LA lineup for more than a month. The quiet, unemotional Hodges was more than the team's hottest hitter, he was also a towering presence in the clubhouse and on the field. In his absence, Alston turned to Norm Larker to handle first base and reinserted Don Demeter into the lineup.

In early August, the newly hot Braves journeyed to the West Coast with designs of knocking San Francisco out of the pennant race. However, after taking game one of their series, the club's offense was knocked into the deep freeze by Jack Sanford and Sam Jones. The Giants took games two and three of the series, further securing their hold on first place. For the Braves, the next stop was southern California, where a previously unknown phenomenon, pennant fever, was raging unabated in Los Angeles. On August 8 and 9, more than 180,000 Angelenos elbowed their way into the Coliseum to watch the Dodgers and the Braves split a two-game series.

As August wore on, the Dodgers and the Braves continued their battle for second place. In game one of a twilight doubleheader on Monday, August 17, the Braves pounded three Dodger pitchers for eight runs. In the nightcap, a home run by Don Zimmer provided the winning margin as Los Angeles edged Milwaukee 4–3. On Tuesday, Don Drysdale carried a 5–4 lead into the ninth inning, when, with two outs, Billy Bruton singled. The next hitter was Aaron, who lofted a routine fly ball to Don Demeter, which he dropped. Hustling on the play, Bruton roared around second and third in a desperate attempt to tie the game. "When I missed the ball, I had enough going for me to realize that I had to throw the ball to home plate to cut down the tying run," Demeter recalls today with a laugh. "When I threw it to home plate, it was a perfect strike. But there was nobody there to catch it, because Roseboro was out at the mound congratulating Drysdale on the victory."

In the tumult, Bruton scored the tying run, forcing the game into extra innings. In the 11th, the Dodgers pushed across another run, only to have the Braves tie it again on Aaron's 33rd homer in the bottom of the inning. That's the way it stayed until the 13th inning, when Rip Repulski blasted a single that drove home Wally Moon from third. Larry Sherry, suddenly making a name for himself out of the bullpen, held Milwaukee scoreless in the bottom half of the inning to preserve the win. It was the biggest victory of the year for Los Angeles and enabled the club to climb within two games of the first-place Giants.

While the Braves and Dodgers were battling one another in LA, the Giants parlayed an Orlando Cepeda home run and a Jack Sanford five-hitter into yet another victory, defeating the Reds at Seals Stadium. With the win, San Francisco's lead over the Dodgers and Braves increased to 1½ and 2½ games, respectively. Throughout the remainder of the month, the Giants continued to play wonderful baseball. Antonelli, Jones, and Sanford shined, racking up win after win. Offensively, the team was in heat. Willie McCovey, in the midst of one of the game's most historic debuts, was feasting on National League pitching, while Mays and Cepeda continued to be among the league's home run and RBI leaders. "Listen. Nobody could ever accuse the '59 Giants of being a finesse club," Stu Miller says with a laugh today. "All our guys were up there swinging for the fences."

On August 10, the Dodgers embarked on a grueling 15-day, 17-game road trip that would pit them against every National League team except the Giants. The trip began badly. Playing without spark, the club dropped two games to the Cubs in Chicago. The next day, the Dodgers, on a brutally muggy afternoon at Wrigley Field, rallied to win behind a gutsy relief performance by young Larry Sherry. However, on August 16, the team again turned in a performance that was marred by the failure of several Dodgers to run out ground balls. Following the game, an angry Walter Alston exploded to the press, ripping Don Zimmer, Ron Fairly, Charlie Neal, and Jim Gilliam for not hustling. "Ballplayers only have to run hard a few times a game," Alston told the press. "Sure, it was hot and humid, but that's no excuse. If a player's too tired to run, we'll get somebody who isn't."

For Alston, using the press as a pipeline to his players was nothing new. Uneasy *mano a mano*, Alston preferred the one-to-many structure of press meetings to convey messages to his players. "Walter never communicated with me personally," Stan Williams recalls:

> I don't know about the rest of them. Anything I ever heard about what he was thinking, I read in the paper. As far as communicating with his players, he was very quiet. Walter Alston was the type of guy that, if he'd been my neighbor, I'd have liked him. But working for him I didn't like.

"He was not very verbal," agrees Don Demeter, "but he'd talk to me quite a bit. He'd talk to the young players and encourage them. Mr. Alston was blessed with having pretty good players most of the time."

Few successful managers in baseball history generate such checkered reviews from their players as Walter Alston. To those he favored, he was the tough but fair tactician, guiding his team with a steady hand. To those who, for one reason or another, did not find his favor, he was a modestly talented manager whose success was more attributable to the contributions of his players and coaches than to any abilities he might possess.

Walter Alston was a great believer in first impressions. If a player shined in his initial appearance before him, he'd forever have the benefit of the doubt. If a player performed poorly, moving heaven and earth might not procure another chance. Alston's handling of Sandy Koufax serves as a prime example. In his autobiography, Koufax blames Alston for delaying his development as a winning pitcher. "Alston began by discounting me," Koufax recalls:

> He fell into the habit of letting his eyes skip right over my name. I was the great unwanted. I was the guy he couldn't afford to take a chance with. That impression carried over a year ... two years ... three years ... four years, can get to be very difficult to shake. Years later — years later — I couldn't put a couple of men on base in the late innings without being pulled right out of there.

"Alston was a guy that always had good coaches," remembers Norm Larker:

> He had Charlie Dressen, Pee Wee Reese, Durocher. He made the decisions, but he asked for a lot of help all the time, which is what makes a good manager. A manager just can't sit there on his own, he needs help from all over. Walt was strict. He was a curfew man, he'd check the curfews, and if he said something, he meant it.

"At that particular time, I don't think there was an awful lot of respect for Walter Alston," says Stan Williams:

He gained some maybe, later on in life. But there just wasn't a lot of respect as far as his managing goes with the ballplayers. The Dodgers always had a topnotch guy to help him out. They had Bobby Bragan one year, Charlie Dressen, he had Durocher. So he always had good people helping him. If a man doesn't know that much about the game and can take advantage of people who do, then it works out fine. I think Walter probably got better and learned how to deal with players a bit more as time went on.

Danny McDevitt also had his problems with Alston but attributes it more to his lifestyle than to Alston's personality:

You can't say anything bad, because he had a lot of success. But we never got along. I don't think he liked my lifestyle off the ballfield. He never talked to me about it, and I never talked to him about it. You remember a girl named June Wilkinson? [Wilkinson was a well-known model and actress during the 1950s.] Well, during one of our road trips, I found out that she wanted to meet me. So we come back to LA, and I'm the first one off the plane and June Wilkinson runs up to me. And Alston was right behind me and saw the whole thing. So, with things like that, Alston probably figured I didn't have much sense.

On Friday, August 28, the Giants arrived in Los Angeles for three crucial games against the Dodgers. With the season winding down and the club still trailing San Francisco by two games, the Dodgers openly spoke of the need to win at least two of the three games to keep their hopes alive. In game one, however, the Giants hammered a struggling Don Drysdale for five runs. But clutch hitting by Wally Moon on Sunday and an 18-strikeout performance by Sandy Koufax on Monday enabled the Dodgers to climb to within one game of first place. Despite the setback, Giants skipper Bill Rigney remained confident. "We're going home for 18 straight days, and we'll have a good home stand," Rigney told the press. "While we've lost our last five of six, we're still in first place."

While Rigney waxed positive, optimism was flagging in Milwaukee. After being shellacked by the Phillies on September 1 and 2, the Braves fell four games off the pace with just three weeks left in the season. Following game two, Braves catcher Del Crandall ruminated on Milwaukee's chances. "We've lost a couple of tough ones here," Crandall told reporters. "But I still think if this team forgets about the pressure and just plays the kind of ball we're capable of, we'll be OK."

In a scheduling quirk, the Dodgers found themselves with back-to-back off days on September 4 and 5. In a move to help ease the pennant pressure his club was feeling, Duke Snider hosted the entire Dodger team at his Fallbrook avocado ranch for two days of swimming, barbecuing, and basking in the late summer sunshine. A fine time was had by all, but once back in Los Angeles, the club struggled to regain its focus. On September 6, the sixth-place Cubs cuffed around Sandy Koufax and Don Drysdale to sweep a doubleheader and drop the Dodgers three full games behind San Francisco.

While the Dodgers floundered, Milwaukee finally began to regain its footing. Between September 6 and September 12, the Braves reeled off seven straight victories to climb into a second-place tie with Los Angeles. With a two-game showdown looming with the Dodgers on September 15 and 16, the Braves now felt that they had the momentum to knock Los Angeles out of the race once and for all.

On Monday, September 15, Bob Buhl took the mound to face Los Angeles in game one. Nobody enjoyed beating the Dodgers more than Buhl, and throughout his career, no one had made it look easier. During one particularly fortuitous year, the crafty right-hander had mastered them an amazing nine out of ten times. And on September 15, Buhl did it again, leading the Braves to a 4–1 victory.

Tuesday, September 16, dawned hot and smoggy in Los Angeles. In game two of their series, Joe Adcock's cannon shot over the Coliseum screen in the first inning to provide Milwaukee with a 2–0 lead. Fighting for survival, the Dodgers scratched back for five runs and chased Braves starter Joey Jay. In the fourth inning, Adcock hammered a towering blast toward left field that appeared to be destined for the left-field stands. However, instead of clearing the screen, the ball careened off a support tower and lodged in the screen's netting. After conferring with his colleagues, home plate umpire Frank Dascoli ruled the ball a ground rule double. Adcock and the Braves howled in protest. "The ball hit the girder over and behind the screen," screamed Braves manager Fred Haney at Dascoli. "It's a home run!" Haney's pleas were to no avail, and the game ground on, deadlocked at 7–7. Finally, in the 13th inning, singles by Wills, Chuck Essegian, and Charlie Neal and a bases-loaded walk issued by Don McMahon handed the Dodgers the victory. Meanwhile, up north in San Francisco, the Giants were keeping pace with their rivals by winning a 13–6 laugher over the Reds.

On September 17, the Dodgers departed Los Angeles for a crucial series against San Francisco, armed with one last opportunity to close the gap between their team and the Giants. "You know, when we left for that last road trip," remembers Norm Larker, "we had to go up to San Francisco and play them three games. And they were leading us by two games. Nobody had to tell us how critical those games were. We knew it."

On Friday, an early fall rainstorm soaked the Bay Area and Seals Stadium, and game one was rescheduled as part of a day-night doubleheader the following day. On Saturday, the Dodgers stunned sellout crowds with a clean sweep behind Don Drysdale and Roger Craig. "Roger had four different pitches he could throw up there," remembers Johnny Roseboro. "And my philosophy has always been, if you've got four different pitches you can throw over the plate, you've got the hitters by the gonads. And he had all of them working against the Giants that day."

On Sunday, the Dodgers again drove a stake into San Francisco's pennant hopes when they beat the Giants for the second consecutive day. Suddenly, Los Angeles was in sole possession of first place. In Philadelphia, a grand slam by Del Crandall powered Milwaukee over the Phillies, and the Braves took over second place.

While the Dodgers and Giants spent Tuesday, September 22, traveling to St. Louis and Chicago, respectively, the Braves were beating up the Pirates in Pittsburgh. A week of transcendent baseball by Los Angeles and Milwaukee had completely transformed the pennant race. With just five days remaining in the 1959 season, the standings now looked like this:

Team	Games Behind
Los Angeles	—
Milwaukee	—
San Francisco	1

On Wednesday, September 23, the Dodgers rolled into St. Louis to confront the Cardinals. In game one, the pitching staff, so steady over the previous two weeks, came unglued, and the club lost 11–10. The Giants, armed with a golden opportunity to regain a share of first place, instead picked this day to begin a terrible decline, which would ultimately spell the end of the team's pennant hopes. Carrying a 4–3 lead into the ninth inning against the Cubs, a dog-tired Sam Jones served up a two-run homer to George Altman, sending San Francisco to its fourth straight loss. "Down the stretch, Rigney had a tendency to use Sam Jones not only as a starter, but in short relief too," recalls Stu Miller. "And I think he just wore poor Sam out. He didn't have much left at the end."

In Pittsburgh, the Braves were the personification of cool confidence as they again manhandled the Pirates. With the victory, the Dodgers and Giants were now one and two games back of Milwaukee, respectively. Following his team's shellacking in St. Louis, Walter Alston's faith in his club appeared shaken. "We're in a tough spot, no question," Alston told reporters. "We'll just have to win all we can. I don't think Milwaukee can go straight through without losing one. They might, though."

On Thursday, the Milwaukee juggernaut hit a speed bump when the Pirates handed them a bitter 5–4 defeat. In St. Louis, Roger Craig shored up his club's pennant hopes with a masterful five-hitter over the Cardinals, which lifted the Dodgers back into a flat-footed tie with Milwaukee. Meanwhile, in Chicago, the Cubs continued to kick dirt over the flickering embers of San Francisco's pennant dreams with a 9–8 victory.

With the pennant race again deadlocked, all three teams took an off day on Thursday, September 24. The following day, the Dodgers would face

Willard Mullin's illustration captures the essence of September 1959. With the American League pennant wrapped up, the Chicago White Sox can't figure out if their opponent in the World Series will be the Dodgers, Braves, or Giants. (Shirley Mullin Rhodes and the Estate of Willard Mullin.)

the Cubs in Chicago, the Braves would square off against the Phillies, and the Giants, playing — and praying — for a miracle, would face the Cardinals in St. Louis.

On Friday, September 25, sterling relief pitching by Larry Sherry and a clutch 11th-inning home run by Gil Hodges lifted the Dodgers over the Cubs. Playing in a steady drizzle in Milwaukee, the Phillies stunned the Braves and a celebrating Milwaukee crowd with a 6–3 victory that lifted Los Angeles into first place with a full game lead. Following the contest, Fred Haney assessed his team's chances for the press: "We just have to go out and win and hope the Cubs help us against the Dodgers. We still have to win ours, but now we have to hope the Cubs take at least one game from the Dodgers."

On Saturday, Haney got his wish. "Saturday, we were blown out by the Cubs, 12–2," remembers Stan Williams with a laugh:

> How bad was it by the end of the game? Well, Earl Averill, Jr., was playing second base in that game, and he was a catcher. We all kind of laughed about it, because you're better off getting blown out, and it's a laugher and everybody's loose, instead of losing a 1–0 heartbreaker.

Against the Phillies on Saturday, the pennant hopes of the Milwaukee Braves were resting squarely upon the able shoulders of Warren Spahn. After surrendering two solo home runs to the Phillies early in the contest, the screwballing lefty settled down and found his groove. Meanwhile, timely hitting by Lee Maye, Johnny Logan, and Eddie Mathews provided the needed offense.

Throughout the contest, updates from the Cub-Dodgers game were relayed to the Braves' bench by the team's equipment manager, who had his ear glued to a radio in the Milwaukee clubhouse. When Gene Frees flied out in the ninth inning, it was over. Spahn notched his 21st victory of the season and his 267th career win. "At a time like this, you don't worry about records," Spahn told the press following the game. "The main objective is to stay in the race." After six months and 153 games, the Dodgers and Braves would carry identical records of 85 wins and 68 losses into the season's final day to determine the winner of the National League pennant.

On Sunday, the masterful Roger Craig, behind the hot hitting of Charlie Neal and Johnny Roseboro, handcuffed the Cubs, 7–1. Over the course of the game, the clubs had waged a gritty battle before the Dodgers finally broke through against Cubs starter Bob Anderson. "We beat a tough pitcher the final day in Chicago," remembers Norm Larker. "He'd beat us all year long. And I remember Duke Snider saying to the bench throughout the game, 'We'll get him. Just stay in there, we'll get this guy now.' And we did."

In Milwaukee, news of the Dodger triumph was posted on the County Stadium scoreboard. The fans, edgy over the tense 1–1 battle being played out on the field, grew deathly silent. Finally, in the seventh and eighth innings, the Phillies' pitching and defense collapsed, opening the door to four unearned Milwaukee runs. When it was over, Milwaukee had defeated the Phillies 5–2. The collapse of the Phillies represented a ticket into the playoffs for Milwaukee, and the Braves weren't complaining. "Hey, with all the hard luck and injuries this club has had this year, we were due for a break," Johnny Logan told reporters following the game.

Back in Chicago, Dodger first baseman Gil Hodges was packing for the 90-mile train ride that would carry the Dodgers to Wisconsin for the fourth sudden-death playoff in baseball history. "Well, we're off to Milwaukee," Hodges said, bag in hand, as he made his way through a gaggle of reporters gathered in the clubhouse. Then just before he reached the door, the big first baseman stopped and looked back at the gathered newsmen. "You know," Hodges told them, "we were hoping the Phillies would help us out today. But that's OK. Now, we'll just have to lick the Braves ourselves."

GAME ONE—MONDAY, SEPTEMBER 28, 1959

After playing lackadaisically through most of the 1959 season, a close brush with elimination had energized the Braves during the season's final weeks. Now at home in Milwaukee to face Los Angeles for game one, the team was hungry to beat the Dodgers and claim its third consecutive National League pennant. So hungry, in fact, that one hour prior to the game, Warren Spahn was dispatched to the Dodger clubhouse with orders to do his best to unnerve starting pitcher Danny McDevitt. "Hey, that was a big game," McDevitt recalls. "And the Braves tried all the tricks. They went so far as to send Warren Spahn over to our clubhouse to speak to me. He wanted to be sure I knew just how big a game it was."

Off-again, on-again rain showers provided a gloomy backdrop to the war of nerves that would characterize the first sudden-death baseball playoff in eight years. In the first inning, the Dodgers parlayed an error by Bobby Avila, an infield out by Moon, and a base hit by Larker into a run. McDevitt looked sharp in the bottom of the first, striking out Mathews and Adcock, but he faltered in the bottom of the second. After he walked Logan, Crandall and Bruton singled to tie the score. Reacting quickly, Alston lifted McDevitt from the game and waved Larry Sherry in from the bullpen. After completing his warmups, Sherry induced Carlton Willey to roll a slow bouncer to Wills who, instead of forcing Bruton at second, booted the ball to load the bases. Wills atoned on the next play with a great stop of Avila's grounder, which forced Willey at second, but Crandall scored on the play to make it 2–1 Braves. Sherry then retired Milwaukee without further scoring.

With the County Stadium lights piercing the autumn gloom, Los Angeles went on the attack in the third inning against Willey. Charlie Neal singled, then was forced at second by Moon. Larker, batting cleanup this day in place of the injured Duke Snider, laced a single for his second hit of the day. "I had a pretty good day," remembers Larker. "See, Carlton Willey had good stuff, but I'd faced him all through Triple A ball in Wichita and St. Paul. Not bragging or anything, but I hit him pretty good down there. And when I came to the big leagues and faced him, it was like old-home week."

With ducks now on the pond, Hodges lined a Willey offering to left field for a hit that drove home Moon. Willey was able to retire the Dodgers without further damage, and after three innings, the score was knotted 2–2. It stayed that way until the fifth when Sherry walked Joe Adcock and then surrendered a single to Lee Maye. However, instead of faltering, Sherry grew stronger, inducing Johnny Logan to ground out. In the sixth inning, Roseboro broke the deadlock when he hammered a Willey fastball over the 355-foot marker in right field for a home run. The score was now 3–2, Los Angeles.

For the remainder of the contest, Sherry was a picture of cool detachment as he utilized a mixture of blazing fastballs, curves, and sliders to handcuff the Milwaukee hitters. After shutting down the Braves in the ninth, the pitcher was mobbed by his teammates, who all but carried him into the clubhouse. The victory over Milwaukee was Sherry's seventh consecutive win and his fifth straight in relief.

"Sherry had great command in that series," Roseboro remembers. "I mean, he was throwing that slider on the outside part of the plate, fastballs up and in, good curve ball. You know, Larry was as mean as Stan Williams out there on the mound. Maybe a little meaner, because he knew where the ball was going."

While reporters continued to pepper Sherry for his thoughts on the game, Walter Alston spoke to newsmen in his office. "In the last month, all our wins have been big. But I guess this one's the biggest." When asked about his pitching plans for game two, he responded, "It'll be Drysdale tomorrow, then if necessary, Roger Craig for game three. But I hope we won't have to look that far," Alston said to reporters, unable to suppress a grin. "I hope we don't have to look beyond tomorrow."

GAME TWO—TUESDAY, SEPTEMBER 29, 1959

On September 29, a game of extraordinary excitement and tension was played at the Los Angeles Memorial Coliseum. For the Milwaukee Braves, the summer-long test of desire versus complacency would finally be answered. For the Dodgers, it was an opportunity to forge a winning tradition in Los Angeles and forsake the grim heritage of 1958.

At 12:55 PM, Don Drysdale walked to the mound with a chance to fulfill his dream of pitching the Dodgers into the World Series. Tall and fearsome, Drysdale struck trepidation into the hearts of the opposition with his hell-bent-for-leather pitching style. Hailing from the "if your grandmother walks up to the plate with a bat, knock her on her ass" pitching school, Drysdale was fearless on the mound. Throughout his career, the big right-hander was renowned for unleashing blazing fastballs in the general direction of opposing hitters, while appearing indifferent as to whether they got out of the way or not.

Today, however, Drysdale was shaky. In the first inning, a walk to Mathews, a double by Aaron, and a single by Frank Torre staked the Braves to a quick 2–0 lead. In the bottom of the first, the Dodgers pieced a Charlie Neal triple and a single by Wally Moon into a run, but the Braves answered back in the second when singles by Logan and Burdette and a throwing error by Snider handed them another run. In the fourth, Burdette hung a breaking ball to Charlie Neal that the second baseman raked over the left-field screen for a home run. The seesaw battle continued in the fifth until Mathews drove Drysdale to the showers with a homer to right. The score was now Braves 4, Dodgers 2.

In the bottom of the seventh, the Dodgers threatened again when Larker opened the inning with a single to left. Then, in a significant play, Larker was forced at second, but in a bone-crushing takeout, he barreled into shortstop Johnny Logan, knocking the wind out of him. Logan was carried off the field on a stretcher, and manager Fred Haney moved second baseman Felix Mantilla to short to play in place of the fallen Logan.

"The big play there was when Larker knocked out Logan on the double play," remembers Danny McDevitt. "Then Mantilla was playing out of position, and that would prove to have a big impact on the game."

"I've played all my life that way," Larker says:

> It wasn't that I wanted to hurt the man, but I learned how to take double plays out when I started playing ball. It's changed now, you can't do that. But I've watched guys go after shortstops, and shortstops hit guys in the face. I saw it all. It's just the way you play ball. You want to win, you want to break

up double plays. I was worried about hurting him when I hit him, but I had to do it.

In the eighth inning, a Del Crandall triple and a Felix Mantilla sacrifice added to Milwaukee's run total. In the ninth, hearts beat quickly in the Coliseum when Milwaukee loaded the bases and threatened to blow the contest wide open, but after strolling in from the Dodger bullpen, Clem Labine fanned Mickey Vernon to end the threat.

Throughout the seventh and eighth innings, Burdette bobbed and weaved like a fighter with a glass jaw, somehow avoiding a knockout blow. With every strike he registered, with every batter he retired, a groan of despair arose from the Coliseum crowd. In the Dodger dugout, the sustained tension of the gritty battle only fueled the belief among Dodger players that today had to be the day. "Who was scheduled to pitch the next day for Milwaukee?" Stan Williams says today. "Bob Buhl, the Dodger killer. I mean, he'd just kind of throw his glove out there, and he'd beat the Dodgers, so we had to win the second game. If we didn't, we'd have to do it against Buhl the following day. A very tough task."

During the top of the ninth inning, a curious event took place in left center field. While waiting out a pitching change, Duke Snider sidled over to Wally Moon and said, "Five straight hits, Wally."

"What do you mean?" questioned Moon.

"I feel it," Snider responded. "I feel we're gonna get five straight hits in the ninth inning."

With the score standing at 5–2 in the ninth, Moon did his part to make Snider's prophecy a reality when he greeted Burdette with a single. The next hitter was Snider, who ripped a shot back through the box that somehow missed Burdette, skidded off the infield grass, and kicked through to center field. When Hodges lined Burdette's 2–2 offering to left for a single, the bases were juiced, and the Dodgers were in business.

With Burdette's tank now reading empty, Fred Haney had to make a move. Emerging from the visitors' dugout, the Braves' manager stopped to confer briefly with home plate umpire Al Barlick, then waved relief specialist Don McMahon in from the bullpen. After taking his warmup tosses and going over signs with Del Crandall, McMahon reached for the resin bag and took the mound to face the Dodgers' most torrid hitter over the past week, Norm Larker.

"We had the bases loaded, and I was the hitter with none out," remembers Larker:

Haney came out to change the pitcher, and he had both Pizarro and McMahon in the bullpen. And I could hear Zimmer hollering from the bench, "Go get 'em, Larker!" See, if Pizarro would've come in, I would've been out of the game, and Alston would've sent one of the right-handed hitters in there. But they brought McMahon in, who'd been tough on me all year. He'd throw that fastball low and away for a strike on the corner. And he had very good control.

Determined not to walk Larker, McMahon unleashed a fastball that started wide, then tailed in over the plate. In a flash, Larker laced the pitch to left field, where it bounced off the left-field screen for the Dodgers' fourth consecutive hit. Larker's drive scored two runs and reduced Milwaukee's advantage to 5–4. With his back now squarely against the wall, Haney again emerged from the dugout and summoned Warren Spahn from the bullpen to face left-handed Johnny Roseboro.

Watching these events unfold with interest from the darkness of the Dodger dugout was veteran outfielder Carl Furillo. At 36, Furillo was the club's elder statesman, his days as a regular player cut short by advancing years and nagging injuries. Throughout 1959, he'd played just 25 games in the field and come to the plate a paltry 93 times. But once the old right fielder had the scent of victory in his nostrils, few men were more treacherous with a bat. Knowing this, and sensing an opportunity to counter Haney's strategy, Walter Alston yelled for Furillo to grab some wood and hit for Roseboro.

At the plate, Furillo took Spahn's first pitch for a ball. On the mound, the crafty left-hander stared at catcher Del Crandall, stretched, and looked once, then twice over his right shoulder at Hodges, who was edging cautiously down the third-base line. Spahn then kicked and delivered to the plate. With a slashing cut, Furillo lifted a deep fly ball to right field, which Aaron hauled in just short of the fence. After the catch, Hodges tagged at third and cruised home with the Dodgers' fifth run to tie the game. The full-throttle pandemonium that erupted in the Coliseum washed over the stunned band of Braves sitting in the Milwaukee dugout.

Maury Wills kept the rally alive when he lashed a single that drove Spahn from the box. Haney then signaled for Joey Jay to come in from the Braves' bullpen. Jay finally restored order when he retired Ron Fairly on a force play and Gilliam on a fly out to right field. But, with its three-run cushion gone, Milwaukee would now be forced to carry its quest for the pennant into extra innings.

In the top of the 10th inning, Stan Williams shut down the Braves without incident. Pitching for the Braves in the bottom of the 10th was Bob Rush, who did the same. In the top of the 11th, Williams set teeth on edge in the Dodger dugout when he walked the bases loaded with two out, yet somehow managed to wriggle free without surrendering a run.

"I walked three or four guys over those three innings of relief I pitched that day, but the funny thing, I was never in trouble, because I never gave in to any hitter," recalls Williams:

> Either they were gonna hit my pitch, or they were gonna walk. I threw one breaking ball in the three innings, I think it was the 10th inning, a slider to Aaron and hung it. I can still see the whites of his eyes. They got very big, and he tomahawked that thing and the ball went straight up in the air and came straight down, right in front of the left-field fence. And that was the last breaking ball I threw. I stayed with fastballs the rest of the time. I was pinpointing extremely well. When I finally got Adcock up in the 11th with the bases loaded, I went after him. He pulled off the ball a little bit, so I pitched him low and away and got him out and out of the inning. But the walks I gave up weren't a matter of being wild, they were the result of not giving in. There's a big difference between the two.

After Rush shut down Los Angeles in the bottom of the 11th, Williams again relied on a steady diet of fastballs to stifle the Braves in the 12th. With their season on the line, the National League's defending champions departed their dugout and took the field for the bottom of the 12th.

As so often happens in baseball's most exciting games, the final inning would begin routinely, yielding no clue that history was about to be made. In the 12th, the Dodgers' first hitter was Wally Moon, who lifted a routine pop fly to second baseman Bobby Avila. The next hitter was Stan Williams, who flied out to Bruton in left center.

Dawdling in an effort to give Williams a chance to catch his breath, Gil Hodges walked slowly to the plate to face Rush. After digging in, the veteran first baseman took Rush's first pitch for a strike, then walked on four straight pitches. After pumping his fist in the direction of on-deck hitter Joe Pignatano, Hodges jogged down to first base. Standing at the plate, Pignatano got a pitch he could handle and promptly singled between short and third base, enabling Hodges to steam into second base with the potential winning run. Now, digging in at the plate to face Rush was the ninth-inning hero, Carl Furillo.

With the shadows of October creeping slowly across the Coliseum playing field, Rush worked the count to 2 and 1. Wigwagging signs behind the plate, Crandall signaled for a curve ball. With a shroud of tension now cloaking the Coliseum, Rush picked off his sign, nodded, slowly rocked into his windup, and delivered. In the batter's box, Furillo watched as the pitch began to break low over the plate. Slashing at it furiously, Furillo pounded the ball into the infield dirt. In a flash, the ball bounded off the turf, then kicked high over Rush's head, seemingly destined for center field. Charging hard from shortstop in a desperate attempt to glove the ball was Mantilla, who after making a sensational grab, gunned an off-balance peg to first base. From his vantage point, first baseman Frank Torre realized that Mantilla's throw would be short and off line. Straining for the ball, Torre came up short, and the pellet skipped off the dirt in front of his outstretched glove, kicked over his head, and struck Dodger first-base coach Greg Mulleavy in the shoulder before finally bouncing into the stands.

With two outs, Hodges had been running on the play. Steaming toward third, the big first baseman saw coach Pee Wee Reese windmilling his right arm in the direction of home plate and screaming, "Go! Go! Go!" Bearing down, Hodges stabbed the outside corner of the third-base bag with his right foot and turned full speed toward home. As he did, he shot a glance over his left shoulder and saw Mantilla's throw kick past Torre and slam into Mulleavy's shoulder. A moment later, Hodges crossed home plate with the winning run.

Somehow, the Los Angeles Dodgers had done it; they'd climbed all the way from seventh place to the National League pennant in just a single year. And it seemed fitting that the two men at the center of the celebration, Hodges and Furillo, had been there when the Dodgers won their only world championship in 1955. If you half-closed your eyes, it was Brooklyn all over again. Only the letters on the caps were different.

Following the game, reporters wasted little time in second-guessing Haney's decision to play Mantilla at shortstop in place of the injured Logan. But today, a number of Dodger players, including Norm Larker, aren't sure that Logan, or anyone else, could've altered the game's outcome:

> Remember that ball that Furillo hit over the mound? Maybe Logan would've never got to that ball. Mantilla was a lot quicker and younger than Logan. When he went to his left to field that ball, that's a hard play when you have to throw it with something on it to first base. You can't come up on top, you throw sinkers. And he threw a hell of a bad sinker to Frank Torre. And Frank was a good first baseman, but the ball had just the right spin and hit and went straight up.

Larker also recalls how fate played a hand in determining his role in game two:

> You know a funny thing about that game? When we left Milwaukee to fly home on Monday to play the next afternoon in the Coliseum, Spahn was supposed to pitch, and when Spahn pitches, I wasn't going to play. It was going to be Demeter in the outfield and Hodges at first. I would be the pinch-hitter. So on Tuesday, my wife and I were driving to the ballpark, and I said, "I'm not going to play today." You have a different kind of a feeling when you know you're not going to play. You're relaxed more, you're not thinking.

Because, usually, if I'm playing, I get up in the morning, and I start thinking about who's pitching, what's this, I go through the whole regimen. I just
relaxed and figured I'd sit on the bench until they need me. And I'll be
damned, we get to the ballpark and Burdette's starting, and I said, "Oh shit,"
because I had to gear up again.

Following game two, many in the jubilant Dodger clubhouse praised
the steely poise shown by Stan Williams in shutting down the Braves during the game's final innings. Looking back, Williams pinpoints the factors
that contributed to his success in 1959:

It was observation and mental planning. I observed pitchers who had half
the physical abilities that I did having great years and being successful. I
started asking questions, finding out what I could do to improve myself. So
I studied different pitchers. Vernon Law, for example. I learned mound presence from him. I learned relaxation from Lew Burdette. And I set up a system for myself called the Three Cs: confidence, control, and concentration.
Something I developed quietly, for myself. I also doubled my running program; whenever [Dodger pitching coach] Joe Becker got done killing us with
his running program, I'd go run another 10 or 15 laps on my own. And when
you put in extra work, you expect to get paid for it when you go to the hill.
And in 1959, I was.

Today, more than 40 years have passed since the Los Angeles Dodgers
bucked the odds and climbed to the top of the baseball world in 1959.
However, the passage of time has done little to dim the amazement of
many observers over the club's success. Noted baseball historian Bill James
still refers to the '59 Dodgers as the weakest championship team in baseball history. The numbers back him up. In 1959, the Dodgers had no one
among the National League's top five in home runs, runs batted in, runs
scored, or hits. Statistically, the pitching staff fared somewhat better, but
the club still had no one among the league leaders in wins, ERA, or winning percentage. And with just 86 regular season victories, their win total
was the lowest for any team in baseball history to that point. In light of
these numbers, explaining exactly how the Dodgers transformed themselves from also-rans to pennant winners takes some doing. To some
observers, it seemed clear that the team had awakened from a slumber of
existential confusion in 1959, finally coming to terms with the loss of
Robinson and Campanella and managing to find a measure of peace in their
bewildering new surroundings. For others, the answer could be found in
the club's unique chemistry: the easy and unlikely blend of veterans and
rookies, which enabled the team to fashion a fulcrum of experience and
youth that lifted it over its opposition.

Catcher Johnny Roseboro has a simpler answer:

We just had a good bunch of guys. We had some guys with experience and some young guys breaking in. We weren't the boys of summer, by any means. We were completely different from the boys of summer, and from that point on, we started playing a different type of Dodger baseball. More aggressive, more defense. When you've got Carl Furillo and Duke Snider and that whole team they had in Brooklyn, you had some guys who could bomb the ball out of the ballpark. We didn't have that in 1959. We just had a good bunch of guys.

SEPTEMBER 28, 1959

LOS ANGELES	AB	R	H	BI
Gilliam 3b	4	0	0	0
Neal 2b	5	1	3	0
Moon lf	4	1	1	0
Larker rf	4	0	3	1
aLillis	0	0	0	0
Fairly rf	0	0	0	0
Hodges 1b	3	0	1	1
Demeter cf	4	0	1	0
Roseboro c	4	1	1	1
Wills ss	4	0	0	
McDevitt p	1	0	0	0
Sherry p	2	0	0	0
Totals	32	3	10	3

aRan for Larker in 7th

MILWAUKEE	AB	R	H	BI
Avila 2b	5	0	0	0
Mathews 3b	4	0	0	0
Aaron rf	2	0	0	0
Adcock 1b	3	0	0	0
Pafko lf	2	0	0	0
aMaye lf	2	0	1	0
Logan ss	3	1	1	0
Crandall c	4	1	2	0
Bruton cf	4	0	1	1
Willey p	2	0	1	0
bSlaughter	1	0	0	0
McMahon p	0	0	0	0
cTorre	1	0	0	0
Totals	33	2	6	1

aBatted for Pafko in 5th
bGrounded out for Willey in 6th
cFlied out for McMahon in 9th

Los Angeles	1 0 1		0 0 1		0 0 0		3		
Milwaukee	0 2 0		0 0 0		0 0 0		2		

Home Runs: Roseboro

Los Angeles	IP	H	R	BB	SO
McDevitt	1⅓	2	2	2	2
Sherry (W)	7⅔	4	0	2	4

Milwaukee	IP	H	R	BB	SO
Willey (L)	6	8	3	2	3
McMahon	3	3	0	1	2

SEPTEMBER 29, 1959

MILWAUKEE	AB	R	H	BI
Bruton cf	6	0	0	0
Mathews 3b	4	2	2	1
Aaron rf	4	1	2	0
Torre 1b	3	0	1	2
Maye lf	2	0	0	0
ªPafko lf	1	0	0	0
ᵇSlaughter	1	0	0	0
DeMerit lf	0	0	0	0
ᵈSpangler lf	0	0	0	0
Logan ss	3	1	2	0
Schoendienst 2b	1	0	0	0
ᶜVernon	1	0	0	0
Cottier 2b	0	0	0	0
ᵉAdcock	1	0	0	0
Avila 2b	0	0	0	0
Crandall c	6	1	1	0
Mantilla 2b, ss	5	0	1	1
Burdette p	4	0	1	1
McMahon p	0	0	0	0
Spahn p	0	0	0	0
Jay p	1	0	0	0
Rush p	1	0	0	0
Totals	44	5	10	5

ªFlied out for Maye in 5th
ᵇPopped out for Pafko in 7th
ᶜStruck out for Schoendienst in 9th
ᵈWalked for DeMerit in 11th
ᵉHit into a force play for Cottier in 11th

LOS ANGELES	AB	R	H	BI
Gilliam 3b	5	0	1	0

LOS ANGELES	AB	R	H	BI
Neal 2b	6	2	2	1
Moon rf, lf	6	1	3	1
Snider cf	4	0	1	0
ᵇLillis	0	1	0	0
Williams p	2	0	0	0
Hodges 1b	5	2	2	0
Larker lf	4	0	2	2
ᶜPignatano c	1	0	1	0
Roseboro c	3	0	0	0
ᵈFurillo rf	2	0	2	1
Wills ss	5	0	1	0
Drysdale p	1	0	0	0
Podres p	1	0	0	0
Churn p	0	0	0	0
ᵃDemeter	1	0	0	0
Koufax p	0	0	0	0
Labine p	0	0	0	0
ᵉEssegian	0	0	0	0
ᶠFairly cf	2	0	0	0
Totals	48	6	15	5

ᵃFlied out for Churn in 8th
ᵇRan for Snider in 9th
ᶜRan for Larker in 9th
ᵈHit sacrifice fly for Roseboro in 9th
ᵉAnnounced as batter for Labine in 9th
ᶠHit into force play for Essegian in 9th

Milwaukee	2 1 0	0 1 0	0 1 0	0 0 0	5
Los Angeles	1 0 0	1 0 0	0 0 3	0 0 1	6

Doubles: Aaron
Triples: Neal, Crandall
Home Runs: Neal, Mathews

Milwaukee	IP	H	R	BB	SO
Burdette	8	10	5	0	4
McMahon	0	1	0	0	0
Spahn	⅓	1	0	0	0
Jay	2⅓	1	0	1	1
Rush (L)	1	2	1	1	0

Los Angeles	IP	H	R	BB	SO
Drysdale	4⅓	6	4	2	3
Podres	2⅓	3	0	1	1
Churn	1⅓	1	1	0	0
Koufax	⅔	0	0	3	1
Labine	⅓	0	0	2	1
Williams (W)	3	0	0	3	3

5

1962: Los Angeles Dodgers vs. San Francisco Giants

choke \'chok\ vb choked; chok-ing: to lose one's composure and fail to perform effectively in a critical situation.

From baseball's earliest days, teams have carried seemingly insurmountable leads into the late season only to watch them dissolve. Sometimes they disappear due to the efforts of another; a hard-charging competitor playing for pride and redemption can often work miracles. (The remarkable late season surge of the 1951 New York Giants to overtake the Brooklyn Dodgers serves as a prime example.) This is called *losing*. At other times, leads evaporate due to a sudden, self-inflicted, teamwide loss of force and effect. This is called *choking*.

Choking is the least satisfactory way for a major league team to lose. Mentioning the word *choke* to a major league player may also be the surest path to a punch in the nose. To the athletic professional, the term suggests a deficiency of courage and cool-headedness, qualities assumed to be *de rigueur* for every major leaguer. Teams may run hot and cold, the refrain goes, but dedicated, experienced professionals do not choke.

Piffle. For if major league teams do not choke, then how are we to explain the 1962 Los Angeles Dodgers, a team superbly talented yet destined for an ignominy almost unparalleled in baseball history. Oh, sure, other teams have choked and grandly: the 1964 Phillies, the 1969 Cubs, and the 1995 Angels are prime examples of first-place teams with august records and shaky hands. But to many, the 1962 Los Angeles Dodgers are *sui generis*; they are to choking what the *Titanic* is to shipwrecks, a pinnacle of perdition, a legend that only grows with the passing years. And, unlike teams whose failure can be traced to the sudden futility of one or two key players, the collapse of the '62 Dodgers was truly a team effort, the manifestation of a collective handiwork so complete that it still retains the capacity to amaze. That it happened is indisputable. How it happened requires us to do a bit of digging.

Entering the 1962 season, the Los Angeles Dodgers was a team in transition. Between 1960 and 1962, the club's focus had shifted toward youth and away from the veteran players who had carried the team for the previous decade. Dodger stalwarts like Clem Labine, Gil Hodges, and Don Zimmer had been traded or left vulnerable to the expansion draft of 1961. Others, like Duke Snider and Wally Moon, remained with the team in reduced capacities, playing supporting roles to emerging stars like Tommy Davis and Frank Howard. So complete had been the club's transformation that, by opening day of 1962, half of the Dodger starting lineup had yet to reach their 25th birthdays.

In truth, there was nothing accidental about the timing of the Dodger youth movement. The completion of Dodger Stadium — the team's new ballpark in Los Angeles's Chavez Ravine — in early 1962 did more than provide the club with a new home, it also signaled an entirely new approach to how the Dodgers would play the game. Unlike the Los Angeles Coliseum, the oblong edifice that served as the team's headquarters between 1958 and 1961, Dodger Stadium was symmetrical, with expansive alleys in right and left center field. The layout mandated that the powercentric approach employed by the club to bludgeon opponents in years past would have to morph into one fashioned around speed and pitching. The task of ensuring that the team's reduced run production would stand up against National League opponents would fall to the able arms of the Dodger pitching staff.

"We had a lot of guys who really made a mark in 1962," recalls Dodger pitcher Stan Williams:

> We had Willie Davis, who could outrun everybody except Secretariat. Maury Wills had come up and carved a notch for himself, in fact, he was MVP that year. There were a lot of guys who had great years. Tommy Davis had a great, great year. Ed Roebuck won 10 in a row in relief at one point. And, of course, Koufax had become Koufax by that time. We were a very strong team.

In stark contrast to the weak-hitting Dodgers stood the formidable presence of the San Francisco Giants. "There was a real difference in styles between us and the Giants," remembers Dodger catcher Johnny Roseboro:

> San Francisco was a potent offensive ballclub, and the Dodgers were a defensive ballclub, dependent on their pitching. We didn't have the power they

had by any means. We couldn't win a ballgame with just one swing of the bat. We were evenly matched, but we weren't evenly matched. The Giants were much more of a power team.

Power was something that San Francisco had in abundance. In 1961, the quartet of Willie Mays, Orlando Cepeda, Willie McCovey, and Felipe Alou terrorized National League pitching by hammering a staggering 122 home runs. By way of contrast, the entire 1961 Dodger team hit just 27 more. But the Giants represented more than just four guys swinging from their heels; the club had pitching too. In 1961, Jack Sanford, Mike McCormick, and Juan Marichal all won in double figures, while bullpen ace Stu Miller won 14 games and saved 17 more.

Since their last pennant in 1954, it had been a long, tough haul for the Giants. Under manager Bill Rigney, the club hit rock bottom in 1956 and 1957, finishing 26 games out of first place each year. The arrival of Orlando Cepeda in 1958 kindled hope, and the team rebounded to third place. The addition of Sam Jones in 1959 helped vault the club into contention, but when the team's pitching collapsed during the season's final week, so did the Giants. Finishing out of the money once again was tough enough for San Francisco, but watching the rival Dodgers capture a world championship in just their second year in California galled the Giants no end.

Seeking to improve his club's fortunes, Giants owner Horace Stoneham fired Bill Rigney in 1960 and installed Tom Sheenan as manager. After showing early promise, the team sputtered in July and by season's end was mired in fifth place. Following the season, Stoneham shuffled his managerial deck once again, firing Sheenan and installing as manager an infielder who the club had just obtained in a trade with the Milwaukee Braves.

"Al Dark was a player with Milwaukee," recalls Giants relief specialist Stu Miller. "A lot of Giants players knew him from around the league and wanted him to manage, so we had to actually trade players to get him to manage our club. We traded Andre Rodgers to the Braves to get him."

With Dark at the helm, things improved in 1961. Powered by the bats of Mays and Cepeda, San Francisco climbed to within 2½ games of first place in July. The club would ultimately stumble, but when the season ended, the Giants finished a respectable third, eight games back of the Reds and four behind the second-place Dodgers. It was an improvement, but Dark wanted more.

So did the people of San Francisco. Support for the club, which had flourished during the team's initial seasons in the Bay Area, was quickly eroding. During 1961, large sections of empty seats had become commonplace at the team's new ballpark at windswept Candlestick Point. Now, eight years removed from their last postseason appearance and entering their fifth season in San Francisco without a pennant, Al Dark and his players were feeling the heat. Merely contending was no longer enough; by the end of the 1962 season, the city of San Francisco fully expected the National League pennant to be flying over Candlestick Park.

THE RACE

In the early weeks of the 1962 season, a particularly tough, aggressive brand of baseball was being showcased by the San Francisco Giants. Led by the hot hitting of Willie Mays and Orlando Cepeda and the pitching of Billy Pierce, Billy O'Dell, and Jack Sanford, the Giants pounded opponent after opponent in the season's early going, and by mid-May, they were in firm control of first place in the National League.

Down south in Los Angeles, the Dodgers were nearly matching the Giants in intensity. Maury Wills, whose knack for stealing bases was about to become the source of sudden fame, was igniting the team with his daring base running.

"Maury was our offense," recalls Stan Williams:

> We didn't score a lot of runs. Our offensive game was that Maury would chop a single, beat it out, then he'd steal second. The catcher would throw the ball into center field, and he'd be on third. Then the next guy would strike out, the following guy would pop out, then Tommy Davis would come up and drive Maury in, and we'd win 1–0. Now, if Maury did this twice in a game, we'd win 2–0. It was that kind of year.

In truth, there was more to the Dodgers than just Maury Wills and Tommy Davis. Ron Fairly and Willie Davis began the season swinging hot bats, and by May, both were hitting over .300. Frank Howard, the 6'7" phenom who'd arrived in Los Angeles three years earlier amidst a chorus of Ruthian hosannas, was awing both fans and opposing players with his towering home runs. Seven weeks into the season, the whole package gelled when the Dodgers reeled off 13 straight victories to climb to within a half game of the first-place Giants. Leading the charge was the National League's best pitching staff, anchored by Don Drysdale and Sandy Koufax. By the end of June, Drysdale had racked up an amazing 13 wins with Koufax close behind with 11. When the starting pitching faltered, steady bullpen work from Ron Perranoski, Ed Roebuck, and Larry Sherry often as not provided the winning edge.

The Dodger pitching staff was so good that discordant voices around the league suspected that factors beyond sound fundamentals might be at work. In midsummer, the Pirates' third baseman, Don Hoak, publicl, accused Larry Sherry, Don Drysdale, Johnny Podres, Ed Roebuck, Ron Perranoski, and Stan Williams of throwing spitballs. Speaking to the press the following day, Philadelphia manager Gene Mauch pronounced Hoak misinformed. "I've never seen Sherry throw one," Mauch said, "but the others I'm certain about."

"I never threw a spitball in my life," says Ed Roebuck today. "I didn't throw hard enough for a spitball to do anything. That's the god's honest truth. If I could've, I'd have tried it. I threw a sinker that was almost like a palm ball; sometimes it would break the other way. But it was a sinker, not a spitter."

By early July, the torrid play of Los Angeles bounced the Giants into second place. By the time the two clubs converged for a crucial head-to-head showdown on August 10, LA's first-place lead over San Francisco had grown to 5½ games. "It's a critical series for us," Al Dark told reporters. "We feel like we have to win two of three against the Dodgers to get back into this race." Coming from a manager whose team had already dropped 8 of its previous 11 games against the Dodgers, it smacked of wishful thinking. The reporters gathered around Dark that day might well have wondered how the Giants hoped to complete such a herculean task.

The following day, a paragraph at the bottom of Frank Finch's sports column in the *Los Angeles Times* provided a clue. "The Phillies," wrote Finch, "report that Candlestick management has let the infield grass grow to a depth where it's virtually impossible to hit a ground ball through the infield." Now, with a crucial series against Los Angeles looming, the first sketchy outline of San Francisco's audacious plan to derail the Dodger pennant juggernaut was becoming clear.

On Friday, August 10, the Giants, in the first of a series of inspired performances, pounded three Dodger pitchers for 12 hits and 11 runs. Giants pitcher Billy O'Dell was in complete control, retiring 24 of the last 25 batters. But the big news, at least as far as the Dodgers were concerned, was the condition of the playing field. An excess of water applied by the Candlestick grounds crew to the areas surrounding first and second base had transformed the basepaths into a muddy, gloppy bog.

"Whenever we came to town, the Giants would try to slow down our running game," recalls Dodger second baseman Larry Burright. "They'd water the field down, and always kept the grass long, trying to slow us down. We always had a problem there with that. They'd do anything they could to beat us."

Throughout the contest, the Dodgers protested to the umpires about the state of the playing field. When O'Dell shut them down for good in the ninth inning, the Dodgers returned to their clubhouse, where they took their case to the press. "It was like playing in a rice paddy," Maury Wills grumbled. "It's ridiculous to play baseball in conditions like that."

The next day, a seething group of Dodger players watched as the Giants' grounds crew did it again. Shortly before game time, workers armed with garden hoses soaked the infield dirt immediately adjacent to first and second bases. The game started without incident, but by the third inning, Maury Wills had had enough. While hitting against Billy Pierce, Wills suddenly backed out of the batter's box and unloaded on umpire Al Foreman over the field's condition. Enraged, Foreman promptly kicked Wills out of the game, much to the delight of Candlestick's taunting throng.

Meanwhile, Pierce was mesmerizing the Dodger offense with a dazzling array of breaking stuff. Backed by a clutch pinch-hit home run by Willie McCovey, the Giants again bested LA, 5–4. Following the game, an angry Wills again complained to the press:

> You all saw it. Before the game, they took four hoses and watered the field down. There was a big mud puddle around shortstop and at first base too. They did the same thing Friday night. The Giants are taking away half of our attack by handicapping our speed.

By Sunday, the marshlike condition of the Candlestick infield and the public bellyaching of the Dodgers had transformed the series into front-page news in San Francisco. Two hours prior to game time, thousands of fans were lined up at stadium ticket offices in hopes of garnering what few unsold tickets remained. Once inside, fans were seen pointing at the field and laughing heartily as the grounds crew went about its pregame ritual of feverishly hosing down the infield. A sign held aloft by a waggish Giants fan along the third-base line provided an appropriate caption to the whole bizarre affair: "Go Mudville!"

At the center of the swirling controversy was the umpiring crew. Complaints to the league office by the Dodgers following Friday's game had escalated the situation, and by Sunday, the umpires were feeling the heat. Finally, prior to the start of the game, they acted. After inspecting the infield and finding an oversurplus of water, they ordered that wheelbarrows full of sod be trucked out and spread over the field to soak up the excess liquid.

But the Dodgers would soon find that the Giants had other ways of rubbing mud in their faces. Spurred on by the partisan, chanting throng in the stands, Juan Marichal completely stifled the Los Angeles offense on

Sunday, surrendering a paltry four hits and leading his team to a sweep of the series. The LA advantage over the Giants, which at its high-water mark had stood at 5½ games, was now reduced to just 2½ games. Suddenly, the Giants and Dodgers were locked in an old-fashioned pennant race.

Following the game, Dodger manager Walter Alston tried to apply a positive spin to the debacle:

> If anyone told me last spring that we'd still be leading by 2½ games after losing three straight to the Giants in August, I'd think seriously of throwing a butterfly net over him. We've still got four games at home with the Giants, and we've taken five straight from them there.

But Alston's confident manner belied a troubled mind. His young players had carried the team this far, but Alston knew what pennant pressure could do to even the most seasoned professional. With the Giants now breathing down his club's neck, Walt thought it might be time to shake up his lineup. As the team packed for a crucial eastern road trip, the Dodger manager weighed his options.

By Monday morning, Alston had decided that a tuneup, not an overhaul, was the answer to the Dodger woes. In an effort to generate more offense, he benched Daryl Spencer and moved Tommy Davis to third base, thus opening a spot for Wally Moon in left field. Moon had finished 1961 with a .328 average and 88 RBIs, but so powerful was the tide of the Dodgers youth movement that more than two months had elapsed since he'd last started a game.

With that decision made, Alston could turn his thoughts to another concern: Sandy Koufax. Since leaving a game on July 17 complaining of pain in his throwing hand, Koufax hadn't pitched an inning. Doctors had initially diagnosed the problem as a minor circulatory ailment involving the index finger and had estimated that the left-hander would miss no more than one or two starts. After being lanced by a Dodger trainer at the end of July, the digit took a turn for the worse and became infected. Days, then weeks, rolled by, and by mid-August, Koufax hadn't thrown a baseball in more than a month. The loss of Koufax would prove to be a devastating blow to the team's fortunes, an event that would ultimately ripple from the pitching mound right into the Dodger dugout, where it would completely destroy the relationship between Walter Alston and third-base coach Leo Durocher.

Trouble had been simmering between Alston and Durocher for a number of weeks, primarily over how best to run the club. "[The 1962 Dodgers] were one of the best teams I was ever associated with," Durocher wrote in his autobiography:

Seven key players having the best seasons of their careers, and we couldn't shake the Giants. Three guys who could run like ring-tailed apes, and we had a manager who sat back and played everything conservatively. Forget the signs. Speed overcomes everything. Let them run. After Koufax went out, I just thought, to hell with it. Alston would give me the take sign, I'd flash the hit sign. Alston would signal to bunt, I'd call for the hit and run. They were throwing the first pitch right there to Maury Wills, knowing he was willing to walk. "Come on," I told him. "Swing at the first one, don't let them get ahead of you. You're not just a runner, you're a hitter. Rip into it." I never "saw" a take sign with any of the speedsters—and how they loved it. The whole team knew what I was doing, and they were saying, "Just keep going, Leo. Goddam, we never played like this before. It was always close to the vest around here, but now, Christ, we're playing wide open."

"There was a lot of animosity between Durocher and Alston," confirms Johnny Roseboro:

And Durocher was right, Alston played by the book all the time. And Leo was two pitches ahead of everybody out there. I do remember Leo saying to Alston in a meeting, "Now, Skip, you're going to give me the signs quick, aren't you?" because Alston had to stop and think about what he had to do, while Leo already knew what he had to do. That is why they didn't get along. I don't know if Leo was trying to take over, but he was aggressive. He was a Billy Martin type. And we all loved him, because he would do anything to win a ballgame. We certainly didn't feel the same way about Walter Alston. Walt Alston was a nice guy, but he sat there back in the corner, and he wouldn't say shit if he had a mouthful.

Unless, that is, he was publicly challenged in front of his players. With the pennant race tightening and Koufax still on the disabled list, tension among the Dodgers had reached a boiling point by mid-August. "We were in Pittsburgh," remembers Larry Burright, "and we'd just taken a beating from San Francisco. Things weren't going well. Then Durocher and Alston really got into it."

A tough loss to the Pirates on August 15 set the stage. Mental errors by Willie Davis and Johnny Roseboro had prolonged a Dodger losing streak, and Durocher, angry over what he viewed as nonchalant play, grew livid. "It's ridiculous to play that kind of baseball in a pennant race," stormed Leo. "Somebody should take some money from those kids." Standing at the far end of the dugout and listening to every word was Walter Alston. For all of his shortcomings as a manager, Alston was rightfully credited with maintaining his composure under fire. But Durocher's insurrection — in plain view of players sitting on the bench — was a direct challenge to his authority. With fire in his eyes, Alston paced the length of the dugout and confronted his coach. "You do the coaching, Durocher, and

I'll do the chewing out and the fining," screamed Alston. "I don't want another word from you on this subject!"

Following the game, a still-seething Alston carried the fight into the clubhouse. Before the entire team, Alston told Durocher:

> I will take complete charge of this ballclub. And Leo, that means you. If I give you a bunt sign, that's what I want. The bunt. And if I give you the take sign, I want that hitter to take. And any sign that I give you and you miss, I will fine you $200 and the player at bat $200.

Instead of being energized by the adrenaline rush that accompanies team friction, the Dodgers faltered. Over the following week, they ran in place, trading wins and losses with the Reds and the Phillies. The only consolation for Los Angeles was that things weren't going much better for the Giants. After winning five straight during the middle of August, the team had stumbled and had been unable to gain any ground. Finally, at month's end, things improved; after winning six of seven games, the Giants climbed to within 2½ games of the first-place Dodgers.

In early September, the Giants and Dodgers met in head-to-head battle at Dodger Stadium in Los Angeles. In response to the aquatic conditions of Candlestick Park the previous month, a rabidly partisan aggregation of Dodger fans arrived at the ballpark armed with duck calls, which would provide a bizarre soundtrack to the four-game series. In game one, steady pitching by Jack Sanford and clutch hitting by Willie Mays provided the edge as the Giants beat the Dodgers 7–3. The Dodgers rebounded the next day thanks to some sterling relief work by Ron Perranoski, but the Giants stormed back on Thursday and Friday to take the final two games of the series. With their near-sweep of the series, San Francisco had sent an unmistakable message to the Dodgers: we can win the big ones.

Smelling blood, the Giants turned tiger. After sweeping the Cubs on September 7, 8, and 9, San Francisco then steamrolled over an overmatched Pittsburgh Pirates to run its winning streak to seven games. "Sanford and O'Dell, those two especially, did great jobs holding the opposition during September," recalls Billy Pierce. "We won a lot of close ballgames, even without the great hitting. Over the year, you have to win some 3–2, 2–1 ballgames and we did. And Sanford and O'Dell were the ones that did it."

Then, without warning, the roof caved in. In the third inning of a game against Cincinnati on September 12, Willie Mays collapsed in the team's dugout and was carried from the field on a stretcher. The sight of team catalyst Mays unconscious on the dugout floor jolted the club, and that afternoon, the team's seven-game winning streak was snapped by the

Reds. That night, Mays underwent a battery of tests at Cincinnati's Christ Hospital as doctors tried to pinpoint what had felled him. The diagnosis proved innocuous enough — acute indigestion — but without their spark plug, the Giants lost their next five games. During the stretch, Los Angeles managed to play well enough to rebuild its first-place lead to four full games.

If the Giants had suddenly fallen on hard times, it was nothing compared to what was about to happen to Los Angeles. After defeating the Milwaukee Braves in an afternoon game on September 19, the Dodgers hopped a plane for Missouri to open a three-game series the following day against the Cardinals. The team's plane touched down in St. Louis by late afternoon, and with an open evening on their hands, a group of Dodger players decided to attend that night's game between the Cardinals and the Giants at Sportsman's Park.

"We went into St. Louis after playing a day game in Milwaukee," remembers Stan Williams:

> We had a 3½–game lead with seven to play, and the Giants had eight to play. The Giants were playing in St. Louis that night, and about half the guys went to the ballgame and the other half went to the race track to just kind of relax a little bit. Anyway, the Giants were leading 2–1 in the ninth inning, but all of a sudden, their pitcher ended up balking home the winning run and wild pitching a run home or something like that, to get beat. We were high as a kite. And when I say "high," it's not in today's meaning of the word. We were elated. We now had a four-game lead with seven to play, and *nobody* can blow a four-game lead with seven to play. Anyway, Alston had a team meeting scheduled the next day. And as I say, everybody was raring to go, couldn't wait to get out on the field. But after what Alston said in the meeting, we all were looking at each other with blank faces. We all walked around like zombies. And from that day on, we struggled.

Observing the "what you see here, let it stay here" maxim of clubhouse etiquette, Williams won't divulge the content of Alston's meeting. But other sources make it clear that the Dodger brass was in full panic mode over the team's pennant chances. And heading the worry brigade was Dodger president Walter O'Malley, who had joined the team in St. Louis to take in the series against the Cardinals. Normally one of baseball's least meddlesome owners, O'Malley had been distressed by the team's recent uneven play. Even more troubling to the owner were the reports of team dissension, which had been triggered by the deteriorating relationship between Alston and Durocher. With just days left in the season and the Giants hot on their heels, O'Malley decided his team needed a wake-up call. And nothing, O'Malley firmly believed, woke people up faster than a little old-fashioned job insecurity.

On September 20, Walter O'Malley convened a meeting in his hotel room with Walter Alston, Leo Durocher, team captain Duke Snider, and club public relations head Red Patterson. After his guests were seated, O'Malley laid it right on the line. "Gentlemen, if we don't win this thing, some heads are going to roll."

A stunned silence gripped the room. To the men in the room, O'Malley's timing made no sense. Compared to the dark days of August and early September, the Dodgers were in clover, sitting atop a four-game lead with just over a week left in the season. And, if they found his timing lacking, they found his methodology to be even worse. With the exception of the Dodger president, every man in the room that day understood that threats and intimidation usually backfire in baseball, creating tension and tightness in a sport that, above all others, requires a relaxed, fluid looseness from its participants.

The following day, Sandy Koufax, in his first start since returning from the disabled list, was hammered by the Cardinals. The Dodgers rebounded on Saturday, but on Sunday, Cardinal hitters notched 12 runs against Don Drysdale. In three days, St. Louis had tallied 37 hits and 24 runs against a tight-as-a-drum Dodger team. "I don't know what our final tab was at the end of the season," says Stan Williams, "but during the last week or two of the season, we just couldn't score any runs. The Cardinals were out imbibing every night, all night long, then they'd come out and shut us down in the daytime. It was amazing."

In Houston, the Giants' long-shot bid for the pennant took on new life when they won two of three games from the Colts. Throughout the series, Giants players peered over their shoulders at the Houston scoreboard, watching for updates on the Dodgers-Cardinals series in St. Louis. The results boosted their spirits, but Alvin Dark was still none too optimistic about his team's chances. "We've got our hands full, no question," he told the press on September 24. "We're three games back with just six to play. But we're going to play hard and see what happens. We're not dead yet."

Monday, September 25, was an off day for both teams. In San Francisco, the Giants relaxed and prepared for their upcoming series against St. Louis. In Los Angeles, Dodger players participated in a mandatory workout at Dodger Stadium. As his players went through their paces behind him, Walter Alston responded to questions about his pitching plans for the season's final days. "It'll be Drysdale tomorrow against the Colts," the skipper told the press:

> I know he just pitched four innings yesterday, but he's strong and he's willing. By using Don Tuesday and Johnny Podres on Wednesday, I can get them both back on the mound against the Cardinals for the final this weekend.

On Tuesday, Drysdale was superb, scattering just six hits over seven innings and yielding only one earned run. However, errors by Maury Wills and Larry Burright and a 10th-inning home run by Al Spangler torpedoed his handiwork, and LA absorbed a crushing 3–2 loss. Up north, Jack Sanford was beating the Cardinals for his 23rd victory of the season. The Dodgers' lead over the Giants now stood at just two games.

On Wednesday, the Dodger offense exploded for 13 runs, and Maury Wills stole his 100th base as LA crushed Houston. It was a critical victory, as the Giants again beat St. Louis, 6–3. On Thursday, under melancholy skies in San Francisco, Stan Musial went 5 for 5 and led the St. Louis Cardinals to a 7–4 win over the Giants. The loss edged the Giants to the brink of elimination; a victory by Los Angeles that night would ensure the Dodgers of at least a tie for the pennant. "It's out of our hands," a downcast Willie McCovey told the press following the game. "All we can do is watch, wait, and see what they do."

That night in Los Angeles, the stakes were as enormous for the Dodgers as the outcome was cloudy. After blowing leads of 3–0 and 4–2, the Dodgers entered the seventh inning deadlocked 6–6 with the Colts. Dodger stopper Ron Perranoski, in a season record 66th relief appearance, was pitching well until errors by Wills and Spencer allowed Houston to push across two unearned runs in the seventh inning, which provided the winning margin. It was a wretched loss, but with a two-game lead and just three games left to play, no one thought the Giants had a prayer of overtaking Los Angeles.

The next day, the two teams changed partners for the final dance of the 1962 season. In San Francisco, an early fall rainstorm forced cancellation of the Giants' game against Houston, and National League president Warren Giles announced that the game would be made up as part of a doubleheader the following day.

That night in Los Angeles, the Dodgers were locked in an edgy battle with St. Louis. With the score deadlocked 2–2, a game but exhausted Ron Perranoski managed to set the Redbirds down in the eighth and the ninth innings. Meanwhile, Cardinal pitcher Larry Jackson was mowing down one Dodger hitter after another. In the 10th inning, Perranoski buckled, surrendering singles to Curt Flood and Stan Musial. When Ken Boyer rolled a grounder to Jim Gilliam, Flood bolted from third base to home, attempting to score. A clothesline peg from Gilliam to Roseboro nailed him at the plate. When Bill White's grounder forced Boyer, Gene Smith advanced to third. The next hitter was Charlie James, who whistled a base hit to right, scoring Smith with the run and staking St. Louis to a 3–2 lead. After being retired without incident in the bottom of the 10th inning, Los

Angeles left the field having blown yet another opportunity to clinch the pennant.

Back in their clubhouse, the stunned Dodger players sat slumped in front of their lockers. In just five days, through a complete lack of offense and poor defense, the team had squandered 3½ games of their league lead. In his office, Walter Alston tried to put the best face on what was clearly the team's most bitter loss yet: "There's no question that we're struggling. No question. Our lead is now just a game and one half. But I'd rather be in our situation than the Giants. We've got Drysdale on the mound tomorrow. He's our ace, and I like our chances against the Cardinals."

Saturday broke as a windswept, cloudy day in San Francisco. In game one of their doubleheader against Houston, the Giants exploded for 11 runs to win a laugher. However, in game two, the team, now showing evidence of pennant jitters, committed three errors. Houston first baseman Norm Larker delivered the *coup de grâce* with a two-run homer, and the Colts nailed down a 4–2 victory. The split assured the reeling Dodgers of at least a tie for the National League pennant. A win against the Cardinals later that evening at Dodger Stadium would grant them clear title to a World Series berth against the New York Yankees.

But that night, the sputtering Dodger offense went into the deep freeze against Cardinal starter Ernie Broglio. Baffling LA with an assortment of rainbow curves and sliders, Broglio allowed just two hits and struck out nine. A misplayed fly off the bat of Dal Maxvill by Frank Howard nullified a gallant performance by Drysdale, who yielded no earned runs in his eight innings. The lead over San Francisco had now crumbled to just a single game. Following the loss, Alston's optimistic facade finally broke, and he went public with his frustration. "If we don't win the pennant," he snapped to reporters, "we've got no one to blame but ourselves. We've had plenty of chances."

The collapse of the Dodgers was now the talk of baseball. Since its seven-game winning streak had been snapped by the Cubs on September 16, the team had lost 9 of 12 games, including 5 of its last 6. During that stretch, the team's offense had dried up like a worm on a hot driveway. "The offense really was the key to the team slump," remembers Ed Roebuck. "The first thing that happens is you don't score runs. I think we had pretty good pitching all the way down, but we just could not score runs. And that really puts pressure on a pitching staff. The young guys on the team were probably feeling the pennant pressure."

Poor defense also contributed to the team's slump, squandering clutch pitching performances so critical to an offense-starved team. Heading into the season's final day, Los Angeles had nothing left but hope. "In order for us to pull off the impossible, which meant catch the Dodgers," remembers Giants catcher Ed Bailey:

> we had to win on the season's final day, and they had to lose. Anything short of that, and the pennant was theirs. And the Dodgers were facing the Cardinals, who were a hot team. And, as everybody knows, the Dodgers were not a hot team at that point.

On Sunday, a rabid throng elbowed its way into Candlestick Park hoping to watch their team nail down the National League pennant against the Houston Colts. Through the first three innings neither side allowed a run. The Giants drew first blood in the fourth when Ed Bailey homered off Houston starter Turk Farrell. Meanwhile, Billy O'Dell was pitching masterfully for the Giants, yielding just one run through the first seven innings. In the bottom of the eighth, with the game deadlocked 1–1, Willie Mays got a pitch in his wheelhouse and rode a Farrell fastball over the left-field fence for his 47th homer. Reliever Stu Miller soft-paced the Colts into submission over the final two innings to clinch the victory for San Francisco. The Giants had done their part. Now, there was nothing left to do but retire to their clubhouse and await the results from southern California.

At Dodger Stadium, Johnny Podres was waging a gritty, lonely battle against the St. Louis Cardinals. Pitching with transcendent concentration, the left-hander had not surrendered a run through the first seven innings. Meanwhile, the flaccid Dodger offense was flailing futilely against Cardinal pitcher Curt Simmons. In the eighth, Podres retired right fielder Charlie James for the first out. Gene Oliver then stepped into the batter's box. Podres worked the count to one and two, then, after picking off his sign, kicked his leg high and delivered. It was a curve ball, in tight. Timing the breaking ball perfectly, Oliver lofted the offering to left field. Spinning on the mound to watch the flight of the ball, Podres saw left fielder Tommy Davis break back hopefully, then drop his shoulders as the ball sailed over his head and crashed into the stands for a home run. It was all the Cardinals needed, as Dodgers hitters surrendered meekly to Simmons in the eighth and ninth. The impossible had happened. On the last day of the season, the Giants had caught the Dodgers.

Following the loss, the Dodgers' clubhouse was shrouded in funereal silence. Players sat in front of their lockers staring blankly into space. The only sounds to break the gloom were the questions murmured by sportswriters to members of the crestfallen team. Amazingly, it was Podres, the man most entitled to righteous indignation over the day's events, who tried to rally his teammates. Standing in front of his locker, he yelled for attention. "Listen, we won it in a playoff three years ago," he said, refer-ring to the team's stirring victory over the Braves in 1959. "So why can't we do it again?" Finally, he slumped down in front of his locker, reached for a beer, then raised his head to the gathered reporters. "I pitched the best game of my life," he said. "Even the pitch to Oliver was a good one, a curve in tight." Then, he fell silent, shaking his head from side to side. There was nothing left to say.

In San Francisco, the Giants celebrated with joy and amazement. Joy at finally overtaking the Dodgers and amazement at their rival's futility. "We couldn't believe that they could drop four straight to the Cardinals," remembers Stu Miller. "They had a three-game lead on us, with four to go, and they lost all four. We backed into it. Of course, we knew after Sunday's game, we hadn't won anything yet. We still had to beat them two out of three in a showdown for the pennant."

GAME 1—MONDAY, OCTOBER 1, 1962

Jocko Conlon was at rapt attention. Standing on the sidelines prior to game one of the National League's fifth sudden-death playoff, the vet-eran umpire's eyes were trained on the Candlestick Park infield, where the Giants' grounds crew was busily at work. Oblivious to the swirl of noise and activity surrounding him on the field, Conlon's full attention was con-sumed by what was taking place at first base. Then, speaking to no one in particular, Conlon said out loud, "It's fixed to hinder one team. This is the same trick they pulled before."

Spying Alvin Dark behind him, Conlon turned and yelled at the Giants' manager, "Get me the groundskeeper!" Dark, suspecting Conlon's motives, screamed back, "Get him yourself!" Finally, head groundskeeper Matty Schwab was summoned. "I want you to fix up the field for regula-tion play," Conlon told Schwab. "It's heavy all over, and I want you to remove the loose dirt from about 20 feet inside of first base. And I want you to do it now." Five minutes later, a workman perched atop a turf roller was dispatched to the first base area to harden the earth around the bag.

Watching all this from the Giants' dugout was Billy Pierce. Having completed his warmup tosses, Pierce was preparing to take the field for the biggest start of his career. In many ways, it had been a fairy-tale sea-son for the 35-year-old right-hander. As a member of the Tigers and the White Sox, Pierce had won 189 big league games between 1945 and 1961. When his win total slipped to 10 games in 1961, the White Sox, figuring him through, shipped him to San Francisco. During spring training, Pierce had struggled, but once the season started, the crafty lefty won eight

straight without a defeat. Perhaps
most incredible was Pierce's seeming
invincibility in baseball's most churl-
ish ballyard, Candlestick Park. From
day one, Pierce seemed to thrive in
the cold, dank, windy edifice, and by
the season's end, he'd remained unde-
feated at the 'Stick. "You know, in
spring training, if you look back at the
record, I think I had an ERA of 16.00,"
Pierce recalls. "Everything went
wrong. Then we opened the season,
and I was fortunate enough to win my
first eight games. And for the rest of
the year, things went well for me."

Facing Pierce in game one was
Sandy Koufax. The circulatory ailment that had plagued him during
the summer had finally healed, but
the long layoff had exacted a heavy
toll on his stuff. Without the blazing

Stylish lefty and playoff hero, Billy
Pierce proved almost unbeatable in
1962 as a member of the San Francisco
Giants. (National Baseball Hall of
Fame Library, Cooperstown, N.Y.)

fastball that had triggered his ascendancy to baseball's pinnacle, Koufax
was a warrior riding into battle with a depleted arsenal. Shackled to a
steady diet of off-speed pitches, Koufax had been unable to effectively set
up hitters. None of this was lost on Walter Alston. However, with Podres
unable to pitch for at least two more days, and the overworked Drysdale
penciled in as the Dodgers' best, maybe last, hope for Tuesday's game, the
Dodger manager had no choice.

In the first inning, Pierce retired the Dodgers without incident. In the
bottom of the first, Koufax ran into immediate trouble. After retiring Harvey Kuenn and Chuck Hiller, he surrendered a double to Felipe Alou.
Pitching carefully to Mays, Koufax worked the count to two and one before
he hung a curve ball that Mays raked over the 390-foot sign in right center field. Back in the dugout, Willie wasted no time in providing his teammates with a scouting report on Koufax's stuff. "I've seen him throw a lot
harder," Mays told the bench. "He doesn't have much. We can get him."

Koufax managed to escape the inning without yielding additional
runs, but in the second inning he was right back in hot water, surrendering a home run to Jim Davenport and then a single to Ed Bailey. Having
seen enough, Alston summoned Ed Roebuck from the bullpen. Roebuck
quelled the rally and then proceeded to hold the Giants at bay until he was

lifted for a pinch-hitter in the fifth. In the sixth inning, new Dodger pitcher Larry Sherry gave up home runs to Mays and Orlando Cepeda. A single by Jim Davenport finally drove Sherry to cover, and Jack Smith was brought in to relieve. Smith set down the Giants without further scoring, but after six innings, the Giants were cruising 5–0.

Meanwhile, Billy Pierce was providing his infielders with a passel of ground-ball outs. After yielding a single to Andy Carey in the third, Pierce wouldn't allow another Dodger to reach base until the sixth. In the eighth inning, the Giants loaded the bases against reliever Phil Ortega, and Alston summoned Ron Perranoski from the bullpen. After six months of bailing Los Angeles out of tight spots, the overworked Perranoski was out of gas. In short order, the left-hander surrendered a single to Jose Pagan. Frank Howard fielded the ball, but his throw from the outfield somehow hit shortstop Maury Wills in the head, allowing another run to score. In the ninth, the punchless Dodgers, now in their 30th inning without scoring so much as a single run, went down meekly against Pierce. The final score: San Francisco 8, Los Angeles 0.

In the clubhouse following the game, the press swarmed around one of the game's heroes, Willie Mays. "Man I'm tired," Mays told the press, as teammates stopped by to shake his hand and offer congratulations. "I'll be glad when this is over. I've had some big days, like when I hit those four homers in a game last year at Milwaukee. But this game today meant a lot more."

The noisy, chaotic scene in the Giants' clubhouse provided a stark contrast to the gloom that permeated the Dodgers' dressing room. Fielding reporters' questions, Alston straddled the line between bewilderment and forced optimism over his club's predicament. "We were second in the league in runs scored, so we must be able to hit better than we did this week. It's been 30 innings since we've scored. We're due to break loose." Indulging in a bit of whistling past the graveyard, Alston actually suggested to the gathered reporters that the pressure was now on San Francisco. "If there's any pressure now, it's on the Giants," he said. "'We have everything to win and nothing to lose, just like they did over the past weekend." A reporter then questioned Alston about his game two starter. "It'll probably be Williams. Drysdale's awfully tired so it'll probably be Williams."

Overhearing Alston's comments, a Dodger veteran rolled his eyes. "Let's go for broke. There's no point now in saving Drysdale for the junior prom." The bluntness of the comment startled reporters and provided a glimpse of a simmering teamwide unrest, which would, in just two short days, explode in full view of the baseball world.

GAME TWO—TUESDAY, OCTOBER 2, 1962

On Tuesday, Don Drysdale walked to the Dodger Stadium mound with the pennant hopes of his team resting squarely on his broad shoulders. During a pregame meeting, the big right-hander had convinced Alston of his readiness to pitch. Alston, aware that Drysdale had worked three times in the previous eight days, told Don to "go as long as you can, then we'll hand it over to the bullpen". As Drysdale took his warmup tosses, a revamped Dodger lineup was settling into position behind him. Alston, in a desperate attempt to kick-start his team's dormant offense, had benched Ron Fairly and Daryl Spencer to make room for Wally Moon and Duke Snider.

Tuesday's matchup between Drysdale and Jack Sanford had been billed as a pitchers' duel, but it would prove to be anything but. After retiring San Francisco without incident in the first inning, Drysdale stumbled in the second, surrendering a run-scoring double to Felipe Alou. Sanford was strong in the early going, holding the Dodger hitters scoreless through the first five innings.

By the sixth inning, Drysdale's fatigue was apparent to everyone on the field. After striking out Alou, he surrendered a walk to Tom Haller. Jose Pagan's single down the left-field line then advanced Haller to third. With Sanford at the plate, Dark signaled for the squeeze play. Unwinding on the mound, Drysdale delivered to Sanford, while at the same moment, Haller broke for the plate. Sanford squared at the last minute and dumped a bunt directly in front of Drysdale. The big right-hander fielded the ball, lost his footing, then slipped, and fell to the grass before he could make a throw. On the play, Haller scored, Pagan advanced to third, and Sanford was safe at first. Hiller then singled to score Pagan. Next, Davenport followed with a base hit, which drove home Sanford. Alston, realizing that Drysdale had finally tapped out, waved Ed Roebuck in from the bullpen. Roebuck induced Mays to ground into a force play, but McCovey's single drove Hiller home. When the smoke cleared, it was San Francisco 5, Los Angeles 0.

Staked to a comfortable lead, Sanford made his way to the mound to pitch the bottom of the sixth. Thus far, he'd been in complete command and was now just 12 outs from pitching the Giants into their first World Series in eight years. Jim Gilliam started the inning with a base hit to left. Watching closely from the Giants' dugout was Al Dark, who apparently saw something in Sanford's delivery that he didn't like. In a flash, Dark bolted for the mound and lifted Sanford from the game.

Against reliever Stu Miller, the moribund Dodgers offense suddenly awoke with a start. Duke Snider ripped a ball that skipped once, skipped twice, then skidded past McCovey at first for a double, with Gilliam advancing to third on the play. After Davis flied out to center, Gilliam tagged up and scored. The spell had finally been broken; after 35 agonizing innings, the Dodgers were finally on the scoreboard. Next, Miller walked Wally Moon and then surrendered a single to Howard which scored Snider.

Going for the kill, Dark summoned Billy O'Dell to the mound. But pinch-hitter Doug Camilli prolonged the rally with a single to left which loaded the bases. O'Dell then forced in another Dodger run when he hit pinch-hitter Andy Carey on the leg. Lee Walls, batting for Roebuck, promptly airlifted an O'Dell fastball into the gap in left center, clearing the bases for Los Angeles.

Exit O'Dell, enter Don Larsen. Larsen, who'd made baseball history six years earlier with a perfect game in a World Series, induced Wills to ground to Cepeda at first. Breaking from third in an attempt to score was Lee Walls. In one motion, Cepeda scooped up the ball and rifled it home. Giants catcher Tom Haller reached for Cepeda's throw, then squared himself to meet the onrushing base runner. Walls, realizing that the ball would easily beat him to the plate, came at the big catcher with spikes high. Walls exploded into Haller, his spikes kicking past Haller's glove and into the flesh of the catcher's arm. When the cloud of dust thrown up by the force of the collision finally cleared, it revealed two men entangled in a twisted pile on the ground, and a baseball in the dirt at Haller's feet. "Safe!" bellowed umpire Al Barlick. Suddenly, it was Dodgers 7, Giants 5.

Haller, who suffered a nasty gash on his arm in the collision with Walls, was removed from the game. When play resumed, Wills stole second, then tried to advance to third when new Giants catcher John Orsino heaved the ball into center field. However, Mays instinctively pounced on the ball and cut Wills down in the attempt. Finally, after one hour and 11 minutes, the inning ended when Gilliam flied out to right field.

In the seventh inning, Ron Perranoski held San Francisco scoreless. After the Dodgers failed to score in the bottom of the inning, Perranoski again took the mound, needing just six outs to force a pennant-deciding third game on Wednesday. But the stylish left-hander faltered, yielding singles to the first two hitters he faced. Wasting no time, Alston summoned Jack Smith from the bullpen to face Ed Bailey. Bailey promptly lined a single to center, which scored Jim Davenport. Now, with the season on the line, Alston lifted Smith and brought in right-handed fireballer Stan Williams to face the Giants.

For more than two weeks, Stan Williams had been the Dodgers' forgotten man, pitching just one inning of relief between September 17 and September 27. While Drysdale and Podres and an insufficiently rehabbed Sandy Koufax had worn down the grass between the Dodger dugout and the pitcher's mound, Williams rode the pine.

"You mean somebody finally noticed that?" Williams asks:

Alston was never in my corner, I'll put it that way. Even when I was, quote, the ace of the staff in 1960 for the first half of the year, Alston never liked me. That probably sounds like sour grapes. But he had his people. In fact, Alston liked Drysdale better than Koufax. If it rained two or three days, Don got the ball every four days, and everybody else would kind of just fill in. I don't think I'd pitched more than an inning or so in the two weeks prior to the playoffs.

Now, with the Dodgers facing elimination, Williams had been "rediscovered" by the desperate Alston. Facing John Orsino, Williams surrendered a fly ball to center that enabled Carl Boles, who was running for Bailey, to tag at third base and score the tying run. Williams then retired the side without further incident. With two innings left to play, the game was deadlocked, 7–7.

In the eighth, neither team scored. Then, in the bottom of the ninth, Bob Bolin committed the cardinal sin of walking Maury Wills. Giants manager Al Dark brought in left-handed pitcher Dick LeMay, who compounded the Giants' woes by walking Gilliam. Dark again emerged from the dugout and signaled to Barlick that he was bringing rookie Gaylord Perry in to pitch. In an effort to check Dark's strategy, Alston called Duke Snider back from the on-deck circle and sent pinch-hitter Daryl Spencer to the plate to face Perry.

With Wills and Gilliam taking their leads, Perry kicked and delivered to Spencer. Suddenly, Spencer squared at the plate and dumped a bunt 20 feet in front of Perry. With cries of "Third base! Third base!" in his ears, the rookie disregarded the advice of his teammates, whirled, and threw Spencer out at first. It would prove to be a costly mistake. After instructing Perry to intentionally walk Tommy Davis, Dark changed pitchers again, this time bringing in Mike McCormick.

Pitching carefully, McCormick notched two quick strikes on left-handed hitter Ron Fairly, before Fairly lifted a soft liner to Mays in medium center field. Standing at third base, Wills was poised to issue a direct challenge to one of the game's great arms. At the instant that Fairly's fly dropped into Mays' glove, Maury broke for the plate. Mays uncorked a strong throw, which sailed a bit as it arched over the infield. Orsino, straining to reach first for the ball and then for Wills, missed both. Kicking up a cloud of dust, Wills swept across home plate with the winning run, bounded to his feet, and fell into the arms of his jubilant teammates. The final score was 8–7.

Following the game, the exhausted Dodgers celebrated in their clubhouse. Players backslapped one another and expressed relief at earning the right to fight another day. Wills, Walls, and the other architects of the Dodger victory spoke to reporters gathered around their lockers. Behind them, a smiling and relieved Walter Alston moved among his players, offering congratulations and pats on the back.

Amid the noise and frivolity of the clubhouse, few people took notice of a strange event taking place in front of Leo Durocher's locker. Durocher had removed his Dodger jersey, and in its place, he was slipping on a T-shirt promoting the Dodgers-Giants playoff series of 11 years earlier. The keepsake — an unsettling reminder of the most ignominious loss in Dodger history — seemed, in the present context, an odd talisman. Whether it represented the possibility of triumph over adversity or, conversely, the pitfalls that await a divided team wasn't entirely clear. Aside from wary glances exchanged between one or two pairs of Dodger veterans, no one seemed much concerned. But the joyous men who celebrated that day in the fading light of the Dodger clubhouse had no way of knowing that inaudible voices were already swirling around them. And they were whispering of the cruel truths of October 1951.

GAME THREE — WEDNESDAY, OCTOBER 3, 1962

On Wednesday morning, Mickey Mantle, Whitey Ford, Yogi Berra, and the rest of the New York Yankees left a darkened runway and walked onto the playing field of Candlestick Park. The American League champions had grown antsy in New York waiting for the start of the World Series and had chosen to fly to California for an advance peek at the home turf of the Giants. "We're here to get a look at this ballpark in case the Giants get into the World Series," Yankee manager Ralph Houk told the press. "We couldn't have practiced in Los Angeles, because of the playoff, so we came here. A workout at Candlestick Park will be valuable to us if the Giants should win. But it doesn't matter to us if the Giants or the Dodgers win."

The partisan throng that was filing into Dodger Stadium at that same moment felt differently. All year long, huge crowds had filled the team's new ballpark, establishing an all-time single-season attendance record. As the team's fortunes waxed and waned, the fans had remained loyal, but even the best relationships reach a breaking point. The astonishing collapse of the Dodgers over the season's final week had strained the union, and by the season's last day, outright hostility had erupted among the faithful. But baseball fans are a charitable lot by nature, and the team's win on Tuesday had done much to heal the schism.

In the Giants' clubhouse, Alvin Dark was engaging his players in a history lesson. "We have bounced back to win tough ones and bounced back to win easy ones," Dark reminded his players. "We can do it again." Listening to Dark's pep talk and absentmindedly flipping a baseball into the air was Juan Marichal. The 25-year-old Dominican had notched 18 wins for the club in 1962 and was rapidly blossoming into one of the game's premier pitchers. In a few minutes, he would walk to the Dodger Stadium mound with a chance to fulfill his dream of pitching his team into the World Series. At the other end of Dodger Stadium, Walter Alston was conducting his usual pregame meeting in the Dodger clubhouse, running down the strengths and weaknesses of opposing hitters with starting pitcher Johnny Podres and catcher Johnny Roseboro.

Unfortunately for Podres, the Dodgers would pick this day to demonstrate to a nationwide television audience of 20 million what Los Angeles fans already knew: the 1962 Los Angeles Dodgers were a perfectly awful defensive team. After setting down the Giants without incident in the first two innings, Podres surrendered a single to shortstop Jose Pagan to start the third. The next hitter was Marichal who, in an effort to sacrifice Pagan into scoring position, dropped a bunt in front of home plate. Podres fielded the ball, but in his haste to cut down Pagan at second, threw the ball into center field.

With runners now at first and third, Kuenn singled sharply to left, scoring Pagan with the game's first run. With Marichal at second, it became Chuck Hiller's task to advance him to third, but when Hiller missed a sacrifice attempt, Marichal became trapped between second and third. Roseboro leaped up from his crouch behind the plate and gunned the ball to second, trying to cut down Marichal. But instead of beating Marichal to the bag, Roseboro's throw sailed into center field, and Marichal coasted to third on the play.

On the next pitch, Hiller lifted a short fly to Snider in left. Snider made the catch, but the crumbling Dodger defense wasn't done yet. On the play, Kuenn had let himself become trapped between first and second. Snider rifled the ball to Gilliam who, in an attempt to relay the ball to first base to nip Kuenn, instead hit Harvey in the back for the Dodgers' third error of the inning. On the play, Marichal cruised home with the Giants' second run. The next hitter was Cepeda, who hit into an inning-ending double play. After three innings, it was Giants 2, Dodgers 0.

The Dodgers scratched back against Marichal in the bottom of the fourth, when two singles and a force play accounted for their first run. Meanwhile, Johnny Podres, tired and working with subpar stuff, was battling just to keep the Giants close. After holding San Francisco scoreless in the fifth, he faltered in the sixth when singles by Cepeda, Bailey, and Davenport loaded the bases. San Francisco now had a golden opportunity to blow the game wide open.

In an effort to avert disaster, Alston lifted Podres from the game and waved in Ed Roebuck from the bullpen. Roebuck, with a record of 10 wins and one loss, had had a sterling season for the Dodgers. But the right-hander had also worked in six of LA's previous eight games and, like the rest of the Dodger staff, was pitching with a dead arm. "I'd relieved in all three games of that playoff, and I came in with the bases loaded and nobody out in the fifth inning," Roebuck remembers. "And let me tell you, I was tired."

After taking his warmup tosses, Roebuck stared at Jose Pagan. With the crowd hushed in anticipation, Roebuck delivered to the plate. The shortstop connected and sent a hard grounder to Maury Wills, who scooped the ball and fired home just in time to snuff out Cepeda. After Marichal grounded into an inning-ending double play, the threat was ended. Once again, Roebuck had bailed the Dodgers out of a tough spot.

In the sixth, Los Angeles clawed back. The first hitter was Duke Snider, who managed to fight off a Marichal offering and punch a single through the infield. Fighting fatigue, Marichal backed off the mound and wiped his brow. Stepping into the batter's box was Tommy Davis, in the midst of one of the greatest single seasons any player has ever enjoyed. Staring at Bailey, Marichal picked off his sign, nodded, kicked, and delivered to Davis. A moment later, the ball arched high over the head of center fielder Willie Mays and crashed into a group of screaming fans sitting in the left center field bleachers for a home run. It was now Los Angeles 3, San Francisco 2. Suddenly, the Dodgers were just nine outs away from the National League pennant.

In the seventh, Roebuck, battling exhaustion, managed to hold the Giants scoreless. In the bottom of the seventh, the Dodgers added to their lead when Wills singled for the fourth time, then stole second. A throwing error by Bailey on Wills' attempted steal of third allowed Maury to score. The Dodger lead was now 4–2. In the eighth inning, Roebuck's high-wire act continued. Exhausted, the right-hander still managed to retire the Giants without scoring. As Roebuck left the mound following the final out, he encountered third-base coach Leo Durocher. "How do you feel, buddy?" Durocher asked. "My arm feels like lead," Roebuck responded. "Man, am I tired."

Alarmed by Roebuck's response, Durocher approached Dodger pitching coach Joe Becker, who was standing with Walter Alston near the dugout back rack. "Get somebody ready," Durocher told Becker. "Don't let this fellow go out in the ninth inning. He can't lift his arm." Neither man responded. Durocher then took his case directly to Alston, "Walt, he told me he was tired. He's through." Alston said nothing for a few seconds, then without looking at Durocher, replied, "I'm going to win or lose with Roebuck. He stays right there."

In the eighth, Marichal also began showing signs of fatigue. After delivering three straight balls to lead-off hitter Tommy Davis, Al Dark called for time and summoned Don Larsen from the bullpen. After completing his warmups, Larsen completed the walk to Davis, who then advanced to second on a sacrifice by Ron Fairly. Frank Howard then struck out, but Davis was able to steal third on the play.

In the Giants' dugout, the wheels in Alvin Dark's head were spinning wildly. Glancing down the lineup card that was posted on the dugout wall, Dark saw that Ed Roebuck was the third batter scheduled to hit. Dark weighed his options. Dark was aware that Alston had no one in the Dodger bullpen that inspired confidence. Dark was also unwilling to concede another run to the Dodgers this late in the game. Finally, he decided to test Alston's hand. Signaling from the dugout to the mound, Dark ordered Larsen to intentionally walk Roseboro, then Davis, gambling that Alston wouldn't pinch-hit for Roebuck, even with the bases loaded.

"In the bottom of the eighth, with us leading 4–2, Dark walked two people to pitch to me as a hitter," remembers Roebuck:

> I guess he wanted me out of the game. Walt had Perranoski down in the bullpen, and Dark had McCovey and Alou on the bench. Probably what Walt should've done is use a hitter for me and let Perranoski work the last inning. But that's second-guessing. I guess Walt felt that I'd carried it that far, and he was going to go right down the line with me. But let me tell you one thing. I was tired.

Dark's strategy worked. Alston stuck with Roebuck, who Larsen induced to ground out, killing the rally and ending the inning. Now, with the ninth inning looming, the Dodger bench was in open revolt over Roebuck's obvious exhaustion. When Durocher reached the bench following the end of the eighth inning, he was met by a committee consisting of Don Drysdale, Sandy Koufax, and Johnny Podres. All three were convinced that Roebuck was tapped out and that sending him out to pitch the ninth was courting disaster. The men encircled Durocher and in hushed tones pleaded with him to again approach Alston. Durocher threw up his arms in frustration. "What the hell do you want me to do? I'm not managing the club," he snapped. "There's not a goddam thing more I can say than what I've said."

Finally, in desperation, Drysdale approached Alston. "I remember Drysdale walking up to Alston and volunteering to go into the game to close it out," recalls Johnny Roseboro, "and I remember Alston saying to Drysdale, 'I'm saving you for tomorrow.'"

Exhausted but resolute, Roebuck marched to the mound to pitch the ninth. Things started ominously for the Dodgers when Alou ripped a base hit to start the inning. Digging in at the plate was Harvey Kuenn. Capable of spraying the ball to any field, Kuenn was a difficult hitter to defend against. Alston's scouting reports told him that Kuenn usually went to right field against Roebuck, and the Dodger manager yelled at second baseman Larry Burright to shift to his left. At the other end of the Dodger bench, Snider, Drysdale, and Podres, feeling certain that Kuenn would hit the ball up the middle, screamed at third baseman Jim Gilliam to wave Burright back to his normal position. "I can't tell him to do that," Gilliam hollered back. "They want him over there."

On the next pitch, Kuenn rolled a grounder between third and short, which Wills gloved. Burright broke for second to take Wills' feed and, after forcing Alou, threw to first — late — enabling the slow-footed Kuenn to beat the throw by an eyelash. The Dodger bench exploded in anger. Instead of having the bases clear and two out, the potential tying run was now walking to the plate in the person of Willie McCovey.

"There was a big controversy about that play," remembers Ed Roebuck:

> Burright was playing second base, and Harvey Kuenn was the hitter. And we had to play for a double play. Harvey always pulled me, believe it or not. He'd always shoot the ball to right field. Anyway, Wills called time out and came to the mound and said to me, "Have him hit the ball to me, and we'll get out of this thing." So, sure enough, he hits a two-hopper to Wills, and Wills goes to give the ball to Burright, and Larry can't get there because he'd been playing over toward right field. That double play would've made it two outs with nobody on. Of course, that's second-guessing again, but we should've got a double play on that ball. Poor Larry Burright couldn't get to the bag because somebody moved him over.

"I was shifted over toward first base," remembers Burright:

> Now, Harvey Kuenn wasn't normally a pull hitter. You know, you always cheat when you make a double play. But, in this instance, they moved me toward first, and then Kuenn pulls the ball in the hole between short and

third, and Wills backhands it. So here I gotta cover second, so when I'm running toward second base, I'm going full steam ahead, and my back's toward first base. We got the guy at second, but I had to turn to make the throw to first. It was a close play, and I think it could've gone the other way, but being a rookie, I'm not going to argue.

Rattled by the turn of events, Roebuck promptly walked McCovey and Alou to load the bases. Now, with Mays striding toward the plate, the Dodgers were on the ropes. A moment later, Mays timed a pitch perfectly and ripped a shot right back through the box, which tore the glove off Roebuck's hand. It was a base hit, scoring Kuenn and leaving the sacks loaded. It was now Dodgers 4, Giants 3.

In the dugout, it finally dawned on Walter Alston that Roebuck had nothing left. In the bullpen, Alston had Perranoski and Stan Williams warming up. Catching Durocher's eye, Alston yelled to Leo that he wanted Williams. Leo, standing with one foot on the bench, looked at Alston in amazement: "What? Did I hear you right? You're bringing in Williams?" Williams was a gritty competitor who could throw a baseball through a brick wall, but he was also plagued by wildness. Dropping him into a situation where one errant pitch could cost Los Angeles the pennant seemed foolhardy to Durocher.

But the only opinion that mattered was Alston's, and Williams was summoned from the bullpen. "I'll get Cepeda," Williams yelled over to Perranoski as he left the bullpen mound, "then you can get Bailey." After completing his warmup tosses, Williams toed the rubber to face Orlando Cepeda. A moment later, Cepeda lofted a Williams fastball to Fairly in right field that was deep enough to score Bowman, who was running for Kuenn. The game was now deadlocked 4–4. Thinking that his job was through, Williams looked to the Dodger dugout, expecting to see Alston emerge and wave Perranoski in from the bullpen. There was no movement. In a flash, Williams realized that the game was now his to win or to lose.

Digging in at the plate to face Williams was Giants catcher Ed Bailey. Williams decided to go after the catcher with high fastballs. Williams' first pitch to Bailey was a ball, then the big righty uncorked a pitch that Bailey swung at and missed. Somehow, the ball kicked off of Roseboro's glove and twisted away from the plate, enabling Mays to scramble to second. With first base now open, Alston signaled to Roseboro to intentionally walk Bailey in order to set up a force play at every base. "I was walked intentionally after Williams threw that wild pitch," remembers Bailey. "You bet I was surprised when they let Williams pitch to me. I thought sure that they'd use Perranoski in that situation. But the thing that I really remember was that Davenport was following me, and we had the winning run at third."

Now, with the bases loaded, the infield in, and Davenport hitting, Williams was in a jam. After missing with his first two fastballs, Williams suddenly realized that he had no place to put Davenport and he started fighting his nerves. He then delivered a strike. It was 2–1. Another ball, and it was 3 and 1. Williams backed off the mound, dried his fingers with the resin bag, and then again toed the rubber. He wound up and delivered to Davenport. Ball four. The go-ahead run crossed the plate.

Silence and disbelief among the Dodger Stadium crowd at the sudden turn of events quickly shifted to anger. Boos rained down from the stands upon Williams and the Dodgers. "You know, when you get your butt kicked out there, every little thing becomes a major problem," says Johnny Roseboro:

> Our manager, we thought, made a major mistake in the pitching. Stan Williams was never a dependable pitcher when he was with us. He could throw hard, but you didn't know where the hell it was going. He didn't know where it was going. When you've got Stan Williams on the mound, he's throwing nothing but heat. He didn't have much of a breaking ball, and if he did, he couldn't get it over anyway. So Walt said a couple of "Hail Marys" and it didn't work.

After the walk to Davenport, Alston called Ron Perranoski in from the bullpen to replace Williams. Facing him was Giants shortstop Jose Pagan. Williams got Pagan to ground to second, but Larry Burright, who appeared to have the play right in front of him, kicked it for LA's fourth error, enabling Mays to score. After Nieman struck out, the disastrous inning was finally over. Now just three outs away from the National League pennant, the Giants, behind new pitcher Billy Pierce, took the field for the ninth inning.

Completely broken by the events of the previous inning, the Dodgers rushed to their fate. Pierce retired Wills on a grounder and then got Gilliam and Walls on routine fly balls. It was all over. In just moments, the Dodger Stadium infield was transformed into a scene of chaotic contrast, as crestfallen Dodgers watched exultant Giants tackle, dogpile, and wrestle one another to the ground in joyous celebration.

Back in the Dodger clubhouse, the anger and frustration of Dodger players over the day's events had turned the atmosphere acrid, with most of the enmity being directed at Walter Alston. "You stole my money!" one player screamed at the Dodger manager. The scene was so tense that team captain Duke Snider felt compelled to bar reporters from entering the clubhouse until tempers had a chance to cool.

"We had the game won, and we ended up losing it," says Larry Burright. "We kept the clubhouse door closed to let guys cool down a little.

In a self-portrait rendered after the Giants finally disposed of the Dodgers in baseball's fifth sudden-death playoff, Willard Mullin has a feeling of *déjà vu.* (Shirley Mullin Rhodes and the Estate of Willard Mullin.)

Right away, when you let press guys in, sometimes things are said, you know, taken out of context, so we were better off if guys would cool down a little before letting the reporters in." When the doors finally swung open, the atmosphere had improved, but not by much. "How the hell would you feel if you just lost $12,000?" Wally Moon snapped, responding to a question about the team's mood.

Today the epochal of the 1962 Dodgers continues to astonish baseball fans. The team's accreditation — league MVP; Cy Young, stolen base, and ERA winners; and seven players in the midst of career years— was of such brilliance that superiority over the opposition was presumed. Baseball is, above all, about athletic superiority and, on paper anyway, the Dodgers were the better team. But today, 40 years after Los Angeles swooned its way into the record books, some players feel that the time has come to finally award San Francisco some credit for what it accomplished in 1962.

"Really, you wouldn't think that we had a chance," says Billy Pierce today. "But we played some good baseball coming down the stretch, without any question. They always look at the team that blew the lead, but if you look at it, you'll see that the team that ended up winning was pretty good too."

"You know it's funny," says Ed Roebuck:

All everybody talks about is how we blew the pennant. But you know what? They had a helluva team too. Have you looked at the team they had? Some of the 1962 Dodgers were playing them in an old-timers game down in Arizona a few years ago, and the Giants were using those metal bats. I think Mays was like 55 at the time, and he was hitting these balls out of the ballpark. Stan Williams and I were standing in the outfield and he looked at me and he said, "You know, they had a pretty good team." And you know what? He was right. They had a pretty damn good team.

OCTOBER 1, 1962

LOS ANGELES	AB	R	H	BI
Wills ss	4	0	0	0
Gilliam 3b	3	0	0	0
T. Davis lf	4	0	0	0
Howard rf	4	0	0	0
Walls 1b	3	0	0	0
Roseboro c	3	0	0	0
Carey 3b	3	0	1	0
W. Davis cf	3	0	0	0
Koufax p	0	0	0	0
Roebuck p	1	0	0	0

LOS ANGELES	AB	R	H	BI
^aMcMullen	1	0	1	0
^bTracewski	0	0	0	0
Sherry p	0	0	0	0
Smith p	0	0	0	0
^cCamilli	1	0	1	0
Ortega p	0	0	0	0
Perranoski p	0	0	0	0
Totals	30	0	3	0

^aSingled for Roebuck in 6th
^bRan for McMullen in 6th
^cDoubled for Smith in the eighth inning

SAN FRANCISCO	AB	R	H	BI
Kuenn lf	5	0	0	0
Hiller 2b	4	0	1	0
F. Alou rf	4	1	1	0
Mays cf	3	3	3	3
Cepeda 1b	4	1	1	1
Davenport 3b	3	2	2	1
Bailey c	2	1	1	0
Pagan ss	3	0	1	2
Pierce p	4	0	0	0
Totals	32	8	10	7

Los Angeles	0 0 0	0 0 0	0 0 0	0
San Francisco	2 1 0	0 0 2	0 3 x	8

Doubles: Alou, Camilli, Pagan
Home Runs: Mays (2), Davenport, Cepeda

Los Angeles	IP	H	R	BB	SO
Koufax (L)	1	4	3	0	0
Roebuck	4	1	0	0	2
Sherry	⅓	3	2	1	0
Smith	1⅔	1	0	0	1
Ortega	⅓	0	2	1	0
Perranoski	⅔	1	1	1	0

San Francisco	IP	H	R	BB	SO
Pierce (W)	9	3	0	1	6

OCTOBER 2, 1962

SAN FRANCISCO	AB	R	H	BI
Hiller	3	1	1	1

SAN FRANCISCO	AB	R	H	BI
[b]Nieman	1	0	0	0
Bowman	1	0	0	0
Davenport 3b	6	1	2	1
Mays cf	5	0	1	0
McCovey lf	2	0	1	1
Miller p	0	0	0	0
O'Dell p	0	0	0	0
Larsen p	0	0	1	0
[c]Bailey c	1	0	1	1
[d]Boles	0	1	0	0
Bolin p	0	0	0	0
LeMay p	0	0	0	0
Perry p	0	0	0	0
McCormick p	0	0	0	0
Cepeda 1b	3	1	1	0
F. Alou rf	4	0	2	1
Haller c	1	1	0	0
Orsino c	1	0	1	1
Pagan ss	5	1	2	0
Sanford p	3	1	0	0
M. Alou lf	0	0	0	1
[a]Kuenn lf	2	0	0	0
Totals	40	7	13	7

[a]Hit into force play for M. Alou in 7th   [c]Singled for Larsen in 8th
[b]Flied out for Hiller in 7th   [d]Ran for Bailey in 8th

LOS ANGELES	AB	R	H	BI
Wills ss	4	1	0	0
Gilliam 3b, 2b	3	1	0	0
Snider lf	3	1	1	0
[e]Spencer	0	0	0	0
T. Davis 3b, cf	3	0	1	1
Moon 1b	2	1	1	0
Fairly 1b	1	0	1	1
Howard rf	3	1	1	1
Roseboro c	2	0	0	0
[a]Camilli c	2	1	1	0
W. Davis cf	2	0	0	0
[b]Carey	0	0	0	1
[d]Burright 2b	0	1	0	0
Drysdale p	2	0	0	0
Roebuck p	0	0	0	0
[c]Walls	1	1	1	3
Perranoski p	0	0	0	0
Smith p	0	0	0	0
Williams p	1	0	0	0
Totals	29	8	7	7

[a]Singled for Roseboro in 4th   [d]Ran for Carey in 6th
[b]Hit by pitch for Davis in 6th   [e]Sacrificed for Snider in 9th
[c]Doubled for Roebuck in 6th   Doubles: Alou, Pagan, Snider, Walls

San Francisco	0 1 0	0 0 4	0 2 0	7
Los Angeles	0 0 0	0 0 7	0 0 1	8

San Francisco	IP	H	R
Sanford	5	2	1
Miller	⅓	2	3
O'Dell	0	2	3
Larsen	1⅔	1	0
Bolin (L)	1	0	1
LeMay	0	0	0
Perry	⅔	0	0
McCormick	⅓	0	0

Los Angeles	IP	H	R
Drysdale	5⅓	7	5
Roebuck	⅔	1	0
Perranoski	1	4	1
Smith	⅓	1	1
Williams (W)	1⅔	0	0

OCTOBER 3, 1962

SAN FRANCISCO	AB	R	H	BI
Kuenn lf	5	1	2	1
Hiller 2b	3	0	1	0
ᵇMcCovey	0	0	0	0
ᶜBowman 2b	0	1	0	0
F. Alou rf	4	1	1	0
Mays cf	3	1	1	1
Cepeda 1b	4	0	1	1
Bailey c	4	0	2	0
Davenport 3b	4	0	1	1
Pagan ss	5	1	2	0
Marichal p	2	1	1	0
Larsen p	0	0	0	0
ᵃM. Alou	1	0	1	0
ᵈNieman	1	0	0	0
Pierce p	0	0	0	0
Totals	36	6	13	4

ᵃSingled for Larsen in 9th
ᵇWalked for Hiller in 9th
ᶜRan for McCovey in 9th
ᵈStruck out for M. Alou in 9th

LOS ANGELES	AB	R	H	BI
Wills ss	5	1	4	0
Gilliam 2b, 3b	3	0	0	0

LOS ANGELES	AB	R	H	BI
Snider lf	3	2	2	0
Burright 2b	1	0	0	0
aWalls	1	0	0	0
T. Davis 3b, lf	3	1	2	2
Moon 1b	3	0	0	0
Fairly 1b, rf	0	0	0	0
Howard rf	4	0	0	1
Harkness 1b	0	0	0	0
Roseboro c	3	0	0	0
W. Davis cf	3	0	0	0
Podres p	2	0	0	1
Roebuck p	2	0	0	0
Williams p	0	0	0	0
Perranoski p	0	0	0	0
Totals	35	4	8	3

aFlied out for Burright in 9th

Doubles: Snider, Hiller
Home Runs: Davis

San Francisco	0 0 2	0 0 0	0 0 4 —	6
Los Angeles	0 0 0	1 0 2	1 0 0 —	4

San Francisco	IP	H	R	BB	SO
Marichal	7	4	1	2	2
Larsen (W)	1	0	0	2	0
Pierce	1	0	0	0	0

Los Angeles	IP	H	R	BB	SO
Podres	5	9	2	1	0
Roebuck (L)	3⅓	4	4	3	0
Williams	⅓	0	0	2	0
Perranoski	⅓	0	0	0	1

6

1978: New York Yankees vs. Boston Red Sox

Conceit in weakest bodies strongest works.
— William Shakespeare

If ever there were a model for how not to win a championship, the 1978 New York Yankees were it. Visualize a team decimated by injuries and torn by jealousy and resentment. Then stir in an owner whose paucity of baseball knowledge was only equaled by his compulsive need to micromanage his field captain. Add a self-absorbed slugger with a hunger for the spotlight and a combative, self-destructive manager with a pathological dislike of criticism, and you have what should add up to baseball's version of a train wreck. Yet somehow, the 1978 Yankees managed to navigate through a mine field of adversity to emerge as world champions. It's the story of a hugely talented team fighting to cleanse itself of its demons or, at least, to find a way to live with them. But mostly, it's a story about Billy Martin and George Steinbrenner.

For Billy Martin, life was a war to be won, and it didn't much matter how you did it. Growing up skinny and scrawny on the wrong side of the tracks in Berkeley, California, Martin resolved early in his life that he wouldn't take crap from anyone. In high school, he was kicked off the basketball team for punching an opposing player. A year later, he was also banished from the school's baseball team after he knocked an opposing player unconscious with three punches to the head. A few years later, Martin carried his bad boy act with him into the U.S. Army, where he once cold-cocked a young recruit who had made the mistake of falling asleep on his bunk.

Fighting wasn't the scrappy Martin's only talent. He also could play baseball. While in high school, he had been spotted by big league scouts, and eventually he was signed by the New York Yankees as an infielder. As a rookie, Martin's wise-guy act rubbed some of the more staid Yankee veterans the wrong way, but it hit the mark with a surprising target, Joe DiMaggio. Everyday, the great Yankee center fielder would enter the clubhouse and begin his familiar pregame ritual, first removing his jewelry and watch and placing them in his locker, then stepping out of his pants without first taking off his shoes. Standing in front of his locker, Martin would mimic the Yankee great's every move to growing laughter from his teammates. When Joe summoned the clubhouse boy to fetch him a half cup of coffee, Martin did too. When DiMaggio swigged the coffee, then spit a portion of it into the spittoon that sat at the back of his locker, Martin did the same. Fighting a smile, DiMaggio finally turned to Martin one day and said, "You fresh little bastard."

Never one to let well enough alone, Martin's pranks soon escalated. One day, armed with a leaky pen filled with disappearing ink, Martin asked DiMaggio to sign a ball. In a flash, Martin's pen emptied itself all over DiMaggio's dress shirt. While Martin collapsed in hysterics, DiMaggio's face reddened with anger. Martin quickly acted to calm the Yankee slugger: Joe, it's disappearing ink. Really. It's OK!" To the amazement of almost everyone in the Yankee clubhouse, DiMaggio and Martin became pals, and before long, the scrappy infielder joined DiMaggio's inner circle. The odd pairing of the dignified, classy DiMaggio with the in-your-face rookie amused Yankee manager Casey Stengel, who referred to Martin as "that fresh kid who's always sassing everybody and getting away with it."

Martin's act may have won DiMaggio over, but his take-no-prisoners approach to the game was proving to be a tough sell where opposing players were concerned. A fight with Jimmy Piersall of the Red Sox and two separate brawls with Clint Courtney of the Browns punctuated Martin's early years with the Yankees. In 1960, as a member of the Cincinnati Reds, Martin engaged in a particularly notorious tussle with Jim Brewer of the Cubs: he charged the mound and threw a battery of punches that broke bones around the pitcher's eye.

When his playing days were over, Martin scouted for a couple of years, but his heart wasn't in it. What he really wanted to do was manage. In 1969, he got his first shot with the Minnesota Twins, a seventh-place team that had finished 28 games back of first place the year before. Martin's players responded almost immediately to his fiery management style, and the club won its division. But Martin, beginning a lifelong pattern of wearing out his welcome, was fired when he sucker-punched the Twins' traveling secretary. His next stop was Detroit, where he took the Tigers from fifth to first place in just two years, but following a dispute with the owner, he was fired in 1973.

Despite his bad-boy persona, Martin was gaining a reputation as a baseball Svengali who could pump new life into dormant teams. With his successes in Minnesota and Detroit, Martin was now able to dangle the promise of victory in front of pennant-hungry owners like a carny hypnotist might swing a watch before a willing subject. "Martin's the kind of guy you'd like to kill if he's on the other team," Indians general manger Frank Lane once said, "but you'd like ten of him on your side. The little bastard."

The next to take a chance on Martin was Bob Short, owner of the Texas Rangers. Reaching Martin by phone, Short told him, "I need you to help turn the Rangers around." In 1974, Martin took the club to second place, but after Martin clashed with Short over player personnel matters, he was fired before the end of the 1975 season. Shortly after the debacle in Texas, Martin was on a fishing trip in Grand Junction, Colorado, when he received a message that Birdie Tebbetts, a scout for the New York Yankees, wished to see him. The following day the two men met for lunch in Denver, where Tebbetts explained that he'd been sent by Yankee president Gabe Paul. Paul wanted to know if Martin were interested in managing the Yankees.

To Martin and many others, the once-proud Yankee franchise had fallen on hard times. Since the team's last pennant in 1964, the club's once-vaunted farm system had grown fallow, turning out a succession of highly touted rookies who ultimately went bust. It was bad enough that the archrival Red Sox were continually finishing ahead of the Yankees in the standings, but what really hurt was the surging popularity of the upstart Mets, whose attendance figures were now eclipsing the Yankees.

When Martin expressed interest in the job, Tebbetts arranged for a meeting with Gabe Paul for the following day. After listening to Paul's pitch, Martin indicated that yes, he was interested in managing the Yankees, and yes the money was adequate. But there were problems with certain clauses in the proposed contract. Most troublesome, Martin said, were the paragraphs that forbade him from criticizing Yankee management and the ones that mandated that he "personally conduct himself at all times so as to represent the best interest of the New York Yankees." If he failed to meet the contract's stipulations, he would be fired. Paul told Martin that the contract reflected the wishes of Yankee owner George Steinbrenner and that there was nothing he could do. Martin then told Paul that his answer was no.

"Billy, don't be so hasty," Paul replied. "Why don't you talk to

George?" With that, Paul reached for the phone and dialed Steinbrenner's number. When the Yankee owner came on the line, Paul handed the phone to Martin. "Billy," Steinbrenner said to Martin, "I'd like to have you as our manager." Martin, who had met Steinbrenner briefly a year or two earlier, was familiar with the Yankee owner's reputation as being difficult to work with. Martin told Steinbrenner that while he would like to manage the Yankees, he was less than excited over some of the contract's clauses.

"If you don't take the offer now, you will never get it again," Steinbrenner replied, turning up the heat on Martin. "Here's your big chance to manage the Yankees, something you've always wanted to do." Martin then told the Yankee owner he needed some time to think it over. Back at his hotel, Martin discussed the offer with his wife. That night, with his mind still not made up, he went to bed, hoping that a good night's sleep might make his choices more clear. The following day, Martin again met with Gabe Paul. Following some persuasive words from the Yankee president, he relented and agreed to take over the club. On August 2, Martin was introduced at a Yankees old-timers game as the team's new manager.

In George Steinbrenner, Martin would confront his most formidable nemesis. As a young man, Steinbrenner had assumed control of his father's ship-building business, and under his stewardship, the company had grown into a $200 million colossus. In January 1973, Steinbrenner, feeling sure that he could translate his business success to professional sports, fronted a 12-member ownership group which purchased the Yankees from CBS, Inc., for a reported $10 million. Declaring to the press that restoring the Yankees to glory was his primary goal, Steinbrenner also made it clear that he would play virtually no role in the club's day-to-day operations.

Driven and unpredictable, George Steinbrenner presented two faces to the world. To friends, he was a sensitive man with a caring and generous nature. To those who worked for him, he could be an arbitrary, demanding perfectionist whose dealings with employees were characterized by impatience and insensitivity. To many in the Yankee organization, Steinbrenner also demonstrated a startling ignorance of the sport that he had just entered. Convinced that a dollar sign was the key to unlocking baseball's mysteries, the Yankee owner could never understand how a pitcher making the major league minimum could strike out a hitter making millions.

After taking over the Yankees, Steinbrenner quickly reneged on his pledge to stay out of the club's day-to-day affairs. While attending his first game as the club's owner, Steinbrenner was dismayed to see the hair of some of his players reaching their collars. Quickly dashing off a note to manager Ralph Houk, Steinbrenner instructed Houk to have his players get a haircut or face fines. The Yankee owner's meddling didn't end with sartorial matters; despite his paucity of baseball experience, Steinbrenner regularly phoned his manager during games with suggestions on who should be playing. Exasperated, Houk quit the team following the 1973 season, telling his players, "I have to leave before I hit the guy."

Seeking increased autonomy, Steinbrenner began buying out his partners in 1973. As he cut checks and people left, the Yankee owner's meddling in the club's affairs grew exponentially. His efforts at remaking the Yankees in his image hit a wall in 1974, however, when he was suspended from baseball for two years over illegal contributions he'd made to the reelection campaign of President Richard Nixon. He may have been in exile, but Steinbrenner was determined to retain control over the Yankees; on frequent occasions, he recorded pep talks for his players and instructed new manager Bill Virdon to play them in the clubhouse before important games. The rah-rah tenor of the messages triggered images of Knute Rockne and George Gipp and were generally a source of humor for the Yankee players.

Under Virdon in 1974, the Yankees improved their win total by nine games and climbed to second place. Still, Steinbrenner wasn't satisfied. With the club hovering at the .500 mark during midsummer 1975 and Billy Martin available, Steinbrenner gave Virdon his walking papers and installed Martin as the club's new manager.

On August 2, 1975, Billy Martin, resplendent in cowboy hat, boots, and western pants, was introduced to the press as the new Yankee manager. "I was out hunting wild animals in Colorado when the Yankees hunted me down," Martin told the press. "I'm very happy to be the manager of the New York Yankees, and I promise you we will have a very good ballclub here very shortly."

With Steinbrenner serving out his suspension, Martin was free from distractions for the remainder of the 1975 season. Standing at his customary spot at the foot of the dugout steps, Martin carefully evaluated his new team. Players that didn't enthusiastically embrace the Billy Martin style of play were designated as trade bait. Those who Martin regarded as "clubhouse lawyers" would also be given their walking papers. When the season ended, the Yankees finished a respectable third, 12 games behind the Red Sox. During the off season, Commissioner Bowie Kuhn decided to commute the remainder of George Steinbrenner's suspension, and in March 1976, the Yankee owner was back, just in time for Billy Martin's first full season as manager.

In 1976, the Yankees began the season like a house afire, winning 15 of their first 20 games. By July, the club had a 15-game division lead, but when it slumped somewhat in August, Steinbrenner panicked. Martin, who had repeatedly rejected requests from the Yankee owner to talk with the team's players, finally relented in August. Marching into the Yankee clubhouse with all of the authority of George Patton, Steinbrenner dressed down his players as if he were speaking to a high school team. "You guys aren't giving it all you've got. Don't you know that you're Yankees? You have to play like Yankees." Martin, cringing in embarrassment, listened in silence as Steinbrenner spoke.

Steinbrenner's speech sorely tested Martin's patience, but an incident a short time later roiled the waters even more. In late August, Martin was negotiating with the club for a long-term contract to remain as the Yankees' manager. The two parties had settled most issues, but a disagreement over salary was threatening to torpedo the negotiations. Standing in the Yankee dugout one night, Martin happened to glance up at Steinbrenner's private box. Sitting with the Yankee owner was Dick Williams. Williams, a successful major league manager and a favorite of Steinbrenner's, had recently been let go by the Angels. To Martin, the message from Steinbrenner was clear: agree to our salary proposal or look for a new job.

Considering the distractions, it's hard to believe how much went right for the Yankees in 1976. Slowly, Martin's message of "we can win" was beginning to sink in, and the results were translated into improved play. Martin's aggressive approach to the game, dubbed "Billy Ball " by the New York media, was based upon a foundation of speed, defense, and solid fundamentals. Contributing to the club's success in 1976 were third baseman Graig Nettles with 32 home runs and 93 RBIs; outfielder Mickey Rivers, who provided spark in the lead-off role; and catcher and team captain Thurman Munson, who was the league's Most Valuable Player. With Ed Figueroa, Catfish Hunter, and Dock Ellis all in double figures in wins, the club's starting pitching was solid, while bullpen ace Sparky Lyle won seven games and saved 23.

Contributing to the club's success was its unique chemistry, as day in and day out, disparate personalities meshed with uncommon ease. Munson and Nettles served as the team's agitators, using sarcasm to spawn friendly rivalries. Mickey Rivers, with his funny walk and garbled syntax, played the role of comic relief. Roy White, all class and quiet dignity, was a stabilizing influence on the team's young players. They laughed together in the clubhouse and played tough, aggressive baseball on the diamond. To be sure, the club wasn't free from challenges to its internal harmony. It was common knowledge, for example, that Thurman Munson had an agreement with Steinbrenner that he would always remain the highest paid

Yankee. But the catcher's good ol' boy demeanor and refusal to hog the spotlight made it all but impossible for his teammates to resent him. To a man, winning was what mattered, and when they coasted to the division title in September and then nailed down the American League pennant a week and a half later, it looked like the first of many winning seasons to come.

In the World Series, the club, still nursing hangovers from its pennant celebration, lost four straight to the Cincinnati Reds. Dismayed at his club's lack of superiority in the series, Steinbrenner vowed to strengthen the club for the coming season. With the Yankee farm system in disarray, the Yankee owner turned to baseball's first free agent draft in December 1976 to obtain the players he needed. Moving to shore up the club's pitching, Steinbrenner quickly signed lefty Don Gullett. He then turned his attention to his next goal: signing Reggie Jackson.

The biggest fish in the free agent pond, Reggie Jackson had been pursued by 13 big league clubs. Never one to shrink from a challenge, Steinbrenner courted Jackson relentlessly, escorting the slugger to trendy night spots like the 21 club and introducing him to his rich and powerful friends. When it came time to talk turkey, Steinbrenner's offer easily eclipsed his competitors, and Jackson was won over. After signing Steinbrenner's contract, the slugging outfielder sat down and wrote the Yankee owner a note. "I will not let you down," it read. It was signed "Reginald M. Jackson."

After the signing of Jackson was announced, the New York Yankees held a press conference to welcome the slugger to New York. With Thurman Munson, Willie Randolph, and Ed Figueroa on the dais behind him, Yankee president Gabe Paul said, "We are very pleased to announced that Reggie Jackson has agreed to join us and very happy to have him in a Yankee uniform." The numbers on the contract were, by 1976 standards, impressive: $2.9 million for five years. When asked by the gathered newsmen if he would become a big star in New York, Jackson raised eyebrows in the room when he declared, "I didn't come to New York to become a star. I brought my star with me."

Following the press conference, speculation began in the New York press over how Jackson would mesh with his teammates. Blessed, or cursed, depending on your point of view, with an unshakable confidence and an unremitting hunger for the spotlight, Jackson had made waves wherever he went. "There's not enough mustard in America to cover Reggie Jackson," a former teammate once said of him. As a teammate of Jackson's in Oakland, Yankee pitcher Catfish Hunter knew that changes were in store for the Yankees. "If you think things are controversial now," Hunter told his teammates following Jackson's signing, "wait until Reggie starts his shit."

Happy days in New York, at least for the moment. *From left:* Yogi Berra, George Steinbrenner, and Billy Martin celebrate the clinching of the 1976 American League pennant. (*The Sporting News.*)

Much of the speculation around New York centered on how Jackson's "take care of number one" approach would jibe with Martin's team-oriented philosophy. Four years earlier, as an Oakland Athletic, Jackson had provided a reporter with his take on the Yankee manager: "I hate Martin because he plays tough. But if I played for him, I'd probably love him."

Not necessarily. In truth, Reggie Jackson and Billy Martin mixed like oil and water. While publicly expressing happiness over Jackson's signing, the Yankee manager fretted over the impact that Jackson's high profile would have on his team's fragile chemistry. In the spring of 1977, Martin's ambivalence over his new slugger only increased when Jackson reported late to the club's training camp in Fort Lauderdale.

Martin may have been unsure of his new slugger, but Thurman Munson was not. He didn't like Reggie Jackson. During the spring of 1977, Munson watched with amazement as the outfielder talked virtually nonstop to reporters, who continually surrounded him. Particularly galling to Munson and some of his teammates was Jackson's habit of anointing himself as the Yankees' savior. "I think Reggie Jackson on your ballclub is part of a show of force," Jackson announced to the press upon his arrival at spring training. "It's a show of power. I help to intimidate the opposition just because I'm here. See this?" Jackson held up his bat for all to see. "Nobody will embarrass the Yankees in the World Series again as long as I'm carrying this."

Watching the performance with thinly veiled annoyance, Munson turned to outfielder Lou Piniella and asked, "Can you believe this shit?"

In many ways the club's heart and soul, Munson was probably the last Yankee who Jackson needed as an adversary. A leader on the field and a stabilizing presence in the clubhouse, Munson found Jackson's flamboyance grating and the size of his contract infuriating. It had been himself, Nettles, Rivers, and the others who had turned the Yankees into winners, not Reggie Jackson. If riches were to be doled out, Munson felt, it should be to them and not to this loudmouth who had yet to play a real game in a Yankee uniform.

Early in the season, Jackson had also incurred the wrath of third baseman Graig Nettles over his lackluster play in the field. An outfielder of below average capability, Jackson had nonetheless been installed in right field at the insistence of Steinbrenner. As Nettles put it in his autobiography:

> Our better outfielders would be DHing [acting as designated hitters]; and Jackson would be in right. It didn't make any sense, except that's what George wanted, and he owned the team. And we resented him for that, because there's one thing a professional ballplayer can't abide and that's a selfish teammate.

Jackson's relations with his teammates would grow worse in May when an interview was published in *Sport Magazine*. "You know, this team …. it all flows from me," Jackson said in the article:

> I've got to keep it all going. I'm the straw that stirs the drink. It all comes back to me. Maybe I should say me and Munson … but really he doesn't enter into it. He's being so damned insecure about the whole thing. Munson thinks he can be the straw that stirs the drink, but he can only stir it bad.

In the Yankee clubhouse, the article landed with a thud. After the magazine hit the stands, Jackson was greeted in the Yankee clubhouse with a leaden silence. Players shot sideways glances at the slugger, whispered among themselves, then turned back to face their lockers. At one point, Munson made a point of slowly ambling by Jackson's locker with the interview protruding noticeably from the rear pocket of his uniform. The following day, Jackson's pariah status was cemented when two of his teammates moved their lockers away from his.

Despite the distractions, the Yankees hit the ground running during the early part of 1977. After besting Milwaukee in their season opener at Yankee Stadium, the club tore through the early weeks of the season, steamrolling opponent after opponent. The announcement on May 5 that a confectionery company would market a new "Reggie" candy bar did little to increase Jackson's popularity among his teammates but did not affect the club's winning ways.

The Yankee juggernaut, pummeled by injuries and an offensive drought, finally slowed in June. Alarmed by the slump, Steinbrenner's calls to Martin in the dugout increased in frequency. Apparently, no detail was too small to escape the owner's attention. "Billy," Steinbrenner told Martin one afternoon, "Thurman's not wearing a cup. I want you to fine him." In late summer, Martin became so enraged over Steinbrenner's repeated phone calls that he ripped the phone from its moorings in the Yankee dugout to prevent any further intrusions.

Martin's relationship with Steinbrenner was going steadily downhill, but the real fireworks were about to take place over Jackson. On June 17, the boiling cauldron that was the New York Yankees finally exploded in view of the entire country. In a game against the Red Sox, Jackson misplayed a routine fly ball off the bat of Jim Rice for an error. From Martin's vantage point in the Yankee dugout, it appeared that Jackson didn't hustle on the play. Armed with a golden opportunity to show Jackson once and for all who really stirred the Yankee drinks, Martin told Paul Blair to vacate his seat on the Yankee bench and replace Jackson in right field.

Standing in right field, Jackson saw Paul Blair leave the dugout and run directly toward him. "You here for me?" Jackson asked. Blair nodded. When the Red Sox fans caught wind of what was happening, the stands began to buzz with excitement. In the Boston dugout, players left the bench and moved to the edge of the dugout to get a clear view of the fireworks that would take place when Jackson reached the dugout.

"What the hell do you think you're doing out there?" Martin screamed at Jackson when he reached the dugout steps.

"What do you mean? What are you talking about?"

"You know what the hell I'm talking about!" Martin screamed. "You want to show me up by loafing on me? Fine. Then I'm going to show your ass up. Anyone who doesn't hustle doesn't play for me!"

"I wasn't loafing Billy," Jackson replied. "But I'm sure that doesn't matter to you. Nothing I could ever do would please you. You never wanted me on this team in the first place. You don't want me now. Why don't you admit it?"

"I ought to kick your ass!" Martin yelled.

"Who the hell do you think you're talking to, old man?" Jackson screamed.

"What?" Martin yelled. "Who's an old man? Who are you calling an old man?"

Enraged, Martin advanced on Jackson. In a flash, Yankee coaches Yogi Berra and Elston Howard jumped between the two combatants. Following the altercation, Jackson showered, then returned to his hotel room, where he was soon joined by Yankee backup catcher and team ally Fran Healy. A short time later, Steinbrenner arrived at the hotel, determined to patch up the differences between the two men.

After listening to Jackson's side of the dispute, Steinbrenner made his way to Martin's room to speak with his manager. After getting Martin's side, the Yankee owner conferred with team president Gabe Paul. Both men believed that Martin had demonstrated an inability to handle Jackson and debated firing him. Finally, they settled on a compromise; if Martin would refrain from speaking to the media regarding the incident, they would ask Jackson to be more solicitous of Martin.

Talking to the press following the incident, Jackson cast himself in the role of victim: "It makes me want to cry, the way they're treating me on this team. The Yankee pinstripes are Ruth and Gehrig and DiMaggio and Mantle. I'm not their lackey. I don't know how to be subservient."

In spite of the tension that was swirling around it, the club won 40 of its final 50 games and stormed to the pennant. When the Yankees defeated Kansas City in the playoffs, they clinched their second consecutive American League title. The victory had been a team effort all the way: Munson, Piniella, and Rivers each hit over .300, while Jackson, Nettles, and Willie Randolph contributed big years. The pitching was led by lefty Ron Guidry and Ed Figueroa with 16 wins apiece, and in the bullpen, Sparky Lyle posted a 13–5 record with 26 saves to nail down the American League Cy Young Award.

Following the victory over the Royals, the Yankee clubhouse was alive with celebration. During the raucous party, Jackson carried a champagne bottle into Billy Martin's office. "Here, skipper," Jackson said. "Have some of this champagne."

"I will if you will," Martin replied.

With that, Jackson downed a huge swallow from the bottle. "You had a helluva year, big guy," Martin told his slugger.

"I love you," Jackson replied.

Following the club's triumph over the Dodgers in the World Series, Lou Piniella spoke to the press regarding the strains of 1977. "This club can't take it for another year. It's been the toughest year mentally I've ever had. If the season had dragged on for another two weeks, I don't think I could have made it. It feels like I've been playing for five or ten years." Lou Piniella had no way of knowing that 1977 was just a preview of the tumult that would threaten to tear the Yankees apart in 1978.

While the Yankees spent much of 1976 and 1977 battling among themselves, the Boston Red Sox were consumed with their own problems. Since their dramatic World Series loss to the Cincinnati Reds two years earlier, the Sox had played also-rans to the Yankees in the American League East. Under manager Darrell Johnson, the club slipped to third place in 1976, finishing a humiliating 15½ games behind New York. Things improved somewhat in 1977, but it was clear that the Sox was a team in search of balance. Throughout the year, the club bludgeoned opposing pitching with the long ball, but more often than not, the power surge was negated by poor starting pitching. Still, the club, under new manager Don Zimmer, managed to close to within 3½ games of the Yankees in August. But when New York shellacked them in a crucial three-game series in September, the bubble burst.

With the announced goal of improving its pitching staff for the 1978 season, the club acquired right-handed starter Dennis Eckersley and Mike Torrez, whose 14 wins for the Yankees in 1977 had helped them to their world championship. The club also bolstered its infield by acquiring line drive–hitting Jerry Remy to play second base.

In New York, George Steinbrenner and the Yankees weren't standing pat. New York may have had Cy Young Award winner Sparky Lyle in the bullpen, but Steinbrenner wanted National League fireballer Rich "Goose" Gossage, and in the fall of 1977, he signed the big right-hander to a contract. Things were changing in the front office too. At a press conference in March 1978, Steinbrenner announced the resignation of team president Gabe Paul and named former Cleveland great Al Rosen to replace him. Following the announcement, Steinbrenner told the press that Rosen's responsibilities would vastly exceed those wielded by Paul, meaning that Steinbrenner's role would be drastically reduced in the coming year. "I'll be less involved with the team in 1978," he told the press. "That's the way I want it."

Steinbrenner's announced intention of being less visible during the coming season was greeted with headlines around New York. On Friday, April 7, the *New York Times*, handicapping the '78 season, ran an article entitled "Martin: No Yank Discord Expected." In the story, the Yankee manager was asked about his problems with Jackson during the previous year. "That's history," Martin replied. When asked how he was getting along with Steinbrenner, Martin answered with just one word, "Sensational."

THE RACE

With their first world championship in 16 years to celebrate, the Yankees' home opener was a festive occasion for New York and its fans. In a ceremony that preceded the game, Yankee greats Mickey Mantle and Roger

Maris hoisted the 1977 world championship banner to the top of the flag pole in center field as a cadre of past Yankee greats looked on. In the opener against the White Sox, Reggie Jackson picked up where he'd left off the previous October by blasting a home run in his first at-bat. As Jackson circled the bases, hundreds of Reggie! candy bars, which had been distributed to fans before the game, were thrown onto the outfield grass. In the dugout, Jackson and Billy Martin were a picture of conviviality, laughing and joking together as the Yankee grounds crew cleaned the candy from the field.

For the Yankees, the joy of opening day would soon be shattered by an onslaught of physical injuries. A game in mid-May proved to be the harbinger. Against the Royals, Goose Gossage was protecting a one-run lead in the ninth when Amos Otis lifted a fly ball to the gap in deep right field, which appeared to be destined for extra bases. Paul Blair and Reggie Jackson converged on the ball, and at the last moment, Blair lunged with his glove and made what appeared to be a game-saving grab. At the same moment, however, he encountered Jackson, running full speed from his position in right. The two men collided, and the force of the impact jarred the ball from Blair's glove. While Blair and Jackson lay prone, Otis steamed home on a game-winning inside-the-park homer. Following the play, the entire New York bench ran out to right center to check on the fallen Yankees. Limping and holding his back, Blair, with the aid of his teammates, slowly made his way back to the dugout.

By month's end, the Yankee trainers' room was beginning to resemble an infirmary. Bucky Dent was nursing a sore knee, and Willie Randolph was sidelined with a bad thumb. With pain in his battered legs, Thurman Munson was forced to abandon his catching post to become the club's designated hitter. The Yankee pitching rotation was also being hard hit as Don Gullett, Andy Messersmith, and Dick Tidrow developed sore arms, leaving only Ron Guidry and Ed Figueroa uninjured from the team's regular starters.

"We did have a lot of injuries," Yankee shortstop Bucky Dent remembered later. "I think we had Rivers out, Randolph, Munson, Catfish. It was a tough time."

Probably most distressing for the defending champions were the woes of Catfish Hunter. Struggling for the past two years with a bad shoulder, the one-time Yankee ace had become maddeningly inconsistent on the mound. Hunter's physical woes began during his first season with the Yankees when, armed with a large contract, he was determined to prove his worth to his new club. When he beat Detroit on September 3, 1975, he had his 19th win and, most amazingly, his 26th complete game tying a Yankee record set nearly 60 years earlier.

With 18 games left in the 1975 season, new manager Billy Martin was determined to impress Steinbrenner with a run to the wire. In late September, Martin approached Hunter and asked him if he could pitch on two days' rest. Hunter, with 310 innings already registering on his arm for the year, said OK. On a bitterly cold fall night, Catfish beat the Indians for his 22nd victory. In his next outing, Hunter went the distance again, beating Baltimore 3–2. Then, in his last start of the season, the pitcher again gave the bullpen the night off when he went the route against Cleveland. By the time the season ended, Hunter had pitched in all but 18 innings of games that he had started. His complete game total of 30 was the most in the American League in more than 30 years.

After the success of 1975, Hunter's confidence was at an all-time high heading into 1976. Things started out fine on opening day when he tossed a three-hitter at Milwaukee, but from there, it was all downhill. He lost his next three games and by mid-May, his record was an anemic 3–5. Throughout the season's initial weeks, Hunter was plagued by an unusual tightness in his pitching arm. The symptoms grew progressively worse, until by May, the pain was so severe he couldn't lift his arm above his chest.

Despite his woes, Hunter continued to trudge to the mound. On some days, he was better than ever, like in May, when he went 11 innings to beat Boston 1–0. But for every good outing, there were two or three when his pitches had no zip and he would be cuffed around by opposing hitters. Hunter did manage to win 17 games during 1976, but from start to start, he was never confident of the stuff he would take to the mound with him. In 1977, inconsistency continued to plague Hunter. Some days he was the Catfish of old, pitching sharply and without pain. On others, he had no control or velocity. Throughout the season, Hunter was a constant presence in the Yankee training room, hoping against hope that the ministrations of trainer Gene Monahan would ease his distress. On June 17, things hit rock bottom when he surrendered four home runs while facing just six batters in a game against Boston.

As it turned out, arm woes weren't the only thing troubling Hunter. Following the 1977 season, the pitcher became aware of an extreme, unyielding thirst and a constant need to urinate. After he arrived in Fort Lauderdale for the Yankees' spring training camp of 1978, Hunter discussed his symptoms with trainer Monahan, who arranged for medical tests for the pitcher. When the results were disclosed, it was determined that Hunter had diabetes. Treatment for the disease eased the pitcher's symptoms but did little to increase his effectiveness on the mound.

While Hunter and the rest of the Yankees battled injuries in early

1978, things were coming up roses for the Boston Red Sox. Despite the addition of new faces, the club had gelled almost immediately and by early summer, led both leagues in hits, runs, home runs, and runs batted in. Potent hitting was just part of the Red Sox story; improved pitching was also proving key to the club's success as Dennis Eckersley and Mike Torrez comprised a solid one-two punch at the top of the rotation, while lefty Bill Lee and Luis Tiant were proving effective as the club's third and fourth starters.

Speaking to the press regarding his team's hot start, Mike Torrez saw even better things to come for his club:

> We've had guys getting hot at different times. Butch Hobson carried us for awhile, then Jim Rice, then Dwight Evans got hot. We haven't had everyone contributing all at the same time. But I see signs of everyone starting to get hot together. If this whole club gets hot in the next two or three weeks, really, you can forget about it.

"We got off to a great start in '78," Bill Lee says today:

> Eckersley, Torrez, and I all got off to a great start. I think we were on the cover of *Sports Illustrated* at one point. And that was probably the kiss of death. As I remember it, we lost our first two games, one in Chicago on the road. But I got off to a great start, and everyone was getting along fine.

The calendar showed it only to be May, but with the Yankees ailing and the Red Sox hitting on all cylinders, George Steinbrenner was preparing to hit the panic button. Contrary to his announced intention of receding into the background, the Yankee owner had continued his badgering of Billy Martin with unsolicited advice over the club's uneven play. "Wait until Dent and Randolph and Rivers and Munson and Hunter all get healthy," Martin begged the Yankee owner. "We'll pick it up then."

Steinbrenner's impatience with his club only increased when a depleted Yankee lineup dropped two of three to Boston in mid-June. With most of his starting pitchers sidelined, Martin had no choice but to start Ken Clay, a still ailing Don Gullett, and Jim Beattie, who had a combined record of 4 and 5, against Tiant, Torrez, and Eckersley, who had fashioned a cumulative 22 and 4 record.

Visits to Boston were proving to be detrimental to Martin's well-being. Just a year earlier, during a similarly unsuccessful series against Boston, he and Jackson had engaged in their near-fight in the dugout. Now, with the latest series of losses to the Red Sox, the Yankee front office was up in arms again. Speaking to the press following the series against

Boston, Al Rosen said, "Billy, being a professional manager, knows what happens to managers who are supposed to win who don't win."

Making matters worse for Martin were rumors that were suddenly swirling around the club regarding pitching coach Art Fowler. According to reports, the Yankee brass held Fowler responsible for the rash of injuries to the pitching staff, and he would be fired shortly. Some observers saw the Fowler matter as another Steinbrenner plot to rid himself of Billy Martin. Steinbrenner, the speculation went, wasn't willing to incur the wrath of Yankee fans by firing Martin directly, but if he could goad Martin into quitting by canning his long-time pitching coach, all the better.

On June 23, Al Rosen left New York and flew to Detroit, where the Yankees were playing the Tigers. In a meeting with Martin the next day, Rosen told the Yankees' manager, "Billy, we're going to have to get rid of Art."

"No you're not," responded Martin. "If you get rid of Art, I want you to get rid of me at the same time."

"C'mon Billy," Rosen shot back. "We'll get Art a job in the minor leagues."

Martin held fast; he would not have his pitching coach fired. With the two men at an impasse, it was decided to delay the matter of Fowler until the club returned from its road trip and Martin could meet with Steinbrenner. After his meeting with Rosen, Martin rode with a disconsolate Fowler back to the team's hotel. "Billy, I'll go," the pitching coach told Martin. "Let them do what they want to do." Martin demurred, "No, Art, it doesn't work that way."

On Sunday, June 25, the Yankees returned home from Detroit. The next morning, Martin, Steinbrenner, and Rosen met at Yankee Stadium to discuss Art Fowler. Before the meeting, Martin had considered marching up to Steinbrenner and quitting on the spot. However, after conferring with friends, he settled on a different approach; he would remain firm while attempting to win the owner over with an appeal to Yankee loyalty.

What Martin didn't know was that Steinbrenner and Rosen had already decided that Fowler could stay. What hung in the balance, however, was Martin's fate as Yankee manager. Martin also didn't know that Steinbrenner had recently made an unsuccessful attempt to lure Dick Williams away from the Montreal Expos. Even when he found out that Williams was unavailable, Steinbrenner remained unconvinced that Martin was the right man to guide the Yankees through the remainder of the year.

In retrospect, Steinbrenner's attempt at blaming Martin for the poor showing of the Yankees during the first half of 1978 is tantamount to blaming a one-legged man for being poor at kickball. With the Yankee roster resembling an emergency ward, it's hard to conceive that Dick Williams or even a reincarnated Joe McCarthy could have done any more with the ailing Yankees than Martin was. For all their woes, Martin's Yankees could still boast of having the fourth-best winning percentage in the major leagues. If Martin were fired, it would be the first time in baseball history that a manager who had won consecutive pennants would be terminated in the succeeding year.

With the Yankee manager's fate still hanging in the balance, the meeting among Steinbrenner, Rosen, and Martin ground on. It was only when Martin vowed to work more closely with the front office that Steinbrenner made up his mind. Martin could stay. With the meeting concluded, Al Rosen met the press and told them that Martin's job was safe, at least for the remainder of the year. When asked why the club considered firing Martin to begin with, Rosen said, "I said at the time there was a danger in falling 14 or 15 games back of a hot club. That's something we wanted to avoid. That's been avoided. At the moment, it's not a reality."

Maybe not a reality to Rosen on June 26, but it soon would be. After being swept by Milwaukee in early July, the Yankees staggered into the All-Star break 11½ games behind Boston. "This is a cancerous situation," one Yankee player told the press. "Guys are just going through the motions. Nobody's doing anything. Everyone is sitting back and waiting for Jackson and Munson to get hot."

On July 19, the Yankees hit their low-water mark when they fell 14 games behind the Sox. Things were tough, but were it not for Ron Guidry, they would have been a lot worse. In their half-season of discontent, Guidry was the Yankees' saving grace, taking the mound every fifth day and shutting down the opposition. With an incredible 13–1 record by mid-summer, the lanky lefty was the talk of baseball. A Yankee teammate summed up Guidry's value to the club when he told the press in July, "Without Ron Guidry, the Yankees would probably be 25 games behind."

But Guidry wasn't the only bright spot for the Yankees. The club's deep bench was also proving key in preventing a collapse that would render any late-season charge at Boston meaningless. While Dent, Randolph, Munson, Blair, and others took their turns on the disabled list through the injury-plagued months of June and July, the Yankee reserves stepped in and kept the team afloat. "When your front-line people get hurt, you have to have guys you're not afraid to put in there," Bucky Dent said later. "And with guys like Brian Doyle, Fred Stanley, and Jim Spencer, you knew that our bench was as strong as anybody's in baseball."

Strong bench or not, no one was giving the Yankees, or anyone else for that matter, much chance of overtaking the Red Sox. With a 57–25 record, the Sox were playing at a nearly .700 clip, and as the summer wore on, an aura of inevitability had settled upon them. "It sure doesn't look like we're going to catch them," Lou Piniella told the press in early July. "I think we can still finish a very respectable second."

In his autobiography, Red Sox pitcher Bill Lee talked about the mood of the club during the heady days of midsummer:

> On July 19, we had been fourteen games ahead of the Yankees and, to be honest, we had figured they were history. We no longer worried about them, we were going to turn our attention to knocking off Milwaukee and Baltimore.

But dame fortune had her own ideas. Almost imperceptibly, in midsummer, the dynamic of the season began to shift. For Boston, it began with an injury to shortstop Rick Burleson. Third baseman Butch Hobson developed bone chips in his throwing arm which severely limited his ability to throw to first. Next, first baseman George Scott began slumping at the plate. And Bill Lee, struggling with a chronically sore arm, stopped winning and was on his way to being dropped from the rotation.

The decline of the Red Sox can be traced to July 20. Boston was in Milwaukee on a humid, rain-soaked night to face the Brewers. After waiting out a 2½–hour rain delay, Bill Lee blew a three-run lead, and the Brewers won the game. Following the contest, the club flew through the night to Kansas City, where the team's plane didn't touch down until 5 AM. That night, they were hammered 9–0 by the Royals, marking the first time the Sox had been shut out all year. The following night, Frank Duffy, playing in place of the injured Burleson at short, kicked a routine grounder which allowed the Royals to tie the score in the eighth. The Sox lost the game in the 10th, 6–5.

The slump continued the following night when the Royals hammered the Sox's pitching for four first-inning runs and went on to win 7–3. Suddenly, Boston had lost four straight. Against Minnesota a day later, a pinch-hit double by Rod Carew sent them down to defeat again. The Sox finally snapped its losing streak the following day, but the wheels were now wobbling themselves off the Boston wagon. After pummeling American League pitching throughout the first half, the Boston offense scored just three runs over their next four games and were shut out three times. Things were so tough that a Boston area priest offered to stop by the Boston clubhouse to bless the team's bats. His offer was politely declined.

Following a fortnight of frustration, Boston catcher Carlton Fisk spoke to the press regarding the team's change of fortune:

> For the last two weeks, every pitcher you face looks like Cy Young. That's the one thing we thought we didn't have to worry about, hitting. Our pitch-

ing this year is good enough so that it doesn't have to be carried by the hitters. It sure as hell ain't being carried by the hitters now.

While the Red Sox pondered their fate, the saga of Steinbrenner, Martin, and Jackson was about to take a strange new twist. On July 16, Dave Anderson of the *New York Times* reported that Billy Martin was battling liver problems and was seriously ill. Anderson reported that the Yankee front office knew of Martin's health problems and would understand if the Yankee manager wished to take some time off and recover his health. Martin, certain that the story had been planted by Steinbrenner to force his ouster, was furious.

Anderson's story wasn't completely fallacious; over the preceding two weeks, Martin had confided to friends that a spot had been found on his liver and that doctors had told him to stop drinking. Martin had no way of knowing it at the time, but the Anderson column would set into motion a chain of events that within days, would cost him his dearest possession: his job as manager of the New York Yankees.

While Martin simmered over the Anderson column, Reggie Jackson was doing some simmering of his own. On July 17, the slugger walked into the office of George Steinbrenner fully intending to get some things off his chest. With Al Rosen and a couple of Yankee vice presidents in attendance, Jackson told Steinbrenner that he and Billy Martin were incapable of working together. The Yankee manager no longer spoke to him, Jackson said, and worse yet, refused to let him play right field. Steinbrenner listened in silence as the slugger spoke, then without a word, rose from his chair and began pacing the room. Finally, he spoke, telling Jackson that his efforts at convincing Martin to make him the everyday right fielder had failed. Besides, Steinbrenner told Jackson, it wasn't just Martin; there were others in the Yankee organization who considered him a defensive liability. The best thing, Steinbrenner told the slugger, would be for him to adjust to being the club's full-time designated hitter.

Angered at Steinbrenner's remarks, Jackson told the Yankee owner that he wanted to be traded. The air suddenly grew foul as Steinbrenner paced the office with increasing agitation, jabbing the air with his index finger to punctuate his remarks. "You're not going anywhere," he shouted.

In his autobiography, Reggie Jackson maintained that Steinbrenner then referred to him as "boy," and that he erupted in anger. Steinbrenner cut him off. "Get out of my office," he screamed. When Jackson refused, Steinbrenner, with Rosen and the Yankee vice presidents in tow, left instead.

Lingering just long enough to make his point, Jackson left Steinbrenner's office at 7:15 PM. He had just enough time to make it to the Yankee clubhouse in time for the team's game that night against the Royals. Point-edly ignoring Billy Martin as he passed him in the clubhouse, Jackson made his way to his locker and suited up. As he left for the playing field, he encountered third-base coach Dick Howser. "Tell Martin I don't want to talk to him anymore," Jackson told the coach, "and tell him I don't want him giving me any more signs."

The game against the Royals was hard fought, with the clubs battling to a 5–5 tie in extra innings. In the Yankee half of the 10th inning, New York tried to rally when Munson led off with a single. As Jackson left the dugout to hit, Martin approached him.

"Can you bunt?" Martin asked.

"Bunt? Yeah, I guess so."

"OK, I want you to bunt."

Whether Martin truly wanted Jackson to bunt, something he'd never asked him to attempt before, or was simply challenging Jackson in response to his comments to Howser is open to conjecture. Martin's question "Can you bunt?" provides a clue; it's hard to believe that so skilled a manager as Martin would direct one of his players to bunt in such a crucial situa-tion without knowing whether or not he was capable of it. What is clear is that Jackson, with a list of perceived slights coursing through his head, squared to bunt reliever Al Hrabosky's first delivery. The pitch was high, and Jackson took it for a ball.

Standing at the foot of the steps in the Yankee dugout, Martin sig-naled to third-base coach Dick Howser to let Jackson swing away. Jackson stared at Howser for his sign, then stepped back in the batter's box, and attempted to bunt again. Howser yelled for time, then ran down the line to speak with Jackson. "Billy wants you to hit away," he told him.

"I was told to bunt. I'm bunting," Jackson replied.

Stunned, Howser tried again. "Reggie, he wants you to hit away."

"Listen Dick," Jackson told Howser. "Nothing against you, but when I left the dugout, he told me to bunt, and I'm going to bunt. I'm gonna get the runner over, and Piniella will come up and knock the run in, and we'll win. I'm a real team guy, right?"

Returning to the plate, Jackson tried twice more to bunt before finally striking out. In the Yankee dugout, Martin couldn't believe it. Eyeing his manager with every step, Jackson slowly walked back to the Yankee dugout. When he reached the dugout steps, Jackson, fully expecting Martin to punch him, removed his eye glasses. The slugger descended the dugout steps and took a seat at the far end. A minute later, coach Gene Michael approached him. "Billy wants you to go inside and take a shower." Ignor-ing the order, Jackson remained on the bench.

While Jackson sat, Martin struggled to maintain his composure. Martin's mood turned even blacker when the Royals rallied in the top of the 11th to win the game. With his jaw clenched, Martin left the dugout, walked into his office, and threw his clock radio against the wall. Determined to have it out with Jackson, he started for the team's clubhouse. Gauging his manager's mood, coach Yogi Berra stepped into Martin's path. "Take it easy, Billy. Don't hit him. Don't do it."

With Berra preventing him from reaching Jackson, Martin reached for the phone. After reaching Al Rosen, he told him, "He defied a direct order to bunt from his manager. He defied me and there's no way he can get away with that. If you don't fine and suspend him, I'm quitting." Martin then told Rosen that he wanted Jackson suspended for the remainder of the season. Rosen thought the suggestion ridiculous. After conferring with Steinbrenner, Rosen countered with a five-game suspension, which Martin grudgingly accepted.

During Jackson's absence, the Yankees regrouped, winning four straight to trim the yawning deficit between themselves and the slumping Red Sox to 11 games. On July 23, Reggie Jackson arrived by taxi at Chicago's Comiskey Park to rejoin his team. During his suspension, Jackson had avoided all contact with the media, fueling a frenzy among the New York press for his side of the story.

As Jackson made his way into the visitors' clubhouse, Billy Martin was in his office filling out the Yankee lineup card, which tellingly, did not contain Reggie Jackson's name. Martin then summoned Dick Howser and instructed him to tell Jackson that he wanted him to take extra batting practice. Passing through the clubhouse on his way to the field a few minutes later, Martin couldn't believe his eyes. Not only was Jackson not preparing to take the field, he was engaged in a full-scale press conference in front of his locker. "Damn reporters," Martin muttered to himself. "Disrupting my team."

After talking at length with the reporters, Jackson suited up and made his way to the field. The Yankees, with Jackson riding the bench, won the game, extending their winning streak to five straight. Even more important, the club had whittled another game from the Red Sox lead; they had lost to Kansas City. Following the game, Martin, who was unable to contain his curiosity, spied a reporter in the Yankee clubhouse.

"What did Jackson say?" Martin asked him.

"Here, read it yourself," the reporter replied, handing Martin his notes.

"I never considered what I did an act of defiance," Jackson's statement read. "I didn't think people would get so upset at what I did. I was surprised at the way they had taken it."

Angered by what he'd read, Martin handed the notes back to the reporter.

"Yeeech, " Martin said.

"Is that a comment on me?" the reporter asked.

"No, him," Martin replied.

Returning to his office, Martin's blood was boiling. How could Jackson contend that he had not defied him? It made no sense. Jackson wasn't the only matter contributing to Martin's foul mood; a recent conversation with White Sox owner Bill Veeck was also on his mind. The two men had bumped into each other during the Yankees' visit to Comiskey Park. After exchanging pleasantries, Veeck laid a bombshell on Martin. "Did you know that you were almost traded to the White Sox?" he asked. Martin said he had no idea what Veeck was talking about. The White Sox owner then told Martin that Steinbrenner had contacted him in June with a proposed trade of managers; White Sox skipper Bob Lemon would be swapped even-up for Martin. Veeck told Martin that he'd listened politely to Steinbrenner's pitch, then declined the offer. Martin was incredulous. With half the Yankee regulars on the disabled list during June and Martin battling to keep the team afloat, Steinbrenner had been working behind the scenes to unload him.

Even in the best of times, Billy Martin saw enemies everywhere he looked. Now, with Jackson seemingly flaunting his insubordination and Steinbrenner maneuvering against him, Martin's paranoid tendencies were at red alert. An hour later, a still-simmering Martin was on the Yankee team bus sitting next to *New York Times* sportswriter Murray Chass. Martin, who avoided reporters he deemed loyal to Steinbrenner, had always found Chass to be fair. Still chewing over the actions of Steinbrenner and Jackson, Martin opened up to Chass. "When we get to the airport, can I see you for a few minutes? George has got some other guys in his pocket. Do you mind if I have you in my pocket?"

When the Yankee bus finally arrived at the airport, Martin and Chass walked into the terminal, where they were joined by two additional sportswriters from the New York media. Suddenly, Martin began speaking as if Jackson were present. "We're winning without you. We don't need you coming in and making all these comments. If he doesn't shut his mouth, he won't play, and I don't care what George says. He can replace me right now if he doesn't like it." The men asked Martin if his comments were off the record.

"No, sir," Martin replied. "It's all on the record." In a flash, the sportswriters left to phone the story into their papers. As they did so, Martin entered the airport bar.

Martin spent approximately 15 minutes drinking scotch. Exiting the bar, Martin saw the reporters he'd spoken to earlier gathered around a newsstand. "Did you get all that in the paper?" he asked the men. When the reporters answered in the affirmative, the Yankee manager grinned. The men picked up their bags and, as a group, began to walk toward the gate where they would await their plane. As they did, Martin told the reporters that Jackson had lied during his statements to them following the game. "He's a born liar. The two of them deserve each other. One's a born liar, the other's convicted."

When the Yankees' plane touched down in Kansas City, Chass immediately contacted Steinbrenner for his response to Martin's remarks. Steinbrenner said he hadn't heard what Martin had said and asked the reporter to read them to him. After Chass did, Steinbrenner, sounding stunned, asked Chass to read them again. Steinbrenner then asked Chass if Martin had been drinking. Chass replied that he had not seen Martin drinking.

After speaking with Chass, Steinbrenner awakened Al Rosen at home. "Did you hear what Billy said?" he asked. Rosen said he hadn't. After Steinbrenner read him Martin's statement, Rosen called a team official in Kansas City and asked him to track down Martin. Martin, who was drinking with members of the Yankee staff when he was located, denied making the remarks. At 1 AM, Martin called Chass. Slurring his words, Martin told the reporter that he was out to get him.

On Monday, June 24, Al Rosen left New York for Kansas City. The Yankee president had been unable to pin down Steinbrenner regarding Martin's future with the club, but to cover his bases, he had contacted Bob Lemon, who had recently been dismissed as manager of the White Sox. "I'm having some problems," Rosen told Lemon. "Stand by and I'll call you tomorrow. I want you to manage the ballclub if we can't get this thing ironed out."

At 1:30 PM, Rosen arrived at the Crown Center Hotel in Kansas City. At the same moment, Billy Martin, nursing a hangover, was writing his resignation on a piece of hotel stationery. Once the statement was complete, Martin made a spontaneous decision to go downstairs, where he would read the statement to the newsmen on the hotel's mezzanine. As Martin was leaving his room, he encountered Rosen in the hallway. Throwing his arms around the Yankee president, Martin told him, "Tell George that I didn't say those things."

Once on the hotel balcony, Martin, disguising his bloodshot eyes behind dark glasses, read from the paper in his hand. "There will be no questions and answers with anyone after the statement is made. That means now and forever, because I am a Yankee, and Yankees don't talk or throw rocks. I would like to thank the Yankee management, the press, the news media, my coaches, my players ..." Choking on his words, Martin halted, reached up to adjust his glasses, then attempted to continue. "And most of all ..." Unable to continue, Martin broke into sobs before being led away by Yankee broadcaster Phil Rizzuto.

Following Martin's statement, Al Rosen announced that Bob Lemon would take over as Yankee manager. Lemon had been a star pitcher for the Cleveland Indians in the 1940s and '50s and, as Billy Martin's pitching coach in 1976, helped guide the Yankees to the pennant. One of the game's prodigious imbibers, Lemon, as he himself often noted, never took the game home with him, preferring to leave it in a bar along the way. Lemon lacked Martin's cunning and keen baseball instincts, but he was knowledgeable, patient, and soft-spoken, qualities that would act as balm on the troubled Yankee team. "He was a big peacemaker," Bucky Dent said of Lemon. "He was just what we needed at the time."

Following Rosen's announcement, Lemon spoke to the press: "I know Billy was a favorite, and he's going to be a tough act to follow. He's been successful. He's always been my friend. I don't think Boston has won it yet. It could be interesting."

In fact, "interesting" was exactly what the 1978 pennant race was about to become. On Tuesday, July 25, the Yankees, behind Guidry's six-hitter, shut out the Royals 4–0, while the Red Sox were losing for the sixth time in their last seven games. The Boston slump was now raising eyebrows around the league. "Our problem's been hitting," Don Zimmer told the press:

> But these guys don't figure to be stopped forever, they're too good. When Jimmy Rice slumps for five or six days, he goes out to the batting cage and works with Johnny Pesky and the other coaches. He's doing the same this time, but nothing's happening.

With losing suddenly becoming a habit for the Sox, Carl Yastrzemski was in a quandary. The Red Sox great had been troubled all year with a bulging disk in his back, which made swinging a bat an agonizing experience. Finally, Yastrzemski could take no more, and in late July, he checked himself into the New England Rehabilitation Center outside Boston for treatment. However, with the Sox staggering, the veteran knew that he belonged with his team. On August 1, he checked himself out of the facility and took a cab to Fenway. Walking into Don Zimmer's office, Yastrzemski told his manager, "I'm ready to go."

At 39, Yastrzemski knew that his playing days were dwindling to a precious few. Too many meaningless Octobers had punctuated the career of one of the game's great players; in Yastrzemski's 19 years with the Red Sox, he'd played in more than 2,000 games, stood at the plate more than 9,500 times, and had appeared in 11 All-Star games and two World Series. He'd also won three batting titles, been chosen the league MVP, and was creeping up on 3,000 hits. What he hadn't done during all that time was play on a championship team.

In the first game back with his team, Yastrzemski lined a single off the left-field wall at Fenway in his first at-bat, but it wasn't enough. The Sox lost again. The Boston lead over the Brewers was now 4½ games and just 8½ over the Yankees. "We've got the best record in baseball," Zimmer told the press. "And we're in a horrible slump."

While Boston's fortunes continued to wane, things were looking up in New York. In early August, injured Yankees finally started returning from the disabled list. "A week or so after Bob took over the ballclub, we started getting some people back," Bucky Dent said later. "Mickey Rivers, Willie Randolph, a healthy Catfish Hunter. We started to get the people we needed to chase the Red Sox."

The resurrection of Catfish Hunter is one of the most amazing events of the 1978 season. After a series of terrible outings, Hunter was finally placed on the club's disabled list in June. Later that month, Hunter entered the Manhattan office of orthopedic surgeon Maurice Cowen. With Hunter under anesthesia, the doctor manipulated the pitcher's arm into the cocked position that allows pitchers to generate velocity. Suddenly, a resounding "pop" came from the joint. "Shit, we broke his arm," a surgical assistant said. But Cowen, feeling otherwise, continued his treatments.

When Hunter awoke from the procedure, he found Cowen standing over his bed with a ball of wadded surgical padding in his hand. "Here," the doctor told Hunter, handing him the padding, "throw this to me. " Hunter did, and for the first time in nearly two years, felt no pain. The awful sound that Cowen had heard was actually a piece of diseased ligament tearing away from Hunter's arm joint. The ligament had prevented the pitcher's arm from moving fluidly in the arm socket and was the source of the pitcher's pain. Showing remarkable improvement, Hunter returned from the disabled list on July 17. By the time he shut down Texas on August 1 by an 8–1 score, the old Catfish was back, and he was instrumental in helping the Yankees climb to within 6½ games of Boston.

On August 2, the reeling Red Sox pulled into New York for a two-game showdown with the Yankees. To a man, the Yankee players viewed the series as a must-win. "We struggled so hard to come from 14 games back to within 6½ of the Red Sox," Bucky Dent remembers. "We considered those games vital."

Prior to the game, Bob Lemon did his best to reduce expectations for the series. "Every game is important now. We play Boston, we play Baltimore, and then we play Milwaukee. They're all right there together. But it isn't critical. We have nine games left with Boston. And anything can happen."

But on August 2 and 3, the resurgent Yankees stumbled. In game one, Boston spotted the Yankees a five-run lead, but when Goose Gossage twice walked batters with the bases loaded, they were able to tie the game. Throughout the contest, the Red Sox bullpen continually pushed back Yankee rallies until the game was suspended by curfew at 1 AM. Nineteen hours later, the game was resumed, and in the 17th inning, Rick Burleson's single through the infield provided Boston with the victory. In the regularly scheduled game, the Sox again manhandled New York, 8–1, rekindling their lead over second-place Milwaukee to six games and their lead to 8½ over the third-place Yankees.

Following the series sweep, a sense of relief washed over the Boston clubhouse. "After we tied them in game one," Fisk told the press, "I started yelling, 'Curfew, curfew!'" Sitting at his desk, looking exhausted and depleted was Boston manager Don Zimmer. When a photographer approached and told Zimmer he wanted "a happy Don Zimmer," the manager put down the sandwich he was eating and broke into a smile.

Amazingly, the losses to Boston did little to dismay the Yankees. With Martin gone, the club was at last liberated from disruptive ego clashes and free to concentrate on what it did best: playing winning baseball. Most relieved of all by Martin's departure was Reggie Jackson. In his first act as Yankee manager, Lemon had restored the slugger to the cleanup spot, and Jackson responded at the plate. Driving in runs with almost equal fervor were Thurman Munson and Lou Piniella. Brian Doyle, the minor league recruit who was filling in for the ailing Willie Randolph, was exceeding everyone's expectations. Even a newspaper strike, which hit the city in the middle of August, seemed a blessing in disguise. "With the papers on strike," Bucky Dent said later, "we couldn't read what somebody else had to say about us. We saw it as a benefit, really."

In late August, the surging Yankees kicked off a seven-game winning streak, which lifted them over Milwaukee and into sole possession of second place. Speaking to the press, Lou Piniella uttered the words that New York fans had waited all year to hear. "We're only 6½ games back now. There's going to be a pennant race. It's going to be tough, no question. But there's going to be a race. And it's now or never."

With the race tightening, both clubs were looking forward to a crucial four-game showdown in Boston on September 7. In early September,

Thurman Munson and Lou Piniella were sitting side by side on the Yankee bench. "I looked at the schedule," Munson told the right fielder. "If we can pick up 2½ games this week, we can go into Boston only four down."

As it turned out, that's exactly what happened. On Saturday, September 2, Figueroa's 14th win and an Oakland victory over the Red Sox carried the Yankees to within 5½ games of first place. After New York split a doubleheader with Detroit and the Red Sox lost to Baltimore on September 4, the lead was down to five games. On September 6, Jim Palmer of the Orioles handcuffed the Sox, while in New York, the Yanks won their 11th in 13 games by manhandling the Tigers. Munson's wish was fulfilled. With a four-game series between the two clubs set to begin the following day, the Yankees were within striking distance of first place.

"You chase a team so far and you tell yourself, 'If we can only get close, we're gonna catch them and we're gonna beat them,'" Bucky Dent said regarding the Yankee surge in early September:

> During the week we were chasing them, we happened to be in Cleveland and some of the players there told us, "The Red Sox were in here a couple of weeks ago, and they were eight games ahead of you. And they were asking everyday, 'What did the Yankees do?'" They more or less felt that we were going to come and that we were going to come hard at the end.

When it came to facing the Red Sox in September, "come hard at the end" was all the Yankees knew. In the words of Tom Boswell of the *Washington Post*, "It's axiomatic in the Northeast that no Red Sox lead is safe. And it is cradle lore that no Boston team ever faced up to a Yankee challenge in September." The year 1978 would prove to be no different. For four days beginning on September 7, a fiery Yankee club delivered a series of body blows to the Boston Red Sox that would forever live in baseball lore as the "Boston Massacre."

On Thursday, New York pounded four Sox pitchers for a total of 15 runs. The win was the Yanks' 13th in 15 games and moved them to within three games of first place, the closest they'd been since May 31. "We got the shit kicked out of us," Zimmer said following the game. "The only good thing is that it counts only as one game. All we can do is come back."

On Friday, a shaky Boston club committed four errors in the first two innings and opened the door to seven unearned Yankee runs. The final score was 13–2. "Everything is going right," Piniella said after the game. "Good hitting, good defense, great pitching. It's snowballing for us."

Following the win, Bob Lemon was exultant: "The way we're playing, I won't be happy with a split in the next two games. I want to win them all. Four straight." The Boston lead was now just two games.

On Saturday, the Yankees, behind Ron Guidry's two-hitter, did it to the Red Sox again, 7–0. The next day, the Yankees completed the sweep by swarming over rookie pitcher Bob Sprowl in the first inning for five runs. Ed Figueroa made them stand up, and the final score was 7–4. The loss, Boston's 9th in 11 games, propelled the Yankees into a flat-footed tie for first place. By the time the series was over, the Yankees had outscored Boston by a total of 42 runs to 9. Things were so lopsided that Willie Randolph was 3–3 in one game and Thurman Munson 3–3 in another before Boston's ninth-place hitter ever got to the plate. Following the series, a columnist in the *Boston Globe* summed up the feeling around New England when he said, "The Sox may still be in first place, but they're chasing the Yankees now."

Twenty-two years later, Red Sox pitcher Bill Lee remembers the impact of those four games on Boston:

> The Yanks had all left-handed hitters up there, and they were gonna hurt you. Except for Piniella. And after being down and doing all the fighting they did earlier in the season, they pulled it together. But they were a "bought" team. A typical Steinbrenner-purchased team. You played against them, and you wished you were on the *Titanic*.

Following the debacle against the Yankees, Don Zimmer spoke with the press:

> Choke is not in my vocabulary. But slump is. I've seen ballplayers go into slumps. If a guy goes into a slump, and you're in a second-division ballclub, you never hear the word choke. But the minute you're fighting for a pennant and a guy goes into a slump or a team goes into a slump, the team choked. I think that's ridiculous.

Fred Lynn echoed Zimmer's sentiments:

> You can tell when a team's choking. They look nervous. They lose their aggressiveness. They become pretty passive. They don't say much. That's not the atmosphere on this club. Besides, we're not out of this thing yet. We're still in first place, and we've got a rematch against the Yankees next week.

By the time the two clubs met for a three-game series in New York the following Friday, the reeling Sox had fallen 1½ games behind the Yankees. "Our only hope is to sweep the series," Don Zimmer said on Thursday. "We can't afford to lose a game."

On Friday, September 15, the Red Sox limped into Yankee Stadium to resume their battle against the Yankees. After a Red Sox error opened the door to four runs in the fourth inning, Ron Guidry had all he needed as he shut down the Sox on two hits. Following the game, Sparky Lyle talked to the press regarding the Red Sox: "I'm not sorry for the Red Sox. But I pity them." The Yankee lead was now 2½ games.

On Saturday, a wired-tight Red Sox squad jumped to a 2–0 lead in the first inning, but a subsequent homer by Jackson tied things up. In the ninth, a triple by Rivers and a sacrifice by Munson produced the winning run. All afternoon, Red Sox hitters fought a losing battle with their nerves, swinging defensively at pitches they normally would have feasted upon. The Yankee win, the club's sixth straight win over the Sox in just 10 days, increased its first-place lead to 3½ games.

The Sox salvaged game three with a 7–3 victory, which snapped New York's five-game winning streak. "We didn't win the two of three here we wanted," Zimmer said later, "but we're not going to quit. Two and a half games behind is better than four and a half. Now we have to get a winning streak going."

Fortunately for Zimmer and the Red Sox, a winning streak was just around the corner. For the next five days, the Sox matched the Yankees in wins. When Luis Tiant beat Toronto on Saturday, September 23, the Sox had scratched to within a game of the Yankees with just seven left to play. Over the next six days, the two clubs stood eye to eye, each matching the other win for win, each daring the other to blink. Entering into the season's final day, the Red Sox needed a win against Toronto and had to hope that the Yankees would find a way to lose.

In Boston on Sunday, a soft rain was falling as Luis Tiant squared off against the Blue Jays. The cagey veteran was in complete command all afternoon, mesmerizing Toronto batters with a mixture of off-speed pitches. At 2:12 PM, a roar went up from the crowd when the Fenway Park scoreboard showed that Cleveland had jumped to a first-inning 2–0 lead over the Yankees. Meanwhile, Tiant finished the task at hand, never allowing a Blue Jay beyond first base. The final score was 5–0.

Back in New York, Catfish Hunter and the Yankee bullpen were having no luck against the Indians. Home runs by Thorton in the first and Alexander in the second signaled the start of the onslaught, and by the time the game was over, Cleveland had pounded out a 9–2 victory.

"Cleveland was playing like they were in a World Series," Bucky Dent said later:

> I still remember walking up the tunnel after the ballgame thinking, we'd played so hard, we've played injured, and now we've got to go play a team on their own ground. We'd lost the coin toss. I was just shaking my head thinking, please God, give us one more chance.

In Boston, word of the Yankees' loss came via a radio in the Boston clubhouse. After being left for dead, the Sox had finally caught the Yankees at the wire. The stage was set for a one-game showdown at Fenway Park on Monday for the American League pennant.

"Choke, choke, choke. That's all any of us were going to hear for the rest of our lives if we hadn't come back to square this thing," said Mike Torrez. "We're a different ballclub than the one the Yanks saw a couple of weeks ago. We were just praying for a shot to prove it to them."

"There may be more interest in this game than the World Series," Jerry Remy told the gathered press. "The whole country's gonna be tuned for this one."

Sitting in front of his locker following his club's big win over Toronto, Carl Yastrzemski told reporters, "This was a big one. We're going to come out swinging against the Yankees and give it our best shot."

Following the game, Yastrzemski received word that Don Zimmer wished to see him. Thanking the media, the veteran player made his way to his manager's office. Once close, the relationship between Yastrzemski and his manager had grown distant since Zimmer had taken over the team. Zimmer never said so, but it was Yastrzemski's feeling that the Boston manager had distanced himself from his players in an attempt to retain his objectivity. But now, with his club one win away from the American League pennant, Zimmer wanted to speak to his team captain.

Entering Zimmer's office, Yastrzemski found the Boston manager surrounded by his coaching staff. Ostensibly, the purpose of the meeting was to determine the club's starting lineup for the playoff game against the Yankees on Monday. However, Yastrzemski quickly realized that the true purpose of the gathering was to showcase Zimmer's decisiveness. The Boston manager would mention a player's name, ask the men in the room for their opinion, then respond with his own answers before they could speak.

"Guidry's pitching tomorrow," Zimmer said. "So who's going to be playing third base?" Through much of the year, Zimmer had platooned left-handed hitting Jack Brohamer with righty Frank Duffy. The percentages suggested that Duffy should play, but Zimmer had his own answer. "Brohamer's doing a hell of a job for us the last few weeks, and I think he should play. What do you think?" To a man, the coaching staff replied, "That's right, Zim."

Yastrzemski, blanching at the charade, spoke up:

Wait a minute. You've got a guy who's 24–3, the best left-handed pitcher in baseball right now. Brohamer's never faced a left-hander like this, and besides, he hasn't faced a left-hander the past month because he's been pla-tooning. Duffy might get his bat on the ball and scoot one into right field. But Brohamer's not going to have a chance against this guy. If they bring in Gossage, then you've got Brohamer to pinch-hit.

"No," Zimmer replied. We're playing Brohamer. That's it."

Zimmer then informed the men in the room that Mike Torrez would be Boston's starting pitcher on Monday. "If he gets in trouble, who do we go with from the bullpen?" Before anyone could speak up, Zimmer pro-vided the answer. "Stanley's been having one hell of a year for us. I think we ought to bring in Stanley." Once again, all the coaches nodded.

"I agree with you on Stanley," Yastrzemski said, "but it all depends. They've got two, three lefty batters in a row. Nettles, Jackson. Andy Has-sler has had a hell of a last two months." Hassler was a left-hander in the Sox bullpen, big and strong but given to wildness. Key to Yastrzemski's mentioning of Hassler was the reluctance of left-handed hitters to dig in against him. "I'd go with Hassler if you've got these left-handed hitters coming up and go to Stanley for the right-handers."

"No," Zimmer shot back. "We're going to Stanley and that's it."

Frustrated at his inability to make himself heard, Yastrzemski left the meeting and returned to the clubhouse for a shower before heading home. As he made his way out of the stadium, he encountered pockets of cele-brating Red Sox fans, savoring the lingering flavor of the club's sweet vic-tory that afternoon. Responding to their shouts of encouragement, Yastrzemski smiled and waved, then ducked into his car for the trip home. His club's historic rendezvous with the New York Yankees was now less than 19 hours away.

Back in New York, the Yankees were packing their bags for the unex-pected and unwelcome trip to Boston. "We know we can win there and we'll have in mind what we did there last time," Ron Guidry told the press. "I'm not worried about pitching with three days' rest. I beat Toronto in my last start with three days' rest. I'm not worried about anything. I've had good luck all year, and I expect to have more tomorrow."

Standing at his locker, Reggie Jackson, who'd gone hitless against the Indians, was in a subdued mood:

> How do you think I feel when we've just been beaten? We've played our ass off and now we're going to have to do it again. The season starts again tomorrow. It's all even. There's no psychological advantage. This is the way it ought to be. One at-bat. One pitch. The fifth game of the playoffs. The seventh game of the World Series. It starts at 2:30 tomorrow, and I hope we'll all be ready.

Once packed, the Yankees boarded a bus for the ride to the airport.

Despite the club's bitter loss to Cleveland, the players were loose and confident. An hour later, they deplaned in Boston. As the players made their way through the terminal, they were booed by passing Red Sox fans. The electricity in the city over the looming showdown was palpable. Boarding a bus that would carry them to the Sheraton Boston, some of the Yankees dozed while others drank or kibitzed among themselves. In a joking reference to the pressure-packed game that would be played the following day, Catfish Hunter turned to Lou Piniella and said, "Don't choke, Lou. Don't choke."

MONDAY, OCTOBER 2, 1978

On October 2, Lou Piniella was sitting in the visitors' dugout of Fenway Park. In less than an hour, the New York Yankees would battle Boston in only the second sudden-death playoff in American League history. Right now, however, Piniella's full attention was on the Red Sox, who were taking batting practice on the field directly in front of him. Intently studying the faces of Carl Yastrzemski, Fred Lynn, Rick Burleson, and the rest of the Red Sox for a few minutes, Piniella realized that this was a transformed club, which little resembled the jittery squad that the Yankees had humiliated with regularity in September. Turning to Reggie Jackson, Piniella said, "We'll have to beat them. They're not going to beat themselves today."

The Red Sox might not beat themselves, but to complete their climb to absolution and the American League pennant, they'd have to find a way to beat Ron Guidry. Rick Burleson summed up the formidable task confronting his team on Sunday. "Now we've got a second chance," the shortstop told the press. "We have the home field. We have the momentum. They … they … they have Guidry."

The Yankees most certainly had Guidry. Following his club's tough loss on Sunday, the fireballing lefty had marched into Lemon's office and told his manager, "I'll take the ball." Guidry had taken the ball all year, parlaying a 95-mile-an-hour fastball and a wicked slider into a 24–3 record. Guidry was a lock for the Cy Young trophy and maybe for the league's Most Valuable Player Award too. Reggie Jackson summed up the Yankees' feeling about Guidry on Sunday afternoon when he told the press, "Guidry's our stud. No doubt about it. He's our stud."

A year earlier, New York had had another stud, Mike Torrez. As a Yankee, the 6'5" 220-pound right-hander had won 14 games and helped his club to the pennant. In the World Series he continued his success when he won two games against the Dodgers. Following the season, Boston had

Armed and ready to fire, Ron Guidry shows the form that made him baseball's premier pitcher in 1978. (National Baseball Hall of Fame Library, Cooperstown, N.Y.)

dangled a $2.7 million free agent contract in front of Torrez, and he had grabbed it.

As a member of the Red Sox, Torrez had pitched extremely well to start the season but slumped when he was most needed, going 0 and 6 down the stretch. The right-hander also hadn't fared well against his former teammates who, fueled by resentment over comments that Torrez had made during the spring about the Yankees, had beaten him three times during 1978. But Don Zimmer, knowing of Torrez's competitive fire when facing his old team, liked the action and at 2:30 PM, Torrez left the Red Sox dugout and walked to the mound to face his former teammates.

In the first inning, hearts around Boston skipped a beat when Reggie Jackson hammered a Torrez fastball to left field. But the wind, always a factor in a ballpark the size of Fenway, was blowing in, and Jackson's drive was carried back toward the field, where it was grabbed by Yastrzemski just short of the left-field wall. After an uneventful first inning, Guidry made a mistake as he pitched to Yastrzemski to start the second inning, and the veteran raked a high, inside pitch around the right field foul pole for a home run. The Sox had drawn first blood. Hard long outs from the bats of Fisk and Lynn ended the inning but also kindled hope in Boston hearts that Guidry might be working with subpar stuff on this day.

While Guidry fought to keep the Sox at bay, Torrez continued to battle the Yankees. In the third inning, Mickey Rivers fired up Yankee partisans when he doubled, but Reggie Jackson lined out to kill the rally. In the fifth, the Yankees threatened again when a tiring Mike Torrez walked Roy White to start the inning. After White moved to second on a ground-ball out by Brian Doyle, Bucky Dent popped out. Torrez worked his way out of the jam by inducing Rivers to roll a grounder to Burleson at shortstop, who threw Rivers out at third to retire the side.

In the bottom of the sixth, Boston finally broke through again against Guidry. After Burleson doubled over third base and was bunted to third by Remy, Jim Rice muscled a single to center to drive in Burleson with Boston's second run. After Yastrzemski rolled out, Guidry walked Fisk intentionally. Now with two out, the hitter was Fred Lynn. Pitching with care, Guidry worked the count to three and two before Lynn lashed a drive to right that looked like a sure bet for extra bases. Breaking with the crack of the bat in right field was Lou Piniella, who somehow fought a blinding sun to make a great running catch. "I was pretty lucky," Piniella said later. "I stabbed it behind me. But I'd been playing the outfield pretty well the last couple [of] seasons. I positioned myself well."

Guarding a slim 2–0 lead, Torrez walked to the mound to face the Yankees in the seventh. Thus far, he'd stymied the New York attack, allowing just two hits over the first six innings. After getting the first out, the big righty yielded singles to Chambliss and White. With two on and time running out, the Yankees were now armed with perhaps their last opportunity to tie the game. But Jim Spencer, hitting for Doyle, popped up for the second out. In the Yankee dugout, Lou Piniella groaned. "If we blow this," he said to Thurman Munson, "we're in trouble."

Digging in at the plate was Yankee shortstop Bucky Dent. From his position in left field, Carl Yastrzemski snuck a glance at the center field flag pole. In a flash, Yastrzemski realized that the wind had reversed direction and was now blowing from home plate toward left field. Yastrzemski shook his head. He knew that a ball popped into the jetstream that was now whistling over Fenway could easily carry over the fence.

Choking up severely on his bat, Dent waited for Torrez to deliver to him. Working carefully, the Boston pitcher was able to get two quick strikes on the shortstop. Dent then chopped the next pitch off of his foot. Grimacing in pain, the Yankee shortstop hopped out of the batter's box. While he was being attended by the Yankee trainer, Mickey Rivers began yelling to Dent from the Yankee dugout. Unable to hear what Rivers was saying, Dent yelled back, "What did you say?" "Your bat is cracked," Rivers replied.

After checking his lumber, Dent realized that Rivers was right and returned to the Yankee dugout to borrow a new bat. Dent limped back into the batter's box and once again prepared to face Torrez. The Boston pitcher kicked at the dirt, got his sign, then wound up to deliver to the plate. To Dent's amazement, it was a hanging slider, out over the plate. Connecting, he lifted the ball skyward where, buoyed by the wind, it carried into the netting atop the wall for a three-run homer. In an instant, a deathly silence enveloped Fenway Park.

"When I fouled the ball of my foot, the trainer came out and sprayed some of that cold stuff on it to keep the swelling down," Dent remembered later:

> And Mickey Rivers told me, "You're using a cracked bat." What had happened was, we only had two bats because it was the last game of the season. And I had broke one, right around the tape. And when I pulled one out of the rack, I pulled the wrong one out. So Mickey said, "You're using a cracked bat, use this one." It wasn't until the game was over, and we were talking about it that I realized that if I'd used the cracked bat, it might've been an out.

While the Yankee dugout celebrated, Mike Torrez was walking Mickey Rivers. Don Zimmer, emerging from the dugout to a chorus of boos, pulled Torrez from the game and waved in Bob Stanley from the bullpen. But

Stanley, so sharp the previous Friday, didn't have it today. After Rivers stole second, Munson hammered a hanging Stanley curve for a double, which drove Rivers home. It was now 4–2 in favor of New York.

In the bottom of the seventh, Guidry, who had struggled to stay loose during the previous half inning, surrendered a single to George Scott with one out. Sensing that his ace was tiring, Bob Lemon signaled that he wanted Goose Gossage from the bullpen. After completing his warmups, Gossage retired the side without incident.

In the top of the eighth, Reggie Jackson led off with a home run into the sun-bleached stands in center field to increase the Yankee advantage to 5–2. In the bottom of the eighth, the Red Sox rallied when a double by Jerry Remy and a single by Yastrzemski made it 5–3. After singles by Fisk and Lynn, Yastrzemski scored to pull the Sox to within one run of New York.

With one out, Gossage was now in deep trouble, but Lemon was making no move to lift him from the game. "He's been the best we've had this year," Lemon would say later. "I wasn't going to make a change." It was fortunate that he didn't. After Hobson popped out to right field, Gossage blew three fastballs by Scott to quell the threat. With eight innings on the books, the Red Sox were still one run short.

In the ninth, Boston made a last, desperate charge at New York. With one out, Burleson drew a walk. After taking two quick strikes from Gossage, Jerry Remy connected on a low inside fastball and lined to right field. Blinded by the sunlight that was peaking just over the Fenway roof, Piniella froze in his tracks, arms outstretched at his sides, looking for all the world like a man testing the sky for raindrops. "I never saw it," Piniella would say later. "I told myself, 'Don't wave your damn arms and let the runner know you've lost it.'"

With his eyes trained intently on the grass in front of him, Piniella caught sight of the ball just as it kicked off the grass in front of him. At the last second he speared the ball with his glove, barely keeping it from skipping by him to the right-field wall. Rifling a throw to third, Piniella prevented Burleson from advancing to third.

"What Lou did," Graig Nettles said later, "was fake it well enough to make Burleson think he might make the catch. Burleson delayed long enough to lose any chance of making it to third."

With runners at first and second, Rice lifted a fly to center for the second out. On the play, Burleson tagged up and went to third. Now with the tying run at third and the season on the line, Yastrzemski, with a homer and a single on the day, was walking to the plate. A dead fastball hitter, Yastrzemski had always done well against Gossage. On the mound, Gossage wound up and delivered. It was a low fastball, which exploded in on Yastrzemski's hands. Unable to turn on it, the veteran popped up to Nettles for the final out. Somehow they'd done it. After being counted out, the New York Yankees had come all the way back to win the American League Eastern Division title.

Back in the Yankee clubhouse, Bucky Dent was the man of the hour. "When I hit the ball," he recalled later:

> I didn't really feel like it was going to be a home run. When I reached first base, the umpire was signaling that it was a home run, and I realized that it had gone over the fence. That was a tremendous ballgame. The pressure was building as the game went on. I think every kid dreams of hitting the ball out of the ballpark to win a big game. When I got to home plate, I finally realized that I'd put the Yankees ahead.

For the Yankees, beating Mike Torrez made the victory all the sweeter Nettles said:

> The only satisfaction in beating them is beating Mike Torrez. Because of the things he said about us. Here is our teammate, a guy we battled hard for last year, and he went out and got a lot of money, and instead of just saying, "Thanks, guys," he said a lot of bad things about individuals on this team. I got a kick out of beating him and I know that other guys did too. It was a very classless thing that he did.

Responding later to Nettles' remarks, Torrez said, "It all goes with the territory. You're in the public eye, and you're going to be a hero for some people and a goat for others. I took it like a man. I made a little mistake. Do you think that I'm going to let it ruin my life?"

Following their clutch win over the Red Sox, the Yankees again beat the Kansas City Royals for the American League pennant and then overcame the Los Angeles Dodgers to win the World Series. Amazingly, the conclusion of the 1978 season did not signal the end of the increasingly strange relationship between George Steinbrenner and Billy Martin. Following Martin's resignation in July 1978, Steinbrenner shocked New Yorkers when he announced that Martin would return as the club's manager in 1980. As it turned out, Martin wouldn't have to wait that long. When the Yankees stumbled during the early weeks of 1979, Steinbrenner's impatience flared again, and after firing Bob Lemon, he installed Martin once again as manager.

The Steinbrenner-Martin saga took a bizarre turn in the fall of 1979 when Martin, who was vacationing in Nevada, managed to get into a fight with a marshmallow salesman. Steinbrenner, making the dubious claim that the resulting publicity embarrassed him and the Yankees, fired Martin yet again.

From that point, you need a scorecard to trace the comings and goings, as Martin was hired, fired, hired, fired, hired, and finally, following yet another nightclub brawl in 1988, fired for the final time as Yankee manager. The cycle was finally broken for good 18 months later, when Billy Martin, riding in the passenger seat of a pickup truck driven by an intoxicated friend, was killed when the truck overturned.

OCTOBER 2, 1978

NEW YORK	AB	R	H	BI
Rivers cf	2	1	1	0
Blair cf	1	0	1	0
Munson c	5	0	1	1
Piniella rf	4	0	1	0
Jackson dh	4	1	1	1
Nettles 3b	4	0	0	0
Chambliss 1b	4	1	1	0
White lf	3	1	1	0
Doyle 2b	2	0	0	0
Spencer ph	1	0	0	0
Stanley 2b	1	0	0	0
Dent ss	4	1	1	3
Totals	35	5	8	5

BOSTON	AB	R	H	BI
Burleson ss	4	1	1	0
Remy 2b	4	1	2	0
Rice rf	5	0	1	1
Yastrzemski lf	5	1	2	2
Fisk c	3	1	1	0
Lynn cf	4	0	1	1
Hobson dh	4	0	1	0
Scott 1b	4	0	2	0
Brohamer 3b	1	0	0	0
Bailey ph	0	0	0	0
Duffy 3b	0	0	0	0
Evans ph	1	0	0	0
Totals	36	4	11	4

Doubles: Rivers, Munson, Scott, Burleson, Remy

Home Runs: Dent, Yastrzemski, Jackson

New York	0 0 0	0 0 0	4 1 0	5
Boston	0 1 0	0 0 1	0 2 0	4

New York	IP	H	R	BB	SO
Guidry (W)	6⅓	6	2	1	5
Gossage	2⅔	5	2	1	2

Boston	IP	H	R	BB	SO
Torrez (L)	6⅔	5	4	3	4
Stanley	⅓	2	1	0	0
Hassler	1⅔	1	0	0	2
Drago	⅓	0	0	0	0

7

1980: Houston Astros vs. Los Angeles Dodgers

Heading into the 1980 season, the Houston Astros were a team on the move. In 1979, they'd won 89 games and finished second in the National League's Western Division, the finest showing in the team's 19-year history. It was a big step forward for a team that just five years earlier had lost 97 games with players so anonymous that the club's marketing department found it easier to sell tickets by promoting the team's ballpark — the cavernous Astrodome — rather than its players.

The sudden success of the Astros can be traced to the arrival of general manager Tal Smith in 1975 and manager Bill Virdon a year later. After watching their predecessors tinker with the Astrodome fences and air conditioning in a futile attempt to generate more offense for the team, Smith and Virdon took a different approach. Because both men believed that pitching and speed, not power, were the keys to bringing winning baseball to Texas, they resolved to build a team that could exploit the Astrodome's unique qualities.

Almost immediately, the strategy paid dividends. In 1977, the Astros finished at .500 for the first time in their history. By 1979, they were the best-kept secret in the National League. When they took over first place and opened up a 10-game lead over the Cincinnati Reds in June, the baseball world took notice. "We knew we had a good team coming out of spring training," Enos Cabell said. "It was just that nobody else did." Ultimately, the better known and more highly favored Reds would catch the Astros in September, but the word was out: the 'Stros were for real.

After its near-miss in 1979, the team, sensing that its moment was at hand, went for broke. In the off-season, the Astros ponied up $4 million to add Nolan Ryan to the already formidable pitching staff of James Rodney Richards, Joe Niekro, Joaquin Andujar, and Joe Sambito. Then, with an eye toward balancing the team's youth and inexperience with veteran leadership, they signed former Cincinnati Red Joe Morgan to play second base. After years of being laughed at for their funny uniforms and their ballpark, the Astros headed into the 1980 season favored by many to win the National League West.

Farther west, in Los Angeles, it had been a different story. Winning was a tradition. Between 1961, the year of the Astros' inception, and 1966, the Dodgers appeared in three World Series and were crowned world champions twice. After lying fallow in the late '60s, the organization regained its footing, and by the early 1970s, the Dodger farm system represented an embarrassment of riches. In one mass orgasm of talent, the Dodgers produced a crop of young players who would enter the major leagues simultaneously, and play together for eight years.

When Tom Lasorda was named manager at the end of the 1976 season, the chemistry seemed complete. The team, an awesome mixture of pitching, speed, and power, won National League pennants in 1977 and 1978. But after failing against the Yankees in the World Series both years, then finishing a disappointing third in 1979, many observers felt that the team lacked the maturity to ever become one of baseball's great teams. To a man, the 1980 Los Angeles Dodgers felt they had something to prove.

The Race

In the spring of 1980, baseball's preseason pundits and prognosticators were divided into three camps: those who thought the Reds would win the National League West, those who thought the Astros would win the division, and those who picked the Dodgers. As late as mid-August, all three had a shot at being right.

April belonged to Cincinnati. The Reds opened the season red hot, winning their first six games. Houston, powered by excellent pitching, also started fast. Los Angeles, perhaps overly eager to dispel memories of its disastrous 1979 season, stumbled out of the gate and, after two weeks, found itself in fourth place. But, by the middle of the month, the players began to mesh, and a 10-game winning streak brought them within range of the Reds and the Astros by month's end.

In May, all three teams took turns atop the division. Then in June, the Astros went on a tear and won 14 of 16. To fans in Texas, it was clear that the team's near-miss of 1979 was no fluke; after two decades of disregard, they felt sure that the baseball world was now ready to take the Astros seriously. Not everyone was convinced, however. How, some observers asked, could a team with players named Terry Puhl, Alan Ashby, Enos Cabell, and Craig Reynolds be beating up on the Dodgers and the Reds? Astros hitting coach Deacon Jones summed up the confusion: "We come into town and nobody knows who we are. Now writers are swarming all over us saying, 'Who's this? Who's that? Who are these guys'?"

"We didn't have a lot of superstars on that team," concedes Astros pitcher Frank LaCorte. "We just all played together. When you'd go into a bar after a game, you'd see the whole team there. If a guy had trouble, we'd take him up to a room and say, 'Hey, let's talk about it.' Everybody really pulled together on that team."

"It's true, we didn't feel like we had superstars," agrees ace reliever Joe Sambito. "But we were a close team, because we had a nucleus of guys who'd played together for five or six years. And remember, we also had four or five guys on that team who had career years in 1980."

The big gun on the Astro pitching staff was James Rodney Richards. Known to everyone as just J.R., the big right-hander had been the National League's strikeout leader in 1978 and 1979. Watching Richards reduce baseball's most powerful hitters into jelly-legged Milquetoasts with his array of dazzling stuff was one of the game's great spectacles. Such total domination over hitters wouldn't be equaled until Randy Johnson hit his stride with the Seattle Mariners more than a decade later.

But in June, something happened that mystified the Astros. Richards, in the midst of shutting out the Cubs at Wrigley Field on June 17, suddenly removed himself from the game, complaining of a dead arm. The Astros' team doctor examined him and, after finding nothing wrong, prescribed rest, but Richards continued to complain of weakness and fatigue.

Then, in late July, an event took place that jolted the Astros and the baseball world. In the midst of a light workout at the Astrodome on July 30, Richards collapsed on the field. He was rushed to a nearby hospital, where emergency room personnel realized that the 30-year-old pitcher had suffered a stroke. Aside from the personal tragedy, it was a devastating blow to Houston. At the time Richards collapsed, the Astros were in first place, enjoying a 2½ game lead over Los Angeles. Two weeks later, they had dropped to third place and were poised for a collapse of their own.

"When it happened, it was almost like disbelief," Astros relief ace Joe Sambito says of Richards' stroke. "Things like that aren't supposed to happen to professional athletes. We were stunned by it ... that it could happen to someone in his early 30s."

The tragedy had jolted the entire Astros team; each day, they carried their shock and sorrow onto the field like an unwanted 10th teammate. Dazed and reeling, the team appeared ready to drop from the race entirely. The turning point came in mid-August. "We were in San Diego, and shit, we'd lost eight or nine in a row," remembers Frank LaCorte. "We were falling pretty hard and Joe Morgan called a meeting. Basically what he told us was 'Hey, this team can win, we're good enough with the guys we have here.'"

Morgan's message of self-reliance did the trick; after finally confronting the loss of Richards head-on, the Astros regained their footing. In a show of character that must have sent shock waves through clubhouses in Los Angeles and Cincinnati, the team kicked off a 10-game winning streak and regained first place.

Just as the Astros threatened to run away with the division, Los Angeles confronted a catalytic event of its own. On a hot, humid night in late August, the Dodgers were facing the Phillies at Veterans Stadium in Philadelphia. In the ninth inning, Philly reliever Tug McGraw, after missing in his first three attempts, beaned Dodger shortstop Bill Russell with a fastball. Now, Russell, in baseball parlance, was the type of player who wouldn't say shit if he had a mouthful. But something snapped this night, and the normally mild-mannered shortstop broke for the mound, tackled McGraw, and started swinging. The incident triggered a melee that took umpires 20 minutes to control. Later, a Dodger player recalled the importance of that night to a reporter: "It's funny how something like that can really wake a team up. Normally, Russell was the most easy-going guy on the club. But, when we saw him go after McGraw, well, it fired the rest of us up. After that incident, we hit our stride."

Following the incident, the Dodgers got hot. In late August and early September, they won 17 of 20 and despite losing power-hitting Reggie Smith to the disabled list, opened up a two-game lead over the Astros. When they arrived in Houston for a two-game showdown on September 9, the Dodgers were talking openly of knocking the Astros from the race.

But on Tuesday, September 9, Houston capitalized on six Dodger errors and won easily. Suddenly, Houston was just one game back of Los Angeles. Wednesday's game was as thrilling and beautifully executed as Tuesday's had been sloppy. The Dodgers tagged Nolan Ryan early and led 3–0 until the Astros tied the game in the seventh. In the 10th inning, right fielder Rick Monday threw out Joe Morgan, carrying the winning run, at the plate.

The game remained deadlocked until the 12th inning, when Dodger pinch-hitter Gary Thomasson rammed a ball through a drawn-in Astro infield to drive in two runs and make it 5–3. In the Astros' half of the inning, Houston loaded the bases against an ineffectual Dodger bullpen, then scored the tying run on an infield hit. Next, Enos Cabell lined out to Dusty Baker in left field, who whirled and threw out Julio Gonzales at the plate. But when Jose Cruz crushed a Rick Sutcliffe offering over the right-field wall for a homer, it was over. Instead of being knocked from the race, the Astros had delivered a clear and unmistakable message to the haughty Dodgers: "We're for real."

For the next three days, neither team blinked. In mid-September, the Dodgers, demonstrating some character of their own, pulled into River-front Stadium and swept three games from Cincinnati. Now 5½ games off the pace, the once-proud Reds were fading fast.

While the Dodgers were driving a stake through the Reds' title hopes, the Astros were sweeping the Giants in the Astrodome. From September 11 to 16, the Astros and the Dodgers matched wins and losses and remained in a flat-footed tie for first place.

On September 15, the Astros began a three-game losing streak, and on September 17, the Dodgers moved one game up by beating the Padres at Dodger Stadium. The lead proved to be short-lived; between September 19 and September 29, the Dodgers, decimated by injuries to Ron Cey, Rick Monday, and Davey Lopes, dropped seven of ten. When the smoke cleared, LA found itself two games behind the Astros with just six games left in the season. To the fans in Los Angeles, it was clear that the Dodgers' title hopes were fading. "I don't care how good you are," says Dodgers third baseman Ron Cey. "If you lose your key guys like we did in 1980, you're gonna be hurting. And that's what happened to us that final week."

Injuries weren't solely responsible for the Dodgers' swoon; the club's inconsistent bullpen contributed mightily to the team's slide. Don Stan-house, the high-priced free agent obtained in the off-season, was ineffectual when he wasn't on the disabled list. Rookie of the Year for 1979, Rick Sut-cliffe, was erratic and undependable throughout the 1980 season. By late September, the Dodgers' only reliable stopper was a teenaged beer drinker from Mexico named Fernando Valenzuela. To make matters worse, the Dodgers would start the final week of the season against a team that would like nothing more than to knock them from the race once and for all: their hated rivals, the Giants.

Unlike the troubled Dodgers, the Astros were basking in good for-tune. For the previous week, the pitching had been outstanding; Vern Ruhle, the amazing rookie who'd replaced Richards in the starting rota-tion, and Joe Niekro had posted consecutive shutouts. And Joe Morgan, who'd slumped most of the year, was suddenly swinging a hot bat. "I came here to help Houston win the championship and to find the Joe Morgan that had been lost the last couple of years," he said. "I have corrected my swing, and I know I will be a good hitter the rest of the way." The high-flying Astros also had a leg up when it came to the remainder of the schedule. Unlike the Dodgers, who would have life and death on their hands in San Francisco, the Astros would face Atlanta, a team they had dominated all year long at the Astrodome.

At Candlestick Park, nothing came easy for the Dodgers. On Tuesday, September 30, they put on a gritty display, scoring two runs in the ninth inning and then three more in the 10th to win. Meanwhile, in Houston, Nolan Ryan and Dave Smith combined to throttle the Braves, 7–3. With just five games remaining, the Astros' lead over Los Angeles remained at two games.

Wednesday was an unseasonably warm night in San Francisco, and shirt-sleeved Giants fans were amazed to see just two Dodger regulars in the starting lineup. Injuries to his club had forced Tommy Lasorda to field a team of second-stringers and rookies in the most critical game of the year. Yet, somehow, they managed to beat the Giants, 8–4. In Houston, the Astros continued their domination over the Braves with yet another win.

Before Thursday night's game, Giants manager Dave Bristol told the press, "I'd give ten years off my life to beat the Dodgers." In a must-win game, the Dodgers carried a 2–1 lead over the Giants into the eighth inning. But the Dodger bullpen flamed out again, yielding two hits and a walk to load the bases. Giants first baseman Darrell Evans hit a soft flare over second base, which scored two runs. It was a brutal loss for LA. It was bad enough to lose so critical a game, but it was particularly galling for the Dodgers to lose to a fifth-place team whose fans celebrated the Giants' victory as if they'd actually won something themselves. To add insult to injury, the Astros continued to roll, beating the Braves 3–2 on a Joe Niekro six-hitter.

With the Astros heading into Dodger Stadium for the season's final three games, the standings told the story. The Dodgers were three games out of first place with three to play. Just to tie for the division title, they'd have to win three straight from a Houston team they'd been unable to sweep all year. Perhaps it was time to face facts. The team, broken by injuries, had done well just to stay in the race. In a statement that didn't exactly resound with confidence, outfielder Dusty Baker caught the mood of the team: "I think we can do it. I really do. But I'm sure the Astros think they can too."

In Houston, where the Astros were packing for their trip to Dodger Stadium, Joe Morgan was brimming with confidence. To a half circle of reporters gathered around his locker, he said, "This team could not have won the championship in April, but we can do it now. May the best team win, and I think we will."

Manager Bill Virdon was a bit more circumspect. "I am confident we can win one of three games," he said, "But it will be tough." As he sat in the clubhouse beneath the stands of the Astrodome that day, Virdon had no idea how prophetic those words would prove to be.

If the Dodgers' cause was hopeless, somebody forgot to tell their fans. Generally reviled in other National League cities for their unfortunate habit of arriving late and leaving early, the noisy throng that packed Dodger Stadium on Friday, October 3, would hang on every pitch and cheer wildly at every Dodger hit. They seemed intent on forever dispelling the image of Dodger fans as apathetic and undemonstrative.

On Friday at 7:30 PM, the Dodgers took the field for game one of their three-game series against the Astros. Veteran curve-baller Don Sutton left the Dodger dugout and headed for the mound to confront the Astros. Sutton, who was in the final year of his Dodger contract, had watched negotiations for a new deal between his agent and the team break down, and the right-hander felt certain that he was pitching his final game as a Dodger. "He never really talked about the contract thing with us," a Dodger teammate said later, "but we all pretty much figured he'd be pitching somewhere else the following year."

In the first inning Sutton was shaky; the Astros loaded the bases with two outs, and a nervous hush fell over Dodger Stadium. But after Sutton induced Art Howe to fly out to center, the threat was ended. In the bottom of the first, the Dodgers went down without incident against Astro starter Ken Forsch. In the second, the Astros got to Sutton for a run, and the pattern for the evening was set: the Astros scratching and threatening virtually every inning, only to have Sutton and the Dodgers beat them back.

In the fourth, the Astros threatened again. With a runner on first, catcher Alan Ashby lined a single off of Sutton's foot, placing runners at first and second with no one out. But Sutton foiled Forsch's sacrifice attempt, then struck out Morgan and Cabell to end the rally. In the bottom of the fourth, back-to-back doubles by Rick Monday and Steve Garvey got the Dodgers on the board. It was now Astros 1, Dodgers 1.

For the next three innings the Astros continued to pressure Sutton, while Forsch, looking strong, cruised. Finally, in the eighth, the Astros broke through again when Ashby's fly ball scored Cesar Cedeno. Forsch retired the Dodgers in order in the bottom of the inning. After eight innings, the score was Astros 2, Dodgers 1. Houston was just three outs away from its first division title.

With their backs against the wall, the Dodgers tried to rally in the ninth. First, Rick Monday singled. The chanting Dodger Stadium crowd groaned when the next hitter, Dusty Baker, rolled a routine double-play ball to second baseman Rafael Landestoy. But, like a croquet ball through a wicket, Baker's grounder rolled right through Landestoy's legs into right field. "When I saw that ball go through Landestoy's legs, I knew we were in trouble," remembers Frank LaCorte. "When the Dodgers get somebody on base and that damn organ starts going in Dodger Stadium, you know shit's about ready to happen."

If Forsch were to pitch the Astros to a title, he'd have to do it against the heart of the LA lineup. With the Dodger Stadium crowd at fever pitch, Forsch bore down against Steve Garvey and got the first baseman to line out to center field. Now, with the Astros just one out from a playoff berth, Ron Cey was coming to the plate for Los Angeles. Cey, who'd delivered in clutch situations for the Dodgers on so many occasions, was playing with an injured right hamstring and hadn't mustered a good swing against Forsch all night.

As Cey made his way from the on-deck circle to the batter's box, Forsch could discern the outline of the heavy, protective wrap around the third baseman's leg. Forsch and catcher Alan Ashby knew that the bandage on Cey's leg impaired his swing, and thus far, they had contained Cey's effectiveness at the plate by feeding him a steady diet of breaking stuff.

Now, with the season on the line, Cey stepped into the box. Forsch, pitching carefully, delivered a strike and then missed with two balls. Forsch stepped off the mound to collect his thoughts, then toed the rubber, and looked at Ashby for the sign. In the batter's box, Cey squinted heavily in a last minute-attempt to clear the stinging Los Angeles smog from his eyes. Forsch kicked and delivered. "A slider, looks like a low strike," Cey remembers thinking to himself.

Just as it reached the plate, it broke sharply toward the dirt. Cey went down and got just enough of the ball to roll it past the mound, beyond the converging gloves of Landestoy and Reynolds and into center field for a base hit. Rudy Law, who was running for Monday, raced around from second to tie the game.

"That was a big moment," remembers Cey. "Forsch made a good pitch, and I was lucky to get wood on the ball. Without that hit, our season was over." Forsch ended the inning without further scoring, but it was a stunned Astros team that prepared to hit in the 10th against Fernando Valenzuela, the new Dodgers pitcher.

In the 10th, Valenzuela retired the Astros quietly, and Ken Forsch, determined to finish this one by himself, took the mound with the score still tied at 2–2. The first Dodger hitter was Joe Ferguson. It had been a tough year for the veteran Dodger catcher. Plagued with injuries at the start of the season, he found himself playing second fiddle to starting catcher Steve Yeager when he returned from the disabled list. Then, in midsummer, the Dodgers brought rookie Mike Scoscia up from the minors and anointed him as the catcher of the future. Suddenly, Ferguson was third in a crowd of three.

In July, Ferguson's season hit rock bottom. On July 13 in Chicago, Ferguson was inserted into right field as a defensive replacement by Lasorda. Late in the game, he lost a ball in the sun and cost the Dodgers the game. Ferguson, frustrated at his lack of playing time and angry at being used out of position, exploded at Lasorda in full view of reporters and fans. "I'm tired of this shit," he screamed. "You've been on my ass all year." He and Lasorda smoothed over their differences, but Ferguson continued to ride the pine. Then, with just a week left in the season, Lasorda suddenly inserted Ferguson into the lineup. Amazingly, Joe found his stroke and started to produce.

Now, with the season on the line, Ferguson stepped into the box against Forsch. Behind the plate, Alan Ashby signaled "curve ball." Forsch nodded and delivered to Ferguson. It was a "hanger," belt high, right over the plate. Ferguson couldn't believe his good fortune. In a split second, the ball exploded off his bat, headed for left center field.

On the mound, Forsch spun around to watch the ball's flight. Out of the corner of his eye, he saw center fielder Cesar Cedeno, in full gallop, racing madly toward the 385-foot sign that adorned the left center field wall. Cedeno and the ball arrived almost simultaneously. In a desperate attempt to save the game, Cedeno leaped skyward, only to see the ball arc just beyond his glove and into the bleachers for the game-winning home run. "I'll never forget that homer," Ferguson later said:

> It was the biggest hit of my career. Forsch had pitched such a great game, but he got a pitch up, and I hit it out. I remember rounding third base after hitting the homer, with my teammates lined up to meet me, and the fans going absolutely berserk.

Marveling at the wonder and delight that resides one step back from the abyss, the city of Los Angeles exploded. People in bars and restaurants leapt screaming from their chairs; on the freeways, horns blared. At Dodger Stadium, pandemonium reigned. Ferguson rounded third base, tore off his batting helmet, and threw it into the air to mingle with the confetti cascading from the stands. Dodger players lined up along the third-base line, waiting to greet the beaming Ferguson. Lasorda, playing Berra to Ferguson's Larsen, leaped into the catcher's arms just as he touched home plate and found himself being carried to the dugout by the man he'd nearly come to blows with just weeks before.

For the Astros, it was a bitter loss. "Forsch pitched a hell of a game," says Joe Sambito. "We should've won that game." But there was no panic. They still led the Dodgers by two games with two to play. Let the Dodgers celebrate tonight; tomorrow the pressure would be on them again. A half hour following the game, Joe Morgan was walking around the Astro clubhouse in a towel, chatting confidently with reporters and announcing to his teammates, "I'll bet anybody we'll be drinking champagne tomorrow. Anybody!"

On Saturday, October 4, Indian summer had descended on Los Angeles, bringing heat and eye-stinging smog, which nearly obscured the hills just beyond Dodger Stadium. Inside the Astro clubhouse, the players were relaxed and confident. Joe Morgan, Nolan Ryan, Joe Niekro, and others were gathered around a television, watching New York and Detroit fight it out for the American League's Eastern Division title. Today's Houston–Los Angeles game was being broadcast nationally as well, and the Astros, neglected for so long by the media, were eager for the exposure. "This is a team that's never gotten recognition," Morgan told reporters before the game. "Today, 50 million people will see what kind of a team we have."

In the Los Angeles clubhouse, the Dodgers were also watching the Yankees-Tigers game, while in Tommy Lasorda's office, the TV was tuned to the UCLA-Ohio college football game. Amidst this backdrop, Dodger trainers attended to the wounded. Davey Lopes, having played for more than a week with a pinched nerve, sat in front of his locker, holding a heating pad to his neck. Ron Cey was on the trainer's table, again having his damaged hamstring tightly wrapped. Bob Welch, today's scheduled starting pitcher, unexpectedly had pulled a groin muscle, and Jerry Reuss, pitching on three days' rest, would start instead.

Outside, excited fans made their way into the park. For Los Angeles, a city always at the vanguard of vogue, the Dodgers were now *au courant*. The events of the night before had filled late-night newscasts and morning papers with images of back-to-the-wall heroics, which had fired the city's imagination. All over LA, there was a palpable sense that something was afoot, that Cey's and Ferguson's clutch hits the night before weren't the final gasps of a dying team but harbingers of grand deeds to come. Through it all, Los Angeles would be watching.

On Saturday, Nolan Ryan would start for the Astros. Ryan, the Astros'

$4 million man, had won 11 and lost nine during the season. While dis-
cordant voices around the league were reporting that Ryan had lost a foot
or two off his fastball over the past two years, he still threw as hard as anyone in baseball. To counter Ryan, Tommy Lasorda announced that lefty
Jerry Reuss would start for the Dodgers. After some big years with the
Pirates in the mid-'70s, Reuss had fallen on hard times by the end of the
decade. Finally the Bucs gave up on Reuss and in 1978 traded him to the
Dodgers. With LA in 1979, Reuss was ineffectual as a starter and was ultimately relegated to the bullpen. Determined to salvage his career, Reuss
undertook an off-season weight training regimen and reported to spring
training in 1980 stronger and in better shape than at any point in his career.
During the spring, Reuss also struck up a fortuitous friendship with a rov-
ing Dodger pitching coach named Sandy Koufax, who convinced him that
a steady diet of well-placed fastballs, not breaking pitches, was the key to
winning ballgames. Once the season was underway, Reuss started winning, and the Dodgers returned him to the starting rotation. By late September, he had chalked up 17 wins, including a no-hitter in July against
the Giants.

But in the first inning on Saturday, Reuss was wobbly. Showing signs
of big-game jitters, he walked Morgan. The next hitter, Cabell, singled.
Morgan, running on a leg that he'd slightly injured the night before, made
it only to second base. Lasorda, wasting no time, immediately rang the
bullpen and told them to get Rick Sutcliffe warmed up. But Reuss settled
down, retired Jose Cruz, and then induced Cedeno to ground into a double play. In the bottom of the first, Ryan was sharp, retiring the Dodgers
in order.

In the bottom of the second, the Dodgers drew first blood. After singles by Steve Garvey and Pedro Guerrero, Derrell Thomas singled and
drove Garvey home to make the score Dodgers 1, Astros 0. In the fourth,
the Astros answered back when Jose Cruz singled and then stole second.
When Cedeno grounded out, Cruz moved to third, and then he scored on
a fly ball by Art Howe, which Dodger center fielder Pedro Guerrero lost
in the haze and smog. The game was tied.

In the fourth inning, Steve Garvey hammered a Ryan fastball deep
into the left-field bullpen for a home run, giving the Dodgers a 2–1 lead.
Ryan retired the next three hitters, but the Astros bench, so loose and
confident during the first three innings, had turned somber. To a man, the
Astros knew that Reuss had commanding stuff this day and that further
scoring against him would be tough.

In the top of the fifth, the Astros tried to rally. After Alan Ashby led
off the inning with a solid single to right field, Ryan laid down a picture-

perfect bunt to advance him into scoring position. Now, with Joe Morgan coming to the plate, the Astros had their best shot of the day against Reuss. Standing at second base, Ashby knew that a base hit would tie the game. Suddenly, Morgan hit a Reuss fastball right on the screws that appeared to be headed to right field. Ashby, thinking that Morgan had a sure double, bolted for third.

What Ashby didn't see, however, was Dodger second baseman Davey Lopes catapult himself high in the air, pinched nerve and all, to somehow snag Morgan's line drive; he descended back to earth and fired to second to double up and choke off the Astro rally. The Astros couldn't believe their luck; Morgan had scorched that ball. An inch higher, and the game would be tied. Instead, the rally was quashed, and the Dodgers returned to their dugout still leading 2–1.

With two out in the ninth, the Astros tried to mount a last-ditch rally. Cedeno blooped a Reuss fastball to center for a base hit, then advanced to third on Howe's single. But Reuss, pacing like a caged animal on the mound, would not be denied. His next pitch was a nasty knee-high fastball, which Gary Woods grounded to second base for the final out. As the crowd erupted, the Dodgers gathered at the mound to congratulate one another.

In the Dodger clubhouse following the game, first baseman Steve Garvey took a shot at "psyching" the Astros: "I've been in their position before, and I'd be concerned if I were them. They've got a one-game lead, but we've got the momentum."

Professional athletes often talk about "momentum," what it is, who has it, who doesn't. Webster's defines momentum as "a property that determines the length of time required to bring a moving body to rest." In this case, the "moving body" was the Dodgers; they were now one game back of the first-place Astros and closing fast. Houston had one more day to bring them "to rest," or the team would confront the indignity of facing the Dodgers in a sudden-death playoff on Monday.

When Tommy Lasorda announced that Burt Hooten would be his starting pitcher for game three against the Astros, he was merely observing formality; Hooten was nursing a sore arm and probably couldn't pitch for more than an inning or two. For Lasorda, Sunday's game would be a staff effort, requiring participation from every available Dodger pitcher.

The Astros would pin their hopes on Vern Ruhle, the rookie phenom who had substituted so ably for J.R. Richards. But in an ominous sign for Houston, Ruhle had cut the index finger on his pitching hand on a tack in the Astro clubhouse the day before. The team doctor had closed the gash but couldn't guarantee that the stitches would hold up under the strain of pitching. "I don't think it will be a factor," Ruhle told reporters before the game, but Virdon wasn't so sure, and he resolved to watch the left-hander closely.

Sunday, October 5, was another hot, brutally smoggy day in Los Angeles. The fans entering Dodger Stadium today would pick up where yesterday's frenzied mob had left off: screaming at anything and everything and doing their utmost to root the Dodgers to another victory.

Sunday's game would prove to be the most exciting contest of the series. In the second inning, the Astros struck first when they parlayed a bunt, a sacrifice, and three singles into two runs. Lasorda, wielding a quick hook, yanked Hooten and brought in screwballer Bobby Castillo to pitch. After getting Ruhle for the first out, Castillo walked Puhl to load the bases. But Castillo struck out Cabell and got Morgan to pop out. After two innings, it was Astros, 2, Dodgers 0.

Ruhle looked sharp in the early going, but fate would intervene. In the third inning, Ruhle felt a sharp pain in his finger. He signaled for time, then called Alan Ashby and manager Bill Virdon out to the mound. When they arrived, they saw that the stitches in the lefthander's index finger had pulled loose and were now spiraling crazily outward. Virdon, wondering if his team would ever catch a break, signaled to the bullpen for Joaquin Andujar.

Andujar had great stuff, but he was fiery and temperamental. When unruffled, his combination of fastballs and breaking stuff was almost unhittable. But if the opposing team pressured him, he often lost his composure. It was a common sight to see Virdon or Joe Morgan screaming at Andujar on the mound in vain efforts to calm him down. But after warming up, Andujar retired the Dodgers without incident in the third. In the fourth inning, the Astros struck again, scoring their third run on base hits by Ashby and Terry Puhl. The lead was now 3–0.

Andujar cruised along until the bottom of the fifth inning. Then, with one out, he surrendered consecutive singles to Derrell Thomas, pinch-hitter Gary Thomasson, and Davey Lopes. It was now 3–1. True to form, Andujar blew his top and began stomping around the mound and swearing at himself in frustration until Virdon and Ashby came out in an effort to cool him off. When that proved futile, Virdon brought in relief ace Joe Sambito to face the Dodgers. Sambito, pitching carefully, got Mickey Hatcher to ground into a 6–4–3 double play to end the inning. In the sixth inning, Fernando Valenzuela, now pitching for the Dodgers, retired the Astros without incident.

In the seventh, the Dodgers rallied. Guerrero and Ferguson opened the inning with singles and advanced into scoring position when Thomas sacrificed. Coming to the plate was Manny Mota. Mota, baseball's all-time pinch-hit leader, was the team's first-base coach and occasional pinch-hitter. Listed in the Dodgers' media guide as being 42 years old, few believed him that young. Christened at birth as Manuel Rafael Geronimo Mota, he'd come to the big leagues years earlier as a strong-armed infielder and outfielder. But his stock-in-trade had always been the pinch hit, the ability to somehow sit idly for two-plus hours, rise from the bench, and deliver a hit in a key situation.

Joe Sambito remembers the scene:

> I was pitching in the seventh inning of that game with runners at second and third, and Mota was coaching first base. And Lasorda calls time out and calls Mota in from the coaching lines to grab a bat and come up and hit against me. He digs in at the plate, promptly proceeds to get a base hit, then he returns to the coaching box. It was something.

Mota had timed Sambito's fastball perfectly and drove it into right field for a solid base hit, which scored Guerrero with the Dodgers' second run. After a runner entered the game in his place, Mota returned to the first-base coaching box to the cheers of 50,000 fans. The Astro lead was now just one run. "Bill Virdon came out to take me out of the game after that at-bat," Sambito remembers, "and as I left the game, I ran past the first-base coaching box and I yelled over to Manny, 'Why don't you just retire?' Many people ask me who my toughest out was, and I tell them Manny Mota."

Frank LaCorte replaced Sambito on the mound. LaCorte was sharp and shut down the Dodgers to end the inning. In the top of the eighth inning, Dodger left-hander Steve Howe retired the Astros without incident.

With time running out, the Dodgers came up to face LaCorte in the eighth. The first hitter was Steve Garvey, who rolled a routine grounder to third base, which Cabell booted. Suddenly, Dodger Stadium was alive. With Ron Cey coming to the plate, the Dodgers had perhaps their last opportunity to catch the Astros.

Since his big hit on Friday night, Cey had struggled with the bat. The tight bandage around his leg continued to hamper his swing, and he'd grown increasingly frustrated. Finally, in the fourth inning, Cey had had enough; between innings, he ducked into the Dodger clubhouse and ripped the bandage from his bruised hamstring. "I figured it was time to go for broke," he recalls. "It was binding me too much. If we didn't win Sunday's game, I figured it would have all winter to heal."

Now, with his right leg liberated and the season on the line, Ron Cey walked to the plate to hit against LaCorte in the eighth inning. Just before he dug in at the plate, the third baseman shot a glance at third-base coach Danny Ozark. Cey couldn't believe his eyes. Ozark was signaling "bunt." To Cey, conservative baseball in this situation made no sense. "It was our time to win the ballgame," Cey remembers. "I don't remember who was following me that day in the lineup, but I didn't want to take it down to that. I felt that we should take a shot at it."

Struggling to mask his annoyance, Cey stepped in. LaCorte went right after the third baseman with fastballs and got two quick strikes. "LaCorte made a couple of good pitches," Cey recalls. "The second strike, he came up and in on me and backed me off the plate. As I was trying to get out of the way, I fouled off the ball. Now the bunt was off."

As the Dodger's fifth-place hitter, Cey had parlayed an almost zen-like patience at the plate and a short, powerful swing into a successful career as a power hitter. "Patient aggressiveness" is what he'd dubbed his hitting style. But now, with two strikes on him and the season hanging in the balance, Cey had to temper his aggressiveness and think about just putting the ball in play.

LaCorte's next pitch was a slider out of the strike zone, which Cey took for ball two. Cey then fouled the next pitch out of play. LaCorte missed again, and the count went to three and two. Then, swinging hard, Cey ricocheted LaCorte's next pitch off his left foot. In excruciating pain, Cey hobbled out of the batter's box to assess the damage. He was quickly joined by Lasorda and Dodger trainer Bill Buhler, who were trying to determine if the third baseman could continue. From the stands, a rhythmic chant of "Cey, Cey, Cey" began to ripple through the crowd. "How's it feel?" Lasorda asked Cey. "Hurts like shit" was the third baseman's reply. After giving himself a minute to test the foot, Cey realized he could continue and stepped back into the batter's box.

When play resumed, the standoff between LaCorte and Cey continued. The hurler delivered another pitch that Cey fouled off. On the mound, LaCorte tugged at his hat as he looked at Ashby for his sign. LaCorte nodded, kicked, and delivered. In an instant, both men knew that he'd made a terrible mistake: the pitch was a belt-high fastball right over the plate. Cey, planting his sore foot and pivoting on his damaged hamstring, timed the ball perfectly. An instant later, the ball crashed into the 15th row of the left-field bleachers for a two-run homer.

As he watched Cey circle the bases, LaCorte was crushed. "I was having a good year, and I just figured I'd go right after the guy in that situation," he remembers. "I threw a fastball, and with Cey's short, quick swing, the next thing I knew, it went out of the goddam park." In an amazing turnaround, the score was now Dodgers 4, Astros 3. LaCorte was able to retire the Dodgers without further scoring, but it was a demoralized Astros team that left the field to prepare for the ninth inning.

In the ninth, Houston tried desperately to rally. After Jay Johnstone made a spectacular catch of Jeff Leonard's foul ball for the first out, Gary Woods took a Steve Howe fastball to right field for a single. Terry Puhl then grounded to Lopes at second base, who forced Woods in a close play. But the next hitter, Enos Cabell, lined a base hit to center, and Puhl advanced to third. With the tying run now just 90 feet from home plate, pulses quickened in the Astro dugout.

Realizing that Howe was out of gas, Lasorda emerged from the LA dugout and made his way to the mound. On the field, Davey Lopes thought Lasorda had lost his mind. From his vantage point at second base, the only person visible to Lopes in the Dodger bullpen was Don Stanhouse. Stanhouse, signed as a free agent early in the year to bring stability to the Dodger bullpen, had done anything but. With his penchant for walking hitters in bunches, he'd spent the year making bad situations worse. Surely, Lopes thought, Lasorda wasn't so desperate as to summon Stanhouse to the mound with the season on the line.

But minutes earlier, something had transpired in the Dodger dugout of which Lopes was unaware. Reggie Smith, the injured Dodger right fielder, who was on the bench in his street clothes, had sensed that the Dodgers' troubled bullpen might falter again in the ninth inning. Between innings, Smith walked by Lasorda and whispered, "The old-timer can give you an inning." Lasorda, turning to look at Smith, saw Reggie pointing a finger toward Don Sutton. Lasorda's eyes lit up at the suggestion, and he signaled Sutton to start warming up.

Dodger fans, who'd grown weary of watching the team's relief corps devise new ways to blow games, booed when they saw Lasorda motion to the bullpen. But when the bullpen gate swung open, and Sutton, not Stanhouse, emerged, a mighty roar of relief went up. With the shadows of fall now creeping slowly across home plate, Sutton met with Ferguson to go over the signs, then took his warmup tosses. Now, he was ready. Stepping in to face him was pinch-hitter Denny Walling. In an instant, it was over: Walling grounded Sutton's second pitch to Davey Lopes, who threw to Garvey to end the game. For the Astros, the unthinkable had happened. The standings two days earlier had looked like this:

	W–L	Games Behind
Houston	92–70	—
Los Angeles	89–70	3

Ron Cey made a career of coming through in the clutch for the Los Angeles Dodgers. Here, he's about to hammer Frank LaCorte's pitch into the left-field bleachers and propel the Dodgers into a sudden-death playoff against the Houston Astros in 1980. (*The Sporting News.*)

Now the standings looked like this:

	W–L	Games Behind
Houston	92–70	—
Los Angeles	92–70	—

Following the game, the Dodger clubhouse was a scene of joyous chaos. Reporters converged around Don Sutton, who deflected the attention by saying, "I only threw two pitches. Go talk to somebody who really did something."

The funereal silence of the Astros clubhouse stood in dramatic contrast to the celebrating Dodgers. Manager Bill Virdon, whose demeanor didn't vary one iota, win or lose, was stoic. "We just have to play one more game," he told the press. But he and the rest of the Astros were shaken by the weekend's events. To a man, they desperately had wanted to win Sunday's game to give the Astro regulars a day to rest up for the National League championship series, which would start on Tuesday in Philadelphia. Now, with their season and their confidence slipping away, the shell-shocked Astros were on the ropes.

"We were thinking, 'Hey, what the hell is going on here, man?' remembers Frank LaCorte. "We were all aware that something just wasn't quite jibing."

Joe Sambito echoes LaCorte's thoughts:

I really remember dragging ass after losing Sunday. There was a real letdown after that game. The tough part was going back to the hotel instead of on to Philadelphia. Knowing we had to stay another day. Now the whole season comes down to one game on Monday.

MONDAY, OCTOBER 6, 1980

On October 6, the seventh sudden-death playoff in baseball history and the second in just three years would be played at Dodger Stadium in Los Angeles. For the first time, a tie for the National League pennant would be decided by a single game due to a rule change implemented in 1969, when the National and American leagues were split into Eastern and Western divisions.

On Monday morning, the Astros and the Dodgers arrived at Dodger Stadium with luggage in tow; the winner today would leave immediately following the game for an all-night flight to Philadelphia to begin the National League championship series on Tuesday.

Prior to the game, Tommy Lasorda's office was crammed with press and various hangers-on listening to the manager of the Dodgers spin a story about a fisherman whose boat had sunk eight miles off shore. "He was determined that he wasn't going to die. He swam and he swam and he fought and he battled," Lasorda continued, "and he made it for seven miles. But with a mile to go, he was exhausted, he gave up and drowned." Pausing a moment for dramatic effect, Lasorda then delivered the kicker: "The stupid jerk would have been better off to drown at the beginning and not waste all that effort." The message to Lasorda's team was clear: don't drown a mile from the beach.

At the conclusion of the tale, Dodger coach Monty Basgall walked into Lasorda's office and said to the Dodger manager, "Have you seen Ron Cey? He can barely walk." As fate would have it, the ball that Cey had fouled off his foot during his eighth-inning at-bat on Sunday had done more damage than first thought. Cey's ankle was sore and badly swollen. "I was in [Dodger team physician] Dr. Jobe's office Monday morning, getting my ankle drained," remembers Cey. "And they injected it with inflammatory drugs. But it was no go. It was just too sore." In the first indication that the Dodgers' luck had finally turned, the hero of Friday and Sunday's games limped into Lasorda's office and told him he'd be unable to play in the most important game of the year.

In the Astro clubhouse, Joe Morgan was engaging in a little whistling-past-the-graveyard. Talking to a crowd of reporters regarding the Astros' three straight losses, Morgan said, "They may have beat us Friday, Saturday, and Sunday. But no one can beat us four straight games." To some of the gathered newsmen, Morgan's bravado sounded slightly ludicrous in light of what had transpired over the past three days. Still, they understood Morgan's motive. He was trying everything in his power to keep his team buoyed. Behind Morgan, hats with "National League Western Division Champs" emblazoned across them sat sealed in plastic, providing mute testimony to what was promised and what had yet to be delivered.

High above the field in the Dodger Stadium offices, the team's administrative personnel were starting to wind down. Somehow, they'd done it; they'd sold and distributed 51,000 tickets in less than 20 hours for a game that a day earlier had seemed unlikely to be played.

In their dugout before the game, the Astros were amazingly loose. Since Sunday's devastating loss, the Astros had engaged in some soul searching. To a man, they had resolved to come out of the chute on Monday playing confident, aggressive baseball and let the chips fall where they may. Better to return home to Texas as vanquished warriors than as the tentative wannabes they'd resembled the previous three days. "There was no team meeting or anything like that following Sunday's loss," Joe Sambito remembers. "We just left everybody to think of what needed to be done. We just felt, 'What the heck, we're out here, let's play the game, let's have a good time, let's play to win.'"

With knuckle-baller Joe Niekro on the mound, the Astros felt confident of finally being able to shut down the Dodgers' offensive attack. The Dodgers countered with right-hander Dave Goltz. Goltz, secured via free agency in the off-season, had turned out to be a bust as a Dodger starter. Arriving in Los Angeles with a million-dollar contract and high expectations, he'd pitched poorly and was regularly and lustily booed by Dodger fans. But, with his pitching staff depleted, Lasorda had no choice but to cross his fingers and hope that Goltz and his sinker ball could contain the Astros.

In the first inning, things began ominously for the Dodgers. After second baseman Davey Lopes booted lead-off hitter Terry Puhl's grounder for an error, Cabell blooped a single to right, which advanced Puhl to third. After Morgan struck out, Cabell, turning the heat up on Goltz and Dodger catcher Joe Ferguson, stole second. The next hitter was Jose Cruz, who rolled a grounder to Mickey Hatcher at third base. Like a shot, Puhl broke for the plate in an attempt to score. Hatcher fielded the ball and threw a strike to Ferguson, which he dropped, allowing the Astros to score their first run. The Dodgers, so sure-handed through the previous three games, had now committed two errors in one-third of an inning. When Cabell scored, the Astros had staked themselves to a 2–0 first-inning lead.

Niekro, mixing his knuckle ball with the occasional fastball and slider, kept LA off balance and retired the first six Dodgers he faced. In the third inning, the Astros struck again against Goltz. With one out, Cedeno singled, then stole second base. Art Howe then lined a hanging Goltz curve ball over the left center field fence for a two-run home run. The Astros, sensing that their nightmarish detour through Los Angeles might at last lead them to Philadelphia, let out a collective yell in their dugout. The next hitter, Alan Ashby, singled. After Craig Reynolds lined a hit to the gap in right field, Ashby was thrown out at the plate attempting to score. In an event that demonstrated the tension and frustration surrounding the series, both dugouts emptied onto the field after Dodger catcher Joe Ferguson roughed up Ashby on the play. Order was restored, and when the dust cleared, the Astros had a 4–0 lead.

After Hatcher and Thomas opened the bottom of the third with hits, the Dodgers tried to work their magic one more time. But the spell was broken, and Niekro induced Law to fly to left, then got Lopes and Johnstone on nasty knucklers.

In the fourth inning, the Astros put the game out of reach. After Terry Puhl bunted perfectly for a base hit, he stole second and third base before scoring on a fly ball. After Cedeno walked, Art Howe ripped a shot to center for his fourth RBI of the day, and suddenly, the Dodgers trailed 7–0.

In the bottom of the fourth, the Dodgers managed to push across a run, but it would be their last. They threatened briefly in the sixth inning, but the well from which they'd drawn three heroic victories had finally run dry. Niekro, growing stronger in the late innings, retired the Dodgers in order in the seventh, eighth, and ninth innings. The final score was 7–1.

Crafty knuckle-baller Joe Niekro finally halted the Houston skid when he beat the Dodgers in baseball's seventh sudden-death playoff. (National Baseball Hall of Fame Library, Cooperstown, N.Y.)

When it was over, the Astros met at the pitching mound in joyous celebration, then broke for the clubhouse to celebrate before heading to Philadelphia that night. Art Howe, wiping champagne from his eyes, said to the reporters gathered in a half circle around his locker, "I'd be a liar if I said there weren't any doubts." Standing nearby, catcher Alan Ashby told a reporter, "It was frustrating to say the least, scary, maybe. We didn't want it to happen the way it did, but the Dodgers took it away from us for three straight days."

For all their effort, the Astros never really had a chance to savor their first division title. "It wasn't like we got a chance to enjoy the victory over the Dodgers," remembers Joe Sambito. "We went right from the stadium to the airport, got on the plane to Philadelphia and by the time we got to Philly, it was about four or five in the morning. We had to forget it pretty quickly and focus on Philadelphia."

Incredibly, the two teams would meet again under virtually the same circumstances a year later. In a playoff to determine the winner of the National League's Western Division in a strike-shortened year, the Dodgers lost the first two games of a best-of-five series to the Astros in Houston and returned home once again to find themselves on the brink of elimination. This time, freed from the crippling injuries that decimated them in 1980, they completed yet another three-game sweep of the Astros to win the division, then went on to defeat Montreal and New York to become the 1981 world champions of baseball.

OCTOBER 6, 1980

HOUSTON	AB	R	H	BI
Puhl rf	5	2	1	0
Cabell 3b	4	2	2	0
Bergman 1b	0	0	0	0
Morgan 2b	2	1	0	0
Landestoy 3b	2	0	0	0
Cruz lf	4	0	1	1
Cedeno cf	4	1	1	1
Howe 1b	3	1	3	4
Ashby c	4	0	1	0
Reynolds ss	4	0	3	0
Niekro p	2	0	0	0
Totals	34	7	12	6

LOS ANGELES	AB	R	H	BI
Lopes 2b	4	0	0	0
Howe p	0	0	0	0
Johnston rf	4	0	0	0
Baker lf	4	1	1	0
Garvey 1b	4	0	0	0
Monday cf	3	0	1	1
Ferguson c	4	0	1	0
Hatcher 3b	3	0	1	0
Thomasson ph	1	0	0	0
Thomas ss	3	0	2	0
Goltz p	0	0	0	0
Law ph	1	0	0	0
Sutcliffe p	0	0	0	0
Beckwith p	0	0	0	0
Castillo p	0	0	0	0
Davallio ph	1	0	0	0
Valenzuela p	0	0	0	0
Perconte 2b	2	0	0	0
Totals	34	1	6	1

Doubles: Reynolds, Cabell
Home Runs: Howe

Houston	2 0 2	3 0 0	0 0 0	7
Los Angeles	0 0 0	1 0 0	0 0 0	1

Houston	IP	H	R	BB	SO
Niekro (W)	9	6	1	2	6

Los Angeles	IP	H	R	BB	SO
Goltz (L)	3	8	4	0	2
Sutcliffe	⅓	1	3	2	0
Beckwith	⅓	1	0	1	0
Castillo	1⅓	1	0	1	2
Valenzuela	2	1	0	0	1
Howe	2	0	0	0	0

8

1995: California Angels vs. Seattle Mariners

Always be a good worker.
"The Cowboy Code" by Gene Autry

Between 1961, when they entered the major leagues, and 1996, when they were sold to the Walt Disney Company, the California Angels did precious little good work for the man who owned them, Gene Autry. During his lifetime, few men could boast of conquering as many fields of endeavor as Autry did. As a young man in the late 1920s, he managed to parlay a pleasant voice and a folksy manner into a role as "Oklahoma's Yodeling Cowboy" on the radio. In 1934, Autry packed his bags and headed west to Hollywood, where, within three years, he soared to popularity as America's singing cowboy. Always seeking a new horizon, Autry next decided to try his luck at making records. The result was a recording career that spanned more than three decades and accounted for sales of more than 40 million records worldwide.

When television became popular in the early 1950s, Autry decided to give the fledgling medium a shot. Almost immediately, "The Gene Autry Show" on CBS became one of television's highest rated programs. When the public's appetite for crooning cowboys began to slacken in the late 1950s, Autry simply shrugged and shifted his focus to another of his interests, business. Demonstrating as much savvy behind a desk as he had in the saddle, he purchased a string of radio and television stations in California whose profits would ultimately make him a perennial on the Forbes list of the 400 richest Americans.

When it became clear by the late 1950s that major league baseball had its eye on installing a new franchise in the Los Angeles area, who could blame the cowboy with the Midas touch for jumping in with both boots? For a man who'd reached the pinnacle of success in four different fields — heck, even his horse was named Champion — building a winning team must have seemed as easy as outdrawing the stiffs he'd faced in his movies.

But, as time and events would demonstrate, Autry's dream of riding into the sunset of his life with a World Series trophy nestled in his saddlebags would prove to be a nightmare. After a heady second season in which his Los Angeles Angels finished a surprising third, poor personnel decisions and a lack of consistent direction hampered the franchise. It would be seven years before the club would finish as high as third again and 19 years before it would win its first division crown.

Throughout their history, the Angels had languished in the looming shadow of their more successful neighbors to the north, the Los Angeles Dodgers. Lacking anything resembling a coherent plan for building and sustaining organizational excellence, the Angels tried to compete with the Dodgers by utilizing a quick-fix approach that too often resulted in promising minor league talent being made trade bait for veterans on the downside of their careers.

If nothing else, the history of the Angels conclusively demonstrates one truism: you can lead All Stars to the field, but you can't make them play as a team. Consistently confusing success with excellence, the Angels of the 1970s and 1980s expended just enough effort to lure fans to the park before turning up AWOL when the real fighting started. Their litany of inefficacy is truly impressive. In 1982, the Halos kissed off a trip to the World Series by becoming the first team to blow a two-games-to-none lead in a league championship series. In 1984, the club seemed a sure bet for a playoff berth until it quit in September, dropping five straight and handing the division title to Kansas City. A year later, the Angels led their division most of the year but dropped three of four to the Royals in the final week to once again kick away the title. In 1987, the club did manage to win its division but then, when it was just one strike away from its first American League pennant, blew the game and ultimately the pennant to the Red Sox.

By the late 1980s, it was clear that age was beginning to catch up with Gene Autry. For some time, he'd been gradually turning over control of the club's day-to-day operations to his much younger wife, Jackie. Diminished responsibility didn't translate into diminished desire, however. At 82, Autry still followed the fortunes of his Angels closely and continued to dream of a World Series title. For the players who genuinely loved him and watched with dismay as the old man slowly faded, the rallying cry of "let's win one for the Cowboy" gradually morphed into the more desperate refrain of "we've got to win one for the Cowboy before it's too late."

For years, Jackie Autry had watched with dismay as the Angels poured millions into free agency in a futile quest to increase the club's competitiveness. As the Angels' new chief operating officer, she resolved to take the club down the road less traveled, at least by them. To cut costs, Autry tightened the Angel purse strings, drastically reducing the amount of money the club spent on promotion and community involvement. Then, heeding the advice of her general manager, Whitey Herzog, Autry shifted the club's focus from free agency to a more traditional approach of relying on its farm system to provide the talent needed to carry the team into the next century.

But nurturing young players takes time, and while they waited for the farm system to pay dividends, the Angels floundered, finishing more than 20 games out of first place in 1992 and '93. The poor showings dismayed the club's fans, but Jackie Autry, hearing nothing but good news from Whitey Herzog regarding the club's revitalized farm system, remained confident. In January 1994, Herzog, feeling that the Angels were at last on the right track, tendered his resignation to Jackie Autry. Before he left, he strongly recommended that assistant general manager Bill Bavasi be hired to replace him.

Bavasi was the son of Buzzie Bavasi, who had successfully guided the Brooklyn and Los Angeles Dodgers to pennants during the 1950s and 1960s. For young Bill, however, dreams of pennants and world championships would have to wait, at least for awhile. The Angels, plagued by weak pitching, poor relief, and an offense that ranked 12th in the league, struggled throughout 1994. As so often happens when a poor team plays up to its potential, the manager was blamed, and in May, Bavasi fired Bob Rodgers and named veteran pitching coach Marcel Lachemann as manager. Under Lachemann, the club compiled a 30–44 record until the season was prematurely ended by a players strike, which also triggered the cancellation of the World Series.

Despite the club's poor showing, the youth movement initiated by Herzog and Autry was finally beginning to show results. In his first full season, right fielder Tim Salmon hammered 31 home runs, racked up 95 runs batted in, and hit .283 to win the Rookie of the Year Award. Other young players, like Garrett Anderson, Jim Edmonds, and Gary DiSarcina, were also maturing quickly and comprised a nucleus of young stars that was expected to keep the Angels in contention for years to come.

By the start of the 1995 season, the Angels were the only franchise extant in 1961 that had never played in a World Series, a fact that had not gone unnoticed by Jackie Autry. Prior to the season, rumors began swirling around baseball that the Angels might be for sale. While not denying the

With the possible exception of Tom Yawkey and Bill Veeck, no owner was more popular with his players than Gene Autry. Here he is shown with Brian Downing and
Juan Beniquez in 1982. (National Baseball Hall of Fame Library.)

reports, Jackie Autry remained steadfast in her belief that a championship
flag would soon fly over Anaheim Stadium: "My focus is on winning a
world championship during Gene's lifetime. It would be very sad for me
if we won it, and he were not here. That would be a real heartbreaker. I'm
not sure I could handle that one."

Putting money where her mouth was, Autry agreed to Bill Bavasi's
plan for revamping the Angel bullpen. In the off-season, the club ponied
up $2 million to sign free agent Lee Smith to a one-year deal. With young
Troy Percival and his 95-mile-an-hour fastball expected to move into the
setup role, the Angels' bullpen, among the league's worst in 1994, now
looked like a potential world beater.

Throughout the winter of 1994, manager Marcel Lachemann eagerly
anticipated the 1995 season. "Part of our preparation during the spring of
1995 was trying to put a rotation together," Lachemann says today:

> We ended up getting [Mike] Bilecki and [Scott] Sanderson and people like
> that out of that spring camp down there. The bullpen was a consideration
> too. Prior to the season, we were concerned with getting everybody into

roles, Smith and [Troy]) Percival, [Mike] James, things like that. All during the spring, we were trying to solidify our lineup. We had just moved Jimmy Edmonds into the lineup the year before as a regular player. J.T. Snow was brought up and given a chance to play first base. We had a lot more role people in '94. When I got there, they were alternating Harold Reynolds and Rex [Hudler] at second. Kind of platooning them. And a platoon in left with Bo [Jackson] and Dwight Smith. And Jimmy Edmonds was actually a bench player at that time. So we intended to go with more of a set lineup in 1995.

By the time the Angels broke camp, it was clear to even the most casual observer that youth would be served in Anaheim. For opening day, the 1995 Angels would field a lineup in which every position would be manned by a player with fewer than three years of major league experience. In baseball's traditional spring handicapping, the consensus among the experts was that the club's talent was real but green. Two, maybe three years, the pundits said, and they might be ready to contend. Until then, Gene Autry would just have to be patient.

In Seattle, patience with the also-ran Mariners was in short supply. Between its inaugural year of 1977 and 1991, the club never finished higher than fifth place and placed dead last five times. By the late 1980s attendance had dwindled to microscopic levels, and discordant voices around Seattle were suggesting that it was time for the Mariners to seek a more suitable home for their struggling franchise.

As the new decade dawned, two forces convened to signal a new direction for the club. In 1992, a group of Japanese businessmen headed by Nintendo Corporation president Hiroshi Yamauchi purchased the team. Armed with deep pockets and an announced goal of transforming the team into a competitive force, the group kindled hope in the Pacific Northwest that the Mariners might at last shake off their loser image.

Also contributing to a sense of optimism in Seattle was the arrival of highly touted rookie Ken Griffey, Jr. Unusually gifted and possessing natural baseball instincts, Griffey had used athletic grace and power to fashion a shortcut to the major leagues, playing only 17 games above class A before he debuted in the spring of 1989. Labeled a "can't miss" prospect with superstar potential, Griffey, at 19, was also untested at the major league level and deeply ambivalent over the expectations people held for him.

As the greenest rookie in the Mariner spring training camp of 1989, Griffey was immediately set upon by his teammates. "We teased him quite a lot in his rookie year," former Mariner second baseman Harold Reynolds recalled:

I remember the day he made the team. It was April 1, 1989. That was the day of the last cuts. And he was real nervous. I mean, he hit about .500 that spring. He shouldn't have been that nervous. But some of us found out he had made the team before he did. When he came into the clubhouse, we told him he had been sent down. He got all upset. Started crying. Then we told him it was an April Fool's joke. Pretty rough, huh?

Rough, but certainly no worse than many other rookies had experienced. Nonetheless, Griffey, feeling anxious and unsure of himself and his abilities, marched into manager Jim Lefebvre's office shortly afterward and told him, "I don't think I'm ready for the big leagues. I think I'd be better off in Triple A." Lefebvre point-blank told Griffey that the decision had been made by the best baseball minds in the Mariner organization: he was ready.

It wouldn't take long for Griffey to prove that they were right. In his first full season, he hit 16 home runs and drove in 61 runs. A year later, he boosted his average 36 points to .300 while hitting 22 homers and driving in 80 runs. But with expectations sky high for his third season, Griffey faltered. By the All-Star break, he'd managed just nine home runs and 36 RBIs, hardly the kind of numbers expected from the game's next great superstar. His fans needn't have worried, however. In the second half, he found his stroke and wound up the season with 22 homers, 100 RBIs, and a .327 average.

"The second half, it was like Junior arrived," said former manager Jim Lefebvre. "His work habits were better. He came to the park prepared. I think he learned to tune out the kidding. He started giving it back. I think we forgot sometimes how young he was when he first came up."

By 1994, Griffey was thrilling fans in the Pacific Northwest with his exploits. Whether using his blazing speed to chase down a ball in the gap or his sweeping stroke to bludgeon opposing pitching, Griffey had captured Seattle's imagination. Not only was attendance up dramatically, but fans who'd once bailed out early hoping to beat the traffic to Puget Sound now stuck around to catch the kid's final at-bats.

The year 1989 signaled the arrival of another baseball nova in Seattle. Claimed by the Expos in the second round of the 1985 free agent draft, 25-year-old Randy Johnson was by his own admission "a thrower," who had no idea how to set up hitters. Blessed with a blazing fastball and devastating slider, Johnson was also cursed by an inability to control where they went. "I can remember a time when he would throw 12 straight balls, and none of them would be close to the strike zone," former teammate Brian Holman recalled. "Then he would come back and strike out the next three batters with nine pitches. He was that kind of pitcher."

After being traded by the Expos to the Mariners in May 1989, Johnson pitched unevenly his first two years, shutting down opposing teams with low-hit games, then lapsing back into the wildness that had always plagued him. Possessed of a tightly wound nature, which made it difficult for him to remain focused, Johnson struggled for the next four years to sharpen his concentration on the mound. In 1993 he finally broke through, winning 19 games and striking out more than 300 hitters.

Armed with a new confidence, Johnson emerged in 1994 as the most feared pitcher in the major leagues. Left handed hitters had a particularly rough time facing the 6'10" Johnson's whiplash delivery. Phillies first baseman John Kruk was so intimidated that he once told a reporter, "If it was the seventh game of the World Series, and he was pitching, I wouldn't play. There is nothing more important than life."

Easy-going, personable, and a prankster in the clubhouse during his off days, Johnson intimidated even his own teammates on days he pitched. "There are times when you have to be careful what you say to Randy and when you say it," former Seattle catcher Dave Valle told a reporter. Seattle shortstop Omar Visquel found out first hand when during a tight game, he approached the mound to speak to Johnson. "Get back to where you belong," the pitcher growled. Visquel did.

With Griffey and Johnson blossoming, bright days appeared to be on the horizon for the Mariners and Seattle. In 1993, the club improved its win total by a full 18 games over the year before. With improved starting pitching, strong defense, and a division downsized to four teams by realignment, the Mariners fully expected to be in the hunt for the Al Western Division title. However, in 1994, the club struggled for most of the year, finally showing a glimpse of its potential when it won nine of its last ten games before a work stoppage shut the game down for the remainder of the season.

THE RACE

The whole business of 1994 and '95 still makes baseball fans queasy. It was bad enough that a dispute between the Players Association and the club owners washed out the second half of the 1994 season and triggered the cancellation of the World Series. Now, with off-season negotiations between the two privileged factions stalled and fears abounding that the season would be cancelled, the owners announced a plan. The 1995 season would indeed start on time, they said, with club rosters to be filled with replacement players recruited from "walk on" tryouts to be held by all 28 major league clubs.

On April 1, 1995, U.S. District Judge Sonia Sotomayor mercifully put an end to the ridiculous charade when she ruled in favor of the players and ordered the owners to restore free agent bidding. With the court defeat and no deal imminent between the two warring sides, Acting Commissioner Bud Selig told a press conference on April 2 that the owners would end their lockout, send the replacement players home, and welcome the regular players to an abbreviated spring training, which was to begin on April 5.

With the announcement, players began changing teams at a dizzying pace as clubs hastened to reshape their rosters in time for the announced opening day of April 25. On one day alone, more than 22 players, including six former 20-game winners, signed contracts to play for different teams.

The impact of all this movement on baseball's competitive balance would prove to be profound, especially in the game's weakest division, the American League West. The Texas Rangers, which had led the division in 1994 with a miserable 52–62 record, moved to dramatically improve their club during the spring by signing nine players. The Angels also made an attempt to bolster themselves when they traded center fielder Chad Curtis to Detroit on April 13 for lead-off hitter Tony Phillips. The move opened up a spot in the Angels' outfield for the promising Jim Edmonds as the everyday center fielder.

Despite the changing face of the American League West, the preseason handicappers were unimpressed. "The only certainty in this mess is that the Angels won't be involved," said the Los Angeles Times, picking California for the cellar, with Seattle, Texas, and Oakland one, two, and three.

But involved the Angels would be. After tinkering with his lineup through much of the season's first month, Marcel Lachemann finally found a combination that clicked. With Tony Phillips setting the table at lead-off and a rejuvenated J.T. Snow providing solid protection for Chili Davis and Tim Salmon in the fifth spot, the Angels began scoring runs in bunches. The pitching rotation of Chuck Finley, Mark Langston, Brian Anderson, and Shawn Boskie was solid, if unspectacular. When the club hammered the Yankees 15–2 on May 26 to win its seventh straight game, its record climbed to 18–9 to equal the best start in the club's history.

Starting the season with almost equal fervor were the Seattle Mariners. Swinging hot bats in the center of the lineup were right fielder Jay Buhner, designated hitter Edgar Martinez (finally injury-free after two years), and Ken Griffey, Jr. To no one's surprise, Randy Johnson immediately jumped to the top of league pitching categories in strikeouts and wins. Speaking to the press regarding the team's best-ever 15–12 start in late May, manager Lou Piniella said, "We're playing well as a team. I like our club's chances. There's confidence in our clubhouse."

On May 27, the club's confident mood was shattered when Griffey fractured his left wrist in a game against the Orioles. The center fielder had just made a spectacular leaping catch of a ball off the bat of Kevin Bass in the seventh inning when he smashed full force into the center field wall. Following the game, the five-time Gold Glove outfielder underwent surgery to have a metal plate and five screws attached to his wrist. Following the operation, Griffey's doctors told the press that the surgery had been a complete success, but that the All Star would likely miss three months of the season.

Devastated at the loss of Griffey, the Mariners spoke cautiously of their team's chances. "This club will be OK," left fielder Darren Bragg told the press. "But everybody on the team is going to have to pick it up a notch."

Manager Lou Piniella tried his best to put on a brave face. "When you lose a player the caliber of Junior, it's not easy," he told the press. "But at the same time, it can be done, and we can't all sit around and lament the fact."

While the Mariners bided their time, the Angels were transforming themselves into an offensive juggernaut. Averaging in excess of six runs per game, the Halos pummeled opposing teams into submission throughout July and early August. The catalyst for the team's amazing run production was lead-off man Tony Phillips, who ranked among the league leaders in runs scored, walks, and on-base percentage.

Phillips was doing more than just leading the team's offense; he was also energizing the young Angels with his no-holds-barred approach to the game. Never one to turn the other cheek, Phillips seldom hesitated to challenge an umpire's call or get in the face of a teammate he felt might be jaking it in the field. A midsummer incident at Boston's Fenway Park served to elevate Phillips to virtual hero status among his teammates. During an on-field brawl in June, the fiery player raced onto the field and challenged virtually any Red Sox player, including hitting instructor Jim Rice, a man twice his size, to a fight.

"Probably the most galvanizing performance and the most important addition to our club in '95 was Tony Phillips," says Angels general manager Bill Bavasi today:

And it's no coincidence that our young guys came of age when he came on board. He was a clubhouse presence, and he led by example. Everything he did was perfect for us that year. We got him with that in mind. I don't know if you remember that deal, but we got ripped for it. We had traded Chad Curtis, who most of the media thought was going to be a big star. But we had a pretty good feel for our own players, and we thought we had enough intelligence to make the deal. Our scouts made it pretty clear that Phillips would help make guys like Edmonds and Anderson and Snow and some of those guys better players. And he did.

With Phillips leading the charge, the Angels became virtually unstoppable following the All-Star break, winning 17 of 20. After the Angel offense hammered Randy Johnson and the Mariners on August 1, the team extended its lead over the second-place Rangers to 11 games, the largest cushion ever enjoyed by the club in its 35-year history. For California, the journey from preseason laughingstocks to runaway division leaders was a heady experience. To many in the Angels' clubhouse, the lack of respect accorded the club early in the year did much to fuel the team's sudden rise to the top.

"No question, we thought we'd surprise some people," says Marcel Lachemann today:

> We had a pretty solid lineup. When we got Tony Phillips as a lead-off hitter, that really helped. And then when he was able to move into the infield and open up a spot for Garrett Anderson, that really kind of put things together. You know, I think we were around .500 or just a little above at the All-Star break, and that's when we kinda hit a hot spell at the same time as those other teams hit a cold spell. And that's when that lead was built up.

"Sure, the fact that we were picked to finish last had an impact on the team," remembers infielder Rex Hudler. "There was no pressure, no sense of overachieving. It's much easier to do it that way than to be on a contending team picked to finish first. Having that expectation from day one, that's pressure. But we had the horses."

The Angels may have had horses, but no one had expected them to run so fast, so soon. "What," many around baseball were asking, "are the young, inexperienced Angels doing leading the American League West by 11 games?"

According to Hudler, it wasn't just baseball's pundits who were surprised. "I think that the team's performance kind of snuck up on Billy Bavasi. He was young, in his second year as GM. He didn't really realize what was going to develop. But we had an excellent ballclub. And when you look at the development of Bavasi's team, it's a beautiful thing."

"I can't tell you we were surprised that they played well," Bavasi says today. "But we were certainly surprised that we were able to build a lead as large as it was. And we were surprised that the pitching held up as well as it had. It wasn't a world beater; it was the offense that was getting us that lead."

As well as they were playing, the Angels also knew that much of the credit for the club's huge lead was attributable to the off-again, on-again play of the Mariners and the Rangers. "We were surprised that Texas and Seattle were not playing better," remembers Bavasi. "But we also knew they would. We were all old enough and experienced enough to realize that it's a long season and that a lot of things could happen."

Seattle, amazed at the rapidity at which California had run up its huge lead and playing without Ken Griffey, Jr., still refused to throw in the towel. While idling at around the .500 mark in late July, the club obtained right-handed starter Andy Benes in a trade with the Padres. Regarding the trade, Lou Piniella told the press, "I think it sends a clear message to the players and fans that ownership is doing everything it can to win. It's the type of deal Seattle hasn't been noted for in the past."

Their gaudy lead notwithstanding, the Angels elected to strengthen their pitching staff with the addition of Jim Abbott. "We were looking for any pitching," Bill Bavasi recalls:

> Jim was one of the guys that was on the available list. There were other guys, but we were successful in getting him. In the end, we gave up a lot, but I look back on it, and that trade was fine for us. I think that was the year that he was ninth in the league in ERA. You'd have to look it up, but I think it was something like that. That's pretty damn good.

Throughout their hot streak, the Angels demonstrated a swagger that bespoke utmost confidence. But beneath the confident veneer existed a real fear common to every winning team: that a key player would get hurt. On August 4, Angel shortstop Gary DiSarcina, dubbed "the heart and soul of this team" by first baseman J.T. Snow, suffered a season-ending injury to his thumb while running the bases. DiSarcina was the one guy who no one felt that the Angels could afford to lose.

"I rode to the ballpark with him everyday because we lived next to each other," recalls Rex Hudler:

> And I remember one day, we're riding to the park and I said, "Disar man, you've got to stay healthy or we're in trouble." Well, that was the jinx. At the time, we both agreed, "Yeah, you're right." And a week or so later, he tears a ligament off his thumb on a simple slide into second base. And there it went. And that was the first little puncture in the tire.

While the Angels were weighing the loss of DiSarcina, events were taking a decidedly positive turn for the Mariners. The acquisition of Andy Benes was increasingly looking like a masterstroke; Seattle had yet to lose a game with him on the mound. A six-game winning streak energized the club, and then on August 16, Griffey returned to the lineup after missing 73 games. "I'm back," Griffey told newsmen upon his return. "It's been a long time, but I'm back. I'm probably more excited than the fans."

Despite the earlier-than-anticipated return of their star center fielder, enthusiasm in Seattle was tempered by the team's predicament. With just six weeks left in the season, the Mariners remained 10½ games behind the league-leading Angels. With the exception of the 1951 New York Giants and the 1978 New York Yankees, no team had ever rallied from such a deficit to win a division or a pennant. If the Mariners were going to make a run at the division title, a winning streak wouldn't be enough. They'd also need the California Angels to do something that they hadn't done all year: stop winning.

Amazingly, the Angels were about to do just that. DiSarcina's loss and a pair of three-game losing streaks in mid-August served as harbingers. By month's end, the Angels were turning in a series of lifeless, punchless performances characterized by a complete cessation of offense. By August 26, the date that Acting Commissioner Bud Selig announced that the Disney Company's proposed purchase of a controlling interest in the California Angels was proceeding "without a hitch," the yawning chasm that had separated the Angels from Texas and Seattle had been reduced to 7½ and 9½ games, respectively.

On August 27, the Angels squared off in the final game of a four-game series against Baltimore. The Halos, whose early season pattern of battering opposing pitchers early in the game had been turned on its ear, were hammered by the Orioles, 11–2. The loss, California's ninth in 12 games and third in a row, particularly troubled manager Marcel Lachemann. Following the game, the Angels' clubhouse door remained locked to reporters, while Lachemann lectured his club on concentration and fundamentals. "It was the most ticked off I've ever seen him," an Angel player told a reporter following the meeting.

Speaking to reporters after the meeting, Lachemann turned the focus for the team's woes directly on himself: "If we don't win this thing, they should get rid of the manager, because this is a good team." That night, the Angels departed for their most important road trip of the year, an eastern swing that would carry them to New York, Boston, and Baltimore.

The road trip began ominously for the Angels. The next day they were battered by the Yankees, 12–4. The club then staggered through their remaining two games against New York, running their losing streak to six straight. On September 1, they were mugged in Boston by the Red Sox, 11–3. During the ugly loss, a cadre of four Angel pitchers gave up a season-high 18 hits as the club suffered its 13th loss in 16 games and 7th in a row.

As the losing streak ground on, the Angels waited desperately for someone in their pitching rotation to act as a stopper. Staff aces Chuck Finley and Mark Langston were ineffectual, and Brian Anderson had lost five straight decisions and was close to being dropped from the rotation. Following the game, designated hitter Chili Davis told the press, "You don't want to panic. You can get an ulcer sitting around and worrying. We're lucky to have a lead while we're going through this. We have some room to breathe, and we have to remember that."

The Angels may have had room to breathe, but the air was growing increasingly thin. While California was being hammered by the Red Sox, the Mariners were squeezing by the Orioles for their sixth win in eight games. Suddenly, Seattle, which had appeared viable for no more than a wild card spot, had leapfrogged over Texas and was just 6½ games back of the Angels and closing.

"I'm sure the Angels are thinking about things right now," Mariner pitcher Tim Belcher told the press following the game. "They had such a big lead a couple of weeks ago, but 6½ certainly isn't insurmountable. It would be nice to catch them."

On Saturday, September 2, the Angels' disastrous road trip continued in Boston. Continuing the recent pattern of falling behind early, Chuck Finley surrendered a three-run homer to Tim Naehring in the first inning to put California in a hole. Throughout the contest, knuckle-baller Tim Wakefield baffled Angel hitters, and when it was over, he had chalked up an 8–1 win. Marcel Lachemann and Tony Phillips, showing the frustration of a club that had now lost 15 of 18, were thrown out of the game for arguing balls and strikes. To make the Angels' dilemma worse, the Mariners, behind Rich Amaral's three-run homer, were manhandling the Orioles in Baltimore, 9–6. With the win, Seattle had closed to within 5½ games of California.

Following the loss to Boston, a number of Angel players spoke with the press regarding the club's collapse. Finley, who had been bombed in his previous start against the New York Yankees, was the most optimistic: "We've got a couple of spokes loose, but we're going to be all right. We've still got a 5½-game lead, and those other teams have to catch us. You lose nine in a row, someone should have caught us by now, don't you think?"

Tony Phillips wasn't quite so upbeat regarding his team's situation: "Yeah, it's slipping away, that's a realization. The only way we can change that is to start winning."

On Monday, the Angels' nine-game skid was finally stopped when a pinch-hit three-run homer by Chili Davis and clutch pitching by Jim Abbott propelled California over Baltimore. Two days later, the Angels became part of baseball history when Cal Ripken played in his 2,131st consecutive game, surpassing the record that had been held by Lou Gehrig for more than a half century.

In front of a standing-room-only crowd, which included the president and vice president of the United States, Ripken received an unprecedented 22-minute ovation when the game became official at the top of the fifth inning. Ripken's feat, a remarkable testimony to durability and perseverance, was a shining moment for Angels infielder Rex Hudler.

"Oh, that was the highlight of my career," says Hudler today:

> Oh, man. Before the game, they passed balls around the locker room, and those balls were going to the Hall of Fame. The fact that Marcel Lachemann, my manager, played me that night against Mike Mussina was a total gift. It was a very tough game, very emotional. One that was hard to play in. I've never been in a World Series game, but that's what it felt like. Like a one-game playoff. I always faced left-handed pitchers during any of my starts. I never faced right-handers. And the manager did me a favor and gave me the highlight of my career.

Unfortunately for the Angels, the historic game also marked yet another loss and the end of a grim 1–8 road trip. As so often happens to slumping clubs, things were going wrong in bunches. During the trip, the pitching staff had run up a collective 6.81 ERA. The offensive tally was just as bleak: during the same stretch, the club had batted .243 and averaged barely three runs per game. To make matters worse, the Angels were undergoing a crisis in fundamentals as outfielders missed cut-off men and infielders threw to the wrong base.

"It's been tough," Marcel Lachemann told the press following the loss to Baltimore. "But we're going home now. We're still in first place by six games, so there's no reason to panic." Lachemann, of course, had no way of knowing that the Angels' nine-game skid was just act one in what would prove to be one of the most historic collapses in baseball history. Act two would begin in just a scant seven days, and it would ring down the final curtain on Gene Autry's 34-year quest for a world championship.

During the following week, the Angels regrouped somewhat and managed to win four of their next six games. Seattle, battling for the division title while simultaneously in the hunt for a wild card berth, had been unable to gain any ground in the race for the division title and remained five games back of the Angels with just 15 to play.

A look at the Western Division schedule for the season's remaining games showed a decided slant toward California. Over the final two weeks, the Angels would take on Kansas City, Texas, Seattle, and Oakland. During the same stretch, the Mariners and Texas would square off against one another a total of seven times, including a season-ending four-game series in Texas. The Angels looked at the season-ending matchups and liked the odds. "That's outstanding," Tony Phillips told the press. "They're the two teams trailing us, so if they can beat up on each other, we'll be in pretty good shape. If they split, it would be great."

Right fielder Tim Salmon agreed: "With everyone playing each other in our division, and teams knocking each other off, it makes it tougher for teams to gain ground. Hopefully, that will be the case. But if we get our jobs done here, it doesn't matter what happens elsewhere."

On September 15, before a festive Friday night crowd at Anaheim Stadium, the Angels' offense remained in the deep freeze against the Royals' Kevin Appier. Allowing only three hits, Appier cruised to an easy 5–0 victory. In Chicago, Andy Benes continued to pay dividends as the Mariners won for their eighth time in his nine starts to sneak by the White Sox, 3–2. The gap between the two clubs now stood at just four games, the Angels' smallest cushion since July 21.

On Saturday, Vince Coleman and Dan Wilson powered the Mariners to a 5–3 victory over Chicago for their fourth straight win. In Anaheim, manager Marcel Lachemann, juggling his lineup in an attempt to shake up his moribund club, could only watch helplessly as the Royals scored six first-inning runs and went on to win, 7–6. Asked about his team's newest losing streak, Lachemann said to the press after the game, "I don't see anything to worry about. But if you guys continue to write about it and make it an issue, it will become an issue."

On Sunday, September 17, 15 game winner Mark Langston took the mound to face the Royals in the concluding game of the three-game series. In the first inning, Langston surrendered a three-run home run to Joe Vitello, the 14th time in the past 26 games that an Angel pitcher had yielded a first-inning homer. The club never recovered, going down 10–8 for its fourth consecutive loss. The only bright spot for the Angels was the news that Seattle had been beaten 2–1 by the White Sox.

With the onset of the new losing streak, the looseness and cama-raderie that had characterized the Angels throughout the heady days of July and August finally crumbled. In its place, backbiting, second-guess-ing, and finger pointing had arisen. Marcel Lachemann seemed to be the target of much of the discord. "Of course, there's second-guessing when you lose," said Tony Phillips:

> Guys are human. Guys say, "Why this? Why that?" But what it all boils down to is you have to look in the mirror and ask what you could have done. I'm not perfect and no one else is, whether he's in the manager's office or general

manager's office. When things are going bad, it's easy to make excuses and point fingers, but the first should be pointed at yourself.

For infielder Rex Hudler, blame for the Angels' predicament rested with the players, general manager Bill Bavasi, and manager Marcel Lachemann:

> When a team goes down like that, it's up to the veterans to step up to a certain extent. At the same time, Billy Bavasi didn't really realize what he had.
> I loved Marcel Lachemann. He was a great pitching coach, but he was not a leader of men. And that's not a knock on him. Everybody has their skills, and that was just not one of them. I don't think Billy Bavasi understood that at the time he hired him. He didn't realize that he was going to need a guy to lead his men to the pennant. And I think it kind of surprised him. In September, with things going bad and you're dropping your lead, you look to your manager. You look to your field general. And I think it's the same in war. When your guys are getting beat in battle, they're looking to the leader to find out what to do. "The ship's sinking. Boss, what are we doing? Are we retreating? Are we attacking?" And Lach couldn't communicate. It was difficult. We had to draw from each other. And Lach was feeling the pressure. I love Marcel. But we're talking about '95 here ... we're talking about the difference between having that one-game playoff and just walking in and playing the Yankees right away. We just didn't have any leadership. Nothing on Lach. I don't want you to make it sound like he was a horseshit manager. But it's the simple truth. I've played the game a long time. I've been on winners and losers. And that was what was happening.

Bavasi understands today how difficult the 1995 season was on Lachemann:

> It was a hurtful season as manager for him. It depends on the kind of person you are, as far as leadership goes. I think that Marcel was not satisfied with his performance as far as team moves. He would always complain to me about that. "I didn't do this. I didn't do that." But that was never an issue with me.
> As far as leadership goes, it's hard for me to comment on that. Because I can look far and wide, high and low, and I can't find a better guy in baseball than Marcel. He is terrific. His brain is excellent. He treats his players like men. And that may be the problem with today's players. That's probably the worst thing that Marcel is guilty of: he treats his players like men. It's hard to imagine that anybody would watch our team play and say, "Hey, he's not good enough." Wasn't our team expected to come in last? Even during the spring, our players expected nothing. Absolutely nothing. Now he gets us a 13-game lead and you know what? I'd like to be able to tell you that if I was playing, that I'm man enough to smell the finish line on my own. Or smell the World Series share or whatever it is that makes you go. Those questions about Marcel's leadership will always be brought up. I'm going to venture

to guess that those comments might have been brought up by the veterans on our club. It might have been Chili. It might have been Tony. But I'll tell you what. Our veterans were the problem on that club, as far as not getting through to the end. We had veterans that absolutely, positively collapsed. The veterans were pointing to kids as the problem, and the problem wasn't the kids, it was the veterans.

On Monday, September 18, the surging Mariners turned up the heat on the reeling Angels when Randy Johnson pitched a three-hitter against Texas. Johnson, in beating the Rangers for the sixth time in seven games, struck out 10 and upped his record to 15–2. Back in Oakland, the Angels' descent into oblivion continued when they were held to two hits by rookie Doug Johns. A sterling pitching effort by Chuck Finley was erased by mental errors on the basepaths by Jim Edmonds and Tim Salmon and continued offensive futility. The loss, the Angels' fifth straight and 23rd of their last 31, pared the club's first-place lead to a meager two games.

"Losing streaks are what happens when a club tries too hard," says Marcel Lachemann today, remembering the slump that gripped his club. "Trying to do more than you have been doing. You don't just let yourself play the game. Everybody's trying to be perfect, not to make any mistakes And when you look at that pair of losing streaks that we had, that's what was happening."

On Tuesday, September 19, the Angels, trying desperately to right themselves, were locked in a bitter struggle with the As in Oakland. The club was down 2–0 in the ninth when a dramatic, two-out, two-run homer from J.T. Snow tied the game. At the very moment that Snow's blast cleared the fence, the Oakland scoreboard flashed the news from Seattle: an RBI single by Ken Griffey, Jr., had accounted for the winning run as Seattle rallied to beat the Rangers, 5–4.

Back in Oakland, where the game had moved into the 10th inning, Angel reliever Troy Percival walked Rickey Henderson. After Henderson stole second, Stan Javier sacrificed him to third. Percival then walked Jason Giambi and Mark McGuire to load the bases. The next hitter was Terry Steinbach, who lofted a fly ball over the drawn-in outfield, which enabled Henderson to score. It was yet another crushing loss for a team that was now completely out of answers. Following the game, the Angels' clubhouse was gripped in a deathly silence as players sat slumped in front of their lockers. Their division lead was now just a single game over the hard-charging Mariners.

On Wednesday, September 20, what was left of the Angels' first-place lead dried up beneath the late summer sun of Oakland. In the top of the first inning, Angel pitcher Shawn Boskie wasted no time, serving up a 465-

foot, three-run homer to Mark McGuire. Never recovering, the Angels lost 9–6, completing a sweep of the series by Oakland and marking California's seventh consecutive loss.

In Seattle, the Mariners continued to manhandle Texas with a 10–1 laugher that was punctuated by the hitting and fielding heroics of Griffey and yet another fine outing from Andy Benes. The win, the Mariners' eighth in ten games, boosted them into a flat-footed tie for first place with the Angels.

When a baseball team meshes, it's a beautiful thing to see. For six weeks, the Mariners had been hitting on all cylinders. When they needed clutch pitching performances, they got them. When they needed someone other than Griffey, Buhner, or Martinez to provide offense, Dan Wilson, Mike Blowers, Tino Martinez, and Luis Sojo stepped up. The contrast with California during the same stretch is striking. Over the previous month and a half, the wheels had wobbled themselves completely off the Angels' wagon. The club, desperately in need of clutch pitching performances during their two slumps, never got them; from August 16 on, Angel starting pitchers went 7–20 with a 6–80 ERA. Lack of steady starting pitching also turned up the heat on an offense that was pressing at the plate. Edmonds, Davis, and Salmon, so crucial to the club's early success, had watched their bats grow cold. And Tony Phillips, named by so many as the key to the Angels' initial wins, slumped terribly when he was most needed, batting just .200 from August 1 through mid-September.

When asked what he did to maintain an even keel during his club's tailspin, Marcel Lachemann says:

> I talked to some people, some good friends of mine, Tony LaRussa, people like that. I just felt that if I altered my style that would show a state of panic. I didn't want to start doing things differently than I'd been doing all year. The people who are in baseball understand it. The ones who aren't locked into it all year don't understand it. Slumps like that happen for a multitude of reasons. One factor is who you are playing. The matchups with who you're playing. You're playing bad teams that you beat often at certain times. And then it turns around, and you're playing the good teams.

On Friday, September 22, the return of shortstop Gary DiSarcina cheered the team but proved to be of little help as Mark Langston once again failed in his role of stopper. A pinch home run by Eduardo Perez had pulled the Angels even with the Rangers in the seventh inning, but Langston immediately surrendered five runs in the eighth inning to seal his club's fate. The amazing losing streak had now reached eight games. In Seattle, the Mariners extended their powerful play when they dramatically rallied from a six-run deficit in Oakland to defeat the As 10–7.

In searching for a quote to describe the Angels in Arlington, Texas, on Saturday, September 23, the following by Stevenson might be most appropriate:

> Under a wide and starry sky,
> Dig me a grave and let me lie

For on this day, Chuck Finley yielded five first-inning runs to the Rangers, and the Angels lost 5–1. Incredibly, the club had now completed its second nine-game losing streak in just three weeks. In Seattle, the Mariners, behind two home runs from Jay Buhner and a powerful performance from Randy Johnson, cruised to victory over the Athletics. It was the club's fifth consecutive win and its 12th in 14 games. Speaking to the press following the game, manager Lou Piniella was relaxed and happy: "Things are going well for us. We had a big crowd on hand tonight to see us, and we came out ready."

The next day, the Mariners were locked in a wild seesaw battle against Oakland. Carrying a 7–6 lead into the eighth, Seattle fell behind 8–7, then rallied in its last at-bat to salvage the victory. The heart-stopping win was the Mariners' sixth straight and was played in front of a pennant-mad crowd of 46,714 in Seattle. It was the ninth time in their past 13 games that the Mariners had surged from behind to win a game.

Following the victory, the Mariner clubhouse was possessed of the magical quality that infuses a team on a hot streak. "We're just playing good fundamental baseball," Jay Buhner told a reporter. "Everyday, someone steps up and does the job. Today it was Tino. Tomorrow it may be somebody else. That's the way it is when things are going well."

Ken Griffey, Jr., whose injury had threatened to torpedo the Mariners' season, said, "No matter what the score is, we've got a chance to win."

Standing in front of his locker with a towel around his midsection, relief pitcher Norm Charlton was talking to the press regarding his team's upcoming series against California:

> They're not playing very well right now, but they're a much better team than they're showing. They're coming here with something to prove, and anybody who thinks they're out of it is crazy. No one thought a month ago that we had any chance of being close to them, but nothing's been clinched.

A couple of lockers away, outfielder Vince Coleman was being much less tactful in discussing their Western Division rivals: "I'm not worried about the Angels. We have to do what it takes to win ballgames. We're just worried about playing consistent baseball. Other teams are the ones who are worrying about the Seattle Mariners."

Earlier that day, Jim Abbott, as he had three weeks earlier, snapped an Angels nine-game losing streak when he pitched a complete game, three-hitter against the Rangers. "In September, we had a couple of nine-game losing streaks," remembers Bill Bavasi:

> and I think if you look it up, Abbott broke both of them. You know, Langston had a chance to break those streaks. There were a lot of guys who had a chance to break those streaks. The point is, if we didn't have Abbott to break those losing streaks, we might never have had a chance to come back and tie Seattle.

Following the game, a drained Marcel Lachemann sat in his office surrounded by reporters. With a well-worn book entitled *Game Time: Motivational Messages for Teams and Life* resting on a table behind him, the manager told the press, "That was a big, big game. Jimmy has put together two outstanding outings on this trip. And he's done it right at crunch time."

In the clubhouse, Tony Phillips was also touting Abbott's role as the club's stopper and waxing optimistic about his club's pending two-game set in Seattle: "Abbott, he's an ace, man. He's got us into a good position now. Two games back with two games up there in Seattle. That's a big lift."

A few feet away, Chili Davis was discussing Abbott's performance and what it meant to the club: "He just grinds and grinds and grinds out there. That's what we've all got to do from here on out. We've got to go out there and perform with that kind of competitive spirit on Tuesday and Wednesday against Seattle."

Standing in front of his locker, right fielder Tim Salmon was asked if the club felt that a sweep in Seattle was critical. "Every game is a must-win now," Salmon responded. "I've never been in a playoff game situation, so it will be interesting to see how we respond to it in Seattle."

A short time later, a humbled but still hopeful band of Angels left their clubhouse to board the plane that would carry them to Seattle for their showdown with the Mariners. In the almost two months since the two clubs had last met, the Angels had watched helplessly as the Mariners surged from 13 games back to a two-game divisional advantage. Now, with two awful losing streaks behind them and their huge lead squandered, the Angels rightly felt that their luck was due for a change.

On Tuesday, September 26, a keyed-up crowd of more than 50,000 packed the Kingdom for game one of the showdown between the Mariners and the Angels. From the start of the contest, Seattle capitalized on every opportunity afforded it by California. In the third, Angel starter Shawn Boskie plunked second baseman Joey Cora with two out and Ken Griffey,

Jr., waiting in the on-deck circle. Griffey then doubled and eventually scored when Angel catcher Grey Meyers was unable to hold a relay throw from Tim Salmon. In the fourth, Griffey did it to the Halos again when he homered to center field. The Mariners never let up, tallying a single run in the fifth, then three more in the sixth. When the onslaught finally ended, the score stood at 10–2, and the win, the Mariners' seventh straight, boosted their lead over the Angels to three games with just five left to play.

"Big win, big win," manager Lou Piniella said to the press following the game. "We're just gonna come out here tomorrow and try to do the same thing. I take nothing for granted, but I like the shape we're in right now."

Desperate to inject life into his moribund team, manager Marcel Lachemann elected to start Rex Hudler at second base for game two of the series. As the club's resident cheerleader, Hudler had done his best to buoy his teammates over the previous week:

> I'd tell them, "Hey, we're in this thing. We're not 15 games out. Come on!" I'll never forget. We'd go to visit the children's hospital in Orange County. These kids are sick and dying of leukemia. A bit later, getting ready to start the last week of the season, seven games left. And I get this Federal Express package full of cards. The kids at the hospital had drawn pictures of themselves, made their own baseball cards, and wished every single player good luck during the final week of the season. I hand-carried those cards to everybody in that locker room and said, "Man, you guys. We're sitting here worried about a pennant race. Look at what these kids who are dying of leukemia, some who won't make it through the summer, look at what they're saying! They're wishing us luck to go win." That was inspirational. Most every guy stopped, grabbed a card, had a moment. Some said, "Whoa, Hud, I feel it."

"So, we kicked it in that last week of the season," Hudler continues:

> And we had to win every game. We were three games back. To me, what I remember most about that season was not losing the one-game playoff, or losing all that ground we had. It was the way we finished. Strong, that last week. That's what a true champion is made of. And Lachemann said, "Hey, forget it, fellows. We're going at it for the last week. Let's duke it out." So Marcel put in his veteran, most scrappy players. And I was very thankful that he chose me that last week.

On Wednesday, a newly energized California Angels finally made some noise. The club jumped on Mariner starter Tim Belcher in the first inning after Tony Phillips walked, Salmon singled, and Chili Davis tripled. For a change, Chuck Finley pitched out of a jam in the bottom of the first, then relied on his forkball to hold the Mariners until Troy Percival and Lee Smith shut them down for the win. The final score was 2–0.

A baseball throwback, no player embraced the game the way that Rex Hudler did.
He's shown in action with the California Angels in 1995. (*The Sporting News.*)

"We may have a faint heartbeat, but we're not dead yet," Tim Salmon
told the press following the game. "We head home now for three against
Oakland, and of course, they [Seattle] head off to Texas for their last four
games We'll just have to watch and see how it turns out. But we'll be out
there playing hard until the final day."

"We played Seattle those two games," remembers general manager Bill
Bavasi:

> On the second game, Finley pitched a 2–0 shutout in the 'Dome, probably
> one of the five best-hitting ballparks in the history of baseball. It was also
> one of the top toilets, too, as far as a ballpark goes. And he goes in there, and
> he shuts them down. That was an awesome lineup he faced that day. They'd
> absolutely crushed us the day before.

On September 28, the Mariners carried their quest for their first division title into Arlington, Texas. In the eighth inning of a 2–2 tie, Griffey
homered into the right-field bleachers with the bases loaded to give Seattle a 6–2 lead, which the team never relinquished. "I'm just trying to do
my small part," Griffey said later of his heroics. "I wasn't thinking homer.

I was just trying to get us a one-run lead. We still have some work to do, but the pressure is on California."

Pressure and the California Angels had been constant companions throughout September. But now, with its goal seemingly out of reach, the club was playing with a looseness characteristic of teams that no longer feel like they have anything to lose. Against the As, the Angels parlayed a throwing error by pitcher Doug Johns into a 4–1 victory at Anaheim Stadium. Starter Mark Langston, who had been ineffective through most of the month, came through with a strong 6⅔–inning performance, surrendering one run and six hits. Leading the cheers as the Angels left the field was Gene Autry, who was on hand to celebrate his 88th birthday. With a scant three days left in the season, the Mariners still clung to their two-game lead over the Angels.

On Friday, the Mariners, coming from behind once more, utilized sacrifice flies from Edgar and Tino Marinez to push across two runs in the eighth inning to up-end Texas, 4–3. With the win, Seattle clinched a tie for the Western Division title. Following the game, Lou Piniella told the press: "I'm going to take a shower and enjoy the win. And I'm not going to worry about what's going on out west tonight. We can control our destiny because we have two games left in the season."

Out in Anaheim, the Angels survived a shaky performance from Jim Abbott and held on to beat the Oakland As. In spite of a minor resurgence, the Angels found themselves in an unenviable position. Just to tie for a division flag that had seemed destined to fly over Anaheim Stadium, they would have to win both of their final two games while the Mariners would have to lose both of theirs.

On Saturday, the Angels, powered by clutch relief pitching from Mike Harkey and home runs from Chili Davis, J.T. Snow, and Rex Hudler, knocked off the As for their fourth consecutive victory. In Texas, the Rangers, behind home runs by Mickey Tettleton and Ivan Rodriguez, overcame Andy Benes and handily cooled off the red-hot Mariners, 9–2. With a single game left, the Mariner lead now stood at one game.

On Sunday, when they could least afford it, the Mariners stumbled. Tim Belcher, working with subpar stuff, yielded a three-run homer to Mickey Tettleton in the first inning, then surrendered two more in the fourth. By the time the Texas hit parade ended, the Rangers had sunk the Mariners by a 9–3 margin. In Anaheim, the bats of Tony Phillips, Jim Edmonds, and J.T. Snow along with a strong outing by Chuck Finley enabled the Angels to complete their unlikely four-game sweep of the As, 8–2. Amazingly, California had caught the Mariners on the season's final day.

In the Angel clubhouse following the game, Angel coach Rick Burleson was sitting in the midst of a swirl of activity. All around him, reporters pressed players for reactions to the club's sudden turn in fortune, while down the aisle, Marcel Lachemann moved among his players, offering congratulations. Burleson, who was on the field at Fenway Park when Bucky Dent hit his famous sudden-death home run 17 years earlier, was discussing the Angels' chances:

> Ideally, we don't want to play this game. But a one-game series is a crapshoot. With the guy the Mariners have going [Johnson], this game is similar to '78. The Yankees had Guidry going in that one. But we've got an opportunity. Let me tell you, it's a great feeling to get on a plane tonight instead of driving home.

A short time later, the Angels were delighted and amazed to see hundreds of fans lining the path between the clubhouse and the team bus. One by one, the still-proud athletes made their way through the throng, some nodding and smiling, others solemn, seemingly drained from the events of the past two weeks. After the last player had made his way up the steps of the bus, the doors slowly closed. Then, carrying the dreams of an old man with one final horizon to conquer, the bus groaned and slowly eased away from the well-wishers who surrounded it, destined for one of baseball's most unlikely rendezvous.

Monday, October 2, 1995

Lou Piniella was on the field of the Kingdome in Seattle. In a short time, the first major league sudden-death baseball game in 15 years would begin. Right now, however, the Mariner manager was standing near the batting cage, speaking to newsmen regarding his starting pitcher for the game against the Angels, Randy Johnson. "We've been riding on his shoulders all year," Piniella was saying. "Take nothing away from the rest of our staff, but Randy's been the guy for us this year."

In the Angels' clubhouse, left-handed Mark Langston was in uniform, standing just inside the door. In a short while, he would take the mound to face the Seattle Mariners. "They'll be waiting for you," a media representative said as he passed Langston. "Good," Langston replied, "Tell them we're coming."

Over the 1995 season, Langston's 15–9 record had made him the ace of the Angel staff. What his record didn't reveal, however, was the label that had been hung on him throughout his career: "can't win the big ones." In a huge game against Seattle during the season's final week, Marcel Lachemann had skipped over Langston in favor of Shawn Boskie. "Tendonitis in his pitching arm" was given as the official reason for the substitution, but Langston took it personally. "It kills me when people say I can't pitch in a big game," he'd told the press a couple of days earlier. "I've only been in one other situation like this, back in Montreal. So it's not like I've been doing it every year."

"How's your arm?" a teammate on his way to the playing field asked Langston. "Great" was Langston's reply. "Physically, I feel great."

Facing Randy Johnson was nothing new for Langston. He and the big lefty went way back. On May 25, 1989, Langston was traded by Seattle to the Montreal Expos for Gene Harris, Brian Holman, and Randy Johnson. No one was more aware of Johnson's record when pitching in the King-dome than Langston. In games that the big lefty had started, the Mariners were 26–3. Despite the odds, Langston was eager for the task. "You can't ask for anything more," he told reporters on Sunday. "I know what Randy Johnson is capable of. I've pitched against him before. I know Seattle. They'll be waiting for all of us, not just for me."

Shortstop Gary DiSarcina was the next to pass Langston. "Ready, Mark?" he asked Langston. "Let's go get them" was Langston's reply; and the two men left the clubhouse together to play in the biggest game of their careers.

Once the game was underway, pitching dominated as Langston and Johnson held opposing batters scoreless through the fourth inning. In the fifth, the Mariners broke through against Langston when a walk, a fielder's choice, and singles by Joey Cora and Vince Coleman made it 1–0.

The tight battle ground on until the bottom of the seventh, when Langston yielded a single to Mike Blowers to open the inning. With Tino Martinez at the plate, the corners of the Angel infield were drawn in, expecting a sacrifice bunt. Reaching his set position on the mound, Langston looked once, then twice at Blowers, who was inching off first. The pitcher then rocked and delivered. In a flash, Martinez dumped a bunt, which rolled directly in the path of Langston, who was charging on the play. The six-time Gold Glove pitcher fielded, then dropped the ball, making a play at second impossible. Looking to first, Langston realized that Rex Hudler, covering on the play from second, was out of position, and the pitcher held the ball. With men at first and second and no one out, Dan Wilson then sacrificed.

With the Angels' season on the line, Langston began fighting his nerves. His next pitch hit second baseman Joey Cora, loading the bases. With Vince Coleman digging in at the plate, Langston backed off the mound to think things over. A moment later, he toed the rubber to face

Coleman. Working deliberately, Langston delivered to Coleman, who promptly lined a shot to right that had base hit written all over it. Then, out of nowhere, a sliding Tim Salmon reached the ball, gloved it, and then fired a throw to the plate that kept the runners from advancing. With the dramatic event, the crestfallen Mariner crowd suddenly turned silent.

With the light-hitting Luis Sojo now walking to the batter's box, it looked as if Langston might be able to escape the inning. Toeing the rubber, the pitcher eyed his catcher, nodded, and delivered to Sojo. Breaking his bat on the swing, Sojo sent a twisting grounder down the first-base line that somehow eluded J.T. Snow's outstretched glove, then bounded all the way down the line to the Angels' bullpen area.

While Tim Salmon chased madly after the ball, Blowers and Martinez scored easily. Finally reaching the ball, Salmon wheeled and fired a perfect strike to the plate in an attempt to cut down Cora, who was attempting to score from first base. Langston, who for some reason was positioned between Salmon and catcher Andy Allanson, inexplicably cut off Salmon's throw. Realizing his mistake, he then turned to fire to Allanson, but the ball had become stuck in the webbing of his glove. Finally dislodging the ball, Langston then threw wildly past Allanson, allowing Cora to score with the Mariners' fourth run.

Sojo, who'd never stopped running on the play, realized that Langston's throw was wild. Rounding third, he headed full speed for the plate. Allanson, who'd by now retrieved the ball, turned and threw to Langston in an attempt to nail Sojo at home plate. Sojo's slide beat Langston's tag, scoring the Mariners' fifth run as the huge Kingdome crowd went wild with glee. When the dust settled around home plate, the prostrate figure of Mark Langston, lying flat on his back over home plate, arms crossed over his chest, staring up at the cement ceiling of the Kingdome, seemed to embody the agonized history of one of baseball's most star-crossed franchises.

Broken by the events, the Angels rolled over. In the eighth, Seattle added four insurance runs, and Johnson had all he needed. The big right-hander lost his concentration only twice the rest of the way: once in the top of the eighth, when he walked Chili Davis and surrendered a double to pinch-hitter Rene Gonzales before retiring the side, and then in the ninth, when he gave up a home run to Tony Phillips. When he reared back and blew a fastball by Tim Salmon with two out in the top of the ninth, it was over. The Mariners had won the first postseason title in their history. The final score was 9–1.

In the midst of the mad crush of media and well-wishers who crowded the Seattle clubhouse following the game, the players spoke of their victory and what it meant to them. "I thought about how fitting it was that it should come down to a single game at home in front of our fans. It couldn't have been written any better," Randy Johnson told a crowd of reporters in front of his locker:

> I was extremely focused in the beginning. It was an extremely tight game, and I maintained my focus until after the floodgates opened a bit. It was the biggest game of my career, and I knew I had to rise to the occasion. I was pitching on adrenaline.

Speaking to a crush of reporters in his office, Lou Piniella said, "Forget the final score. For three-quarters of the game, this was a real nail biter. Randy proved today why he's the best pitcher in baseball."

In the Angels' clubhouse, players struggled to make sense of the latest setback in a season of disappointments. Standing in front of his locker, first baseman J.T. Snow was discussing Luis Sojo's broken-bat hit, which had ignited the Mariners' four-run rally in the seventh inning. "I don't know if it hit a seam or had a cue ball effect," Snow told reporters, "but I couldn't believe I didn't come up with that ball. That's a play I should make."

Regarding Randy Johnson, right fielder Tim Salmon told a reporter, "He was as good as ever, which means great. You get the crowd behind him like that, and it pumps him up even more. You could actually feel the momentum he had."

"What a force," Angel shortstop Gary DiSarcina said of Johnson. "From the first inning, every pitch was a great pitch. We've seen him a lot, but today he was really in a groove."

No one felt worse over the day's events than Mark Langston:

> It was hard to watch them celebrate when it should have been us. But they did it in the game that counted, and we didn't. We had that huge lead, and we let it slip through our hands. When I was laying there on home plate [following Sojo's seventh-inning hit], the whole game flashed before my eyes, right there.

Today, Marcel Lachemann looks back on the final game of the 1995 season and thinks how different it all could have been:

> You know, the final score wasn't really indicative of what the game was. Because it was 1–0 going into the seventh. And then Sojo hits a broken-bat ball past J.T., and he never saw the ball. Then three runs score, and it kinda got out of hand. And it ended up 9–1, or whatever the hell it was. It's hard to tell them that, but I was very proud of the way they came back and didn't fold the tent. You know, everybody was pretty hard on that team at the end

of the year. When you lose a lead that big, it becomes kind of a media event. But to me, the thing that really showed the character of the club was when we went into Seattle. We lost the first game of a two-game series. At that point, we were three games behind, five games to go. We very easily could've folded up the tent and ended up eight games behind.

Rex Hudler also looks back and wonders "what if." "Had it been anybody else on their staff," Hudler says:

we'd have won. We would've whacked them. We'd have killed him. Because we were running like wildfire. And we battled the Big Unit! We battled him! I finally broke up his no-hitter in the seventh inning when I punched one through the right side. Had they pitched anybody else, we'd have won, because we were riding such a streak. But that's the way it happened, and it was a good learning experience. And I was grateful that I got to be a part of that.

Like Lachemann and Hudler, Bill Bavasi also feels proud of the way his club finished:

I'll always be proud of that team. I know that losing that big lead was just awful, and I feel as bad as anybody about it, but I also know that team was expected to come in last. But we didn't. We thought we'd made a couple of good trades with Phillips and the Abbott thing. That got us over the hump. We had a guy, Bob Fontaine, our scouting director, those were his guys. And those kids that you saw playing and that you still see playing today, those are his guys.

Unfortunately for the California Angels, the 1995 season became just one more entry in the team's chronicle of failure, the latest notation in a litany of regret. One win away in 1982. One strike away in 1986. An 11-game lead squandered in 1995. In 1996, the Walt Disney Company completed its purchase of a controlling interest in the California Angels. With the sale, the book was finally closed on Gene Autry's last great dream. A player standing in the Angels' clubhouse following the team's season-ending loss to the Seattle Mariners summed it up best: "It's too bad. It's sure too bad. It would have been nice to have won it for the Cowboy."

OCTOBER 2, 1995

CALIFORNIA	AB	R	H	BI
Phillips 3b	4	1	1	1
DiSarcina ss	3	0	0	0

CALIFORNIA	AB	R	H	BI
cOwen ph	1	0	0	0
Edmonds cf	3	0	0	0
dPerez ph	1	0	0	0
Salmon rf	4	0	0	0
Davis dh	2	0	0	0
Snow 1b	3	0	0	0
Anderson lf	2	0	0	0
aGallegher lf	1	0	0	0
Allanson c	2	0	0	0
bGonzales ph	1	0	1	0
Fabragas c	0	0	0	0
Hudler 2b	3	0	1	0
Totals	30	1	3	1

aLined out for Anderson in 8th
bDoubled for Allanson in 8th
cFlied out for DiSarcina in 9th
dGrounded out for Edmonds in 9th

SEATTLE	AB	R	H	BI
Coleman lf	5	0	2	1
Sojo ss	3	1	2	3
Griffey cf	3	0	0	0
Martinez dh	3	1	2	0
Buhner rf	4	1	1	0
Blowers 3b	3	2	2	0
T. Martinez 1b	2	2	1	1
Wilson c	3	1	1	2
Cora 2b	2	1	1	1
Totals	28	9	12	8

Doubles: Gonzales, Sojo, Wilson
Home Runs: Phillips

California	0 0 0	0 0 0	0 0 1	1
Seattle	0 0 0	0 1 0	4 4 x	9

California	IP	H	R	BB	SO
Langston (L)	6⅔	8	5	3	2
Patterson	⅓	0	0	0	1
James	0	2	3	1	0
Holzemer	0	1	1	0	0
Habyan	1	1	0	1	1

Seattle	IP	H	R	BB	SO
Johnson (W)	9	3	1	1	12

Bibliography

BOOKS

Boswell, Tom. *The Heart of the Order*. Penguin, 1989.
_____. *How Life Imitates the World Series*. Penguin, 1982.
_____. *Why Time Begins on Opening Day*. Penguin, 1984.
Durocher, Leo, and Ed Linn. *Nice Guys Finish Last*. New York: Simon and Schuster, 1975.
Gallagher, Mark. *Day by Day in New York Yankees History*. Leisure Press, 1983.
Golenbeck, Peter. *Bums: An Oral History of the Brooklyn Dodgers*. New York: Putnam's, 1984.
Halberstam, David. *Summer of '49*. Avon, 1989.
Hunter, Jim, and Armen Keteyian. *Catfish: My Life in Baseball*. New York: McGraw-Hill, 1988.
Jackson, Reggie, and Mike Lupica. *Reggie*. Villard, 1984.
Kahn, Roger. *The Boys of Summer*. New York: Harper and Row, 1971.
Koufax, Sandy, and Ed Linn. *Koufax*. New York: Viking, 1966.
Lee, Bill, and Dick Lally. *The Wrong Stuff*. New York: Viking, 1984.
Martin, Billy, and Peter Golenbeck. *Number 1*. Delacorte, 1980.
Nettles, Graig. *Balls*. Pocket Sports, 1984.
Peary, Danny. *We Played the Game*. New York: Hyperion, 1994.
Piniella, Lou, and Maury Allen. *Sweet Lou*. New York: Putnam's, 1986.
Snider, Duke, and Bill Gilbert. *The Duke of Flatbush*. Zebra, 1988.
Turner, Frederick. *When the Boys Came Back*. New York: Holt, 1996.
Veeck, Bill, and Ed Linn. *Veeck: As in Wreck*. New York: Putnam's, 1962.
Yastrzemski, Carl, and Gerald Eskenazi. *Yaz*. Garden City, NY: Doubleday, 1990.

PERIODICALS

Sport Magazine 29, no. 2 (Feb. 1960).

VIDEOS

The Greatest Comeback Ever. Vid America.
The Golden Decade of Baseball. SVS.

Index